a RIVER CALLING

a RIVER CALLING

a CHRISTIAN FATHER AND HIS SONS

a CANOE ADVENTURE

a SPIRITUAL JOURNEY THAT WOULD LAST A LIFETIME

by GLENN FRONTIN

TATE PUBLISHING & *Enterprises*

Published by Tate Publishing & Enterprises, LLC
127 E. Trade Center Terrace | Mustang, Oklahoma 73064 USA
1.888.361.9473 | www.tatepublishing.com

Tate Publishing is committed to excellence in the publishing industry. The company reflects the philosophy established by the founders, based on Psalm 68:11,
"The LORD *gave the word and great was the company of those who published it."*

Book design copyright © 2007 by Tate Publishing, LLC. All rights reserved.
Cover design by Leah LeFlore
Interior design by Kellie Southerland

Published in the United States of America

ISBN: 978-1-60247-858-9
1. Christian Living   2. Relationships
07.08.10

For Dustin, Joshua, and Emma

SPECIAL THANKS

To my family for always encouraging me as a boy to follow my dreams.

To my fellow River Rats, John Davis, Steve Streadwick, and Tim Farley. You guys were the best.

To all the wonderful people along the river who reached out and helped us. We never could have done it without you.

To Karen, for loving me and choosing to go down all those "river miles" of life together.

To my brothers and sisters in Christ. Your friendship and your fellowship have always been an inspiration.

TABLE OF CONTENTS

PROLOGUE

FEBRUARY 1979

It was late in February and the temperature outside our dorm window had dropped well below zero. It was one of those typical Wyoming winter nights: totally still and extremely cold, with millions of stars filling the clear night sky. The smoke that rose above the roof from our wood stove hung in the air, as if too cold to move. The windows that lined our room were glazed over with a thin coating of ice, the crystals forming symmetric designs and patterns of white and silver. It was the kind of night that would make your lungs ache just breathing in the cold air walking from the mess hall to the men's dorm, about fifty feet.

We called it "Yaacland," our camp made up of three buildings: a mess hall, men's dorm and the women's dorm. YACC, the Young Adult Conservation Corps, was a program for young people to spend a year working and living in national parks. I had been hitch hiking through Montana looking for work when I ran into the program recruiter in Great Falls. Room and board and about eighty dollars a week sounded great to a nineteen-year-old young man with little direction in his life and even less money in his wallet.

Our camp was situated six miles inside the north entrance to the park, just three miles from the Montana/Wyoming border. The beau-

11

tiful Mammoth Hot Springs with their mineral terraces were just over the hill, and to the east of camp one could see all the way down to the Gardiner River and the road that led to Lamar Valley, where herds of bison still roamed freely. That eastern view provided an endless display of gorgeous sunrises from the steps of the men's dorm.

I arrived in Yellowstone in mid-September, while the bull elk were challenging each other in duels of strength to see who was in charge for yet another year. By the end of October snow began to fall and it was the last time I saw bare ground. Though Yellowstone in winter is a wonderland of natural beauty and perfect isolation from the rest of the world, on this particular night, we were all somewhat tired of snow. We were all suffering from a case of cabin fever.

There I sat on my bed, the top bunk of bunk beds, my legs dangling off the side, my back against the wall, thumbing through a U.S atlas. Steve and Tim were playing cards at the one round table that sat in the center of the room. The eight track player played Neil Young's Greatest Hits for the third time through without anyone really listening.

My roommates were originally from Illinois, not far from Chicago, and had come out to Yellowstone together. They were both twenty years old, a year older than me. Steve had a medium frame, neither tall nor short. I suppose you would call his hair dirty blond and he sometimes sported a goatee that had a hint of red through it. Steve had a child-like enthusiasm for life that I found easily contagious. Tim was over a foot shorter than most of the guys, and even many of the girls. He had flowing blonde hair and a handsome face that never failed to attract the girls wherever he went. I liked how he was so laid back and easy to get along with. The three of us became close friends quickly As I studied the maps of the western states, I don't know if the cabin fever inspired me but I finally said out loud, "We oughta do something big."

There was no response from the card players.

"Hey, guys," I repeated, "we should do something big!"

"Like what?" Steve asked, looking up from his cards.

We all agreed a big adventure was just what we needed. We thought about walking the entire Appalacian Trial from Maine to Georgia, but the idea of carrying everything you need on your back, walking every day for months with aching shoulders and sore feet…well, the idea lost its appeal rather quickly.

I looked at the map of Montana and noticed the Missouri River ran off the page in Montana and then in North Dakota, and continued through a number of state maps, finally ending at the Mississippi River, just north of St. Louis, Missouri. The three of us agreed almost immediately that a canoe trip from Three Forks, Montana, down to St. Louis would be quite a trip.

Instead of the idea being dismissed as days went on, it seemed to stay on our minds. We did some research to find the river is 2500 miles long, with sixteen dams to portage around. There were also a few gigantic lakes to contend with, the result of the dams. How long would it take to paddle the whole river? Could we really make it the whole way? We were willing to give it a try.

With only three of us, we needed a fourth paddler to help man two canoes. We found it somewhat strange that we couldn't find a fellow adventurer willing to take on the river. Did everyone know something we didn't? I made a phone call to a high school buddy of mine back in New Jersey. John had a love for the outdoors and we had shared many great times hiking and camping in PA and upstate NY. John was eighteen, out of high school but with as much direction as I had, and no commitments to keep him in N.J. With one phone call and few details, John agreed to be our fourth man.

We all pitched in to purchase two seventeen-foot Coleman canoes. They were a burnt red color, made of molded ABS plastic, comfortable and quiet in the water. We tried to imagine what we might encounter on the trip, which led to some boat modifications. We attached hooks down the sides of the canoes and fashioned canvas covers that could be used to cover the gear in the center of the boats, just in case we tipped.

Even on the maps we purchased from the Army Corps of Engineers, the lakes in North and South Dakota looked immense so we decided to build sails, which might come in handy since there would be no current to help our progress. The sails were simple enough. We secured a foot long piece of PVC pipe in the center of each boat. A mast made of PVC pipe would fit inside the larger first piece. The mast was about eight feet tall with a horizontal top and bottom pipe that we attached with butterfly nuts. One of the girls in camp had a sewing machine and sewed two rectangular sails about six feet high and four feet wide, made of bright blue ripstop nylon fabric. When we were done the boats resembled Viking ships! We attached ropes to each bottom corner so someone in the front or back of the boat could turn the sail, depending on the direction of the wind. We painted "Missouri River Rats '79" on each sail and the canoes were ready.

Not one of us had any idea what supplies we might need for the trip. We had all camped and canoed, but this was quite different. We thought of the basics: two collapsible five-gallon water containers, two two-man tents, an assortment of cooking gear, sleeping bags, a .22-caliber pistol, clothes with some cold weather and rain gear…and large black rubber canoe bags to keep everything dry. We brought life vests for use as seat cushions during the day and bed pillows at night.

Our initial food supply consisted of dry goods like potatoes, pasta, rice, flour, and oatmeal, with canned stews, tuna, and yes, even some Spam. We had some freeze dried meals but not much due to the cost. We also brought an assortment of drink mixes like Tang. We probably spent the least amount of time thinking about food before the trip, never considering how much we would think about it during the trip!

On July 29, we packed up all our gear and said goodbye to our friends in Yaccland. Though they were trying to be supportive, I think the consensus in camp was we would all be back within a week, having given up on such a silly idea.

Steve's old, beat up, light blue Chevy Impala was weighted down with the two canoes strapped on top, all our gear in the trunk, and a motorcycle tied to the front bumper and grill. Somehow we made it safely to Steve's dad's house in Three Forks, an hour and a half drive. Steve's dad had moved there a few years earlier. That night we would all sleep on the small living room floor, our first night without a bed, something we would grow accustomed to.

Though the plan was to go to bed early to get an early start in the morning, we ended up staying awake talking well past 11:30 p.m. As we lay there on the floor in the small living room, I'm sure each of us had our own thoughts about the next day. The adrenaline was pumping already with the possibilities that lay ahead, so sleep came slowly. Each of us was committed to having a great adventure and having fun, but perhaps we struggled a bit with how committed we were to our goal of paddling 2500 miles, the entire length of the longest river in America, reaching that glorious Gateway Arch on the waterfront in St Louis.

We were about to follow in the footsteps of Lewis and Clark, paddle past sites made famous during the westward expansion of our then very young country, travel through the homeland of the Sioux and other tribes of the plains people. Those dramatic images flooded my mind as I drifted off to sleep, sensing the four River Rats were about to forge their own history, their own story, with events, memories, and lessons that would last a lifetime.

THOSE RIVER MILES

I stood on the bank of the Missouri River and just savored the moment. My two sons were loading the gear in our canoes while I gazed downstream, my eyes fixed on the bend in the river up ahead. I've always felt a river has a way of enticing a paddler to head downstream to discover what's just around the bend up ahead. If what you find disappoints you, there's always the next bend coming up.

It was one o'clock in the afternoon and I was anxious to get some miles in before dark. The sun was almost directly over us, the temperature in the high 90s. I put the last of the gear in the boats, double checking we had emptied everything from our rented Ford Explorer. I joked that we had more supplies for our three-day trip than we had for our three-month trip years ago, but Karen, my wife, made it clear she wasn't letting her boys canoe through one of the most remote areas of the country without being prepared. As long as we could fit it, it went. I had no objections about making this trip more comfortable than the last. Karen greased up the boys with sun tan lotion while my dad kept our three-year-old, Emma, busy throwing rocks in the water. When everything was done and it was time to shove off, we gathered together as a family and we prayed.

God knows the Missouri River trip of 1979 was a milestone event in my life. I grew to cherish the memories of those days on the river. It was no surprise that after I was married and had two sons I would start dreaming of the day I could take them both on a trip down at least a favorite section of the Missouri. They had heard enough about the trip growing up, whether they were interested or not, but I wanted them to have a taste of the adventure for themselves.

By far, my most favorite section of the river was through Montana. The incredible beauty of the river carving its path through rolling hills dotted with pine trees, rugged rocky valleys, and the mountain peaks in the distance has changed little from the time Lewis and Clark traveled through in 1805. If there was a small section of river that captured the adventure of the River Rats of 1979 and the spirit of the Lewis and Clark expedition of 1804–1806, it was central Montana. There, the sheer beauty of the place is surpassed only by its absolute remoteness.

While the boys were little it was easy for my river reunion to remain just a dream, but in September of 2001, Dustin turned sixteen and Joshua turned eleven. It was about time. Karen listened patiently as I shared my idea of a three-day trip. Though she was somewhat apprehensive, she had to admit, what better opportunity for male bonding than a dad and his sons on a three-day canoe trip in Montana?

After we had prayed, it was time for hugs and kisses, and we climbed into our boats and shoved off. Dustin would start out paddling solo in the canoe with most of the supplies. Josh and I had the other boat, with him up front and me steering in the back. I had to promise Josh he'd get a chance to paddle solo as well. As the current led us down the river, everyone waved and shouted, "Bye!" "I love you!" or "See you in a few days!"

I paddled a few strokes but mostly watched Karen, Emma and my father get smaller as we floated away till the river turned to the east and they were out of sight. With all the excitement of the moment, I felt an uneasiness leaving them there.

Karen had about a forty-minute drive back to the small town of Fort Benton. The tiny town is surrounded by miles and miles of prairie and range land. As you drive along the paved road that seems to go on forever, ignoring any notion of a speed limit, the road dips down into a valley, and the sleepy town appears, straddling the west side of the river.

It's quiet now, but Fort Benton was a busy, noisy place in the mid 1800s. This was the farthest the steamboats could chug up the Missouri, bringing goods and people heading west. With all the commerce going on and little law enforcement, the town, especially Front Street, was a wild place. Shootouts were such a common occurrence that the street was dubbed "The deadliest street in the west."

Front Street consisted of buildings on the west side of the street, mostly old brick two story store fronts, many dating back well over one hundred years. One of these buildings was the Pioneer Lodge, an old quaint hotel we had stayed at the night before.

On the opposite side of the road there was only one building on the south side of town, the Grand Union Hotel. The square brick structure had three stories, with ornate brickwork along the top trim and around each oversized window. It was the first landmark that I remembered after all these years. It was the oldest hotel in Montana, going back to 1882, when steamboats filled the levee in town.

An old weathered metal bridge spanned the river at the end of town, now closed to motor vehicles, but part of the lovely walking trail. The rest of that side of the street was a grassy stretch of park, with a strolling path and benches looking out on the Missouri River flowing by. An immense statue of Lewis and Clark and Sakajawea, the Shoshone Indian girl, stood in the park with a life-sized replica of the keelboat the explorers used for part of their journey. I recalled back in '79 we ate ice cream under the statue after a hot day of paddling. If memory served me right, Fort Benton had not changed a bit in twenty-three years.

Karen and I fell in love with the town and the pleasant folks we met that day and evening. If I had known I would have planned differently, but I had decided Karen, Dad, and Emma should drive another hour to the much larger town of Great Falls. They would spend two nights there while we were gone.

The real challenge for Karen would be meeting up with us in three days on the river at a place called Judith Landing. She would retrace her trip back to where we had launched our boats at Coal Banks Landing but would then drive two or three more hours on a gravel road that would eventually intercept the river. The plan was to meet there around noon.

What a woman! How many wives would agree to such a trip with a three-year-old baby? There would be no towns, no gas stations, probably not even signs. If you look at a map of Montana, you'll notice the north central part is blank with no towns or highways, just the river. That's where Karen would be traveling. I felt justified in feeling somewhat apprehensive. If Karen was, she didn't show it. But this wasn't the time for apprehension. Here we were, Dustin, Joshua, and I, floating down the Missouri River, just the three of us and my river.

Dustin's boat took the lead right away, since I was probably looking around more than paddling. The rolling hills on both sides of the river were mostly treeless. Stands of cottonwood trees clustered up here and there near the water's edge in the fertile ground. The sky was a perfect cloudless blue.

Dustin suddenly turned back toward us and whispered as loudly as he dared, "Look! Look up there!" pointing towards the shore on our right. It was easy to spot the large bald eagle sitting in a tall dead tree, perched on one of the remaining branches. We stopped paddling and floated by him, his suspicious eyes following our every move. Just when we thought we had passed without disturbing him, his huge wings stretched out, his claws came right off the branch, and in one incredibly loud flap, he flew downstream and out of our view. The boys and I were thrilled. We'd been on the river less than ten minutes and had already seen our first eagle!

The sense of the current carrying us along, the warm sun on my skin, the feel of the paddle in my hands, the sound of the water as we stroked through it; all felt so good. I'm sure I was smiling as I let my mind drift back over the years and back upstream a few hundred miles to the morning the River Rats launched their canoes just outside Three Forks, Montana. The span of years had not changed the river or my connection to it.

Missouri River Rats '79

Day 1 through Day 7 July 30–August 5, 1979

It was a warm, still morning with clear skies as we launched our canoes just outside Three Forks, Montana. The river there at its humble beginnings was only about thirty or forty feet wide with a shallow swift current of crystal clear water. Snow was still melting in the highest peaks of the mountains nearby, making the water extremely cold.

The road ran parallel to the river for a short time, but then we had only the rugged, barren hills to enjoy on the left and the right. We paddled about fifteen miles to our first obstacle, Toston Dam. It consisted of a concrete wall barrier just a few feet above the water's edge. The water level on the other side dropped about twelve feet or so, with small waterfalls rushing through slots between wooden boards. There was a concrete structure attached to one side of the dam with what seemed to be an office where we supposed they would control water flow. There wasn't a soul around with just a gravel road that led into the hills.

The carry around the dam was quick and easy, not even fifty yards. We took some of the heavier gear out of the canoes and just carried them without putting them up on our shoulders, then went back for the remaining gear. The water seemed even more clear and colder on the downstream side of the dam. As we paddled on, there was a sense of accomplishment. One dam down and we figured another fifteen to go!

The first few days were spent paddling through the barren rocky hills, unpacking and packing gear in and out of the boats, setting up and breaking down camp. A large fire became the first thing to do each night, for cooking and also for smoking out the mosquitoes and other flying bugs that attacked almost immediately. Some nights the mosquitoes were unmerciful while other nights a slight breeze would keep them away and we could sleep out under the stars.

At first we all pitched in doing the cooking each night, but after a few nights we decided to take turns. Every meal, whether breakfast, lunch if we had one, and dinner, always seemed to be just enough but never fully satisfying our hunger. There was always room for seconds, but there weren't any to serve. We all got in the habit of having a hot tea around the fire. That seemed to help satisfy not having enough to eat.

Lunches at times consisted of crackers, peanut brittle, or trail mix. To ration the trail mix we had a simple rule: you could reach into the bag and grab as much as one hand would hold. It seemed fair though we did argue over whose hands were unfairly larger or smaller than others.

Both sunsets and sunrises filled the sky with hues of purple and pink highlights. The night sky was brilliant with millions of stars shining from east to west. There is no wonder why Montana is called "Big Sky Country."

It wasn't long before we had the opportunity to try out the sails. The river was straight and we had a great tail wind. Once we pulled them out from under the gear, we placed the masts in the bases and straightened out the horizontal bars and tightened them. I have to admit, on the open water, the boats looked pretty impressive!

There was a moment of anticipation as we waited to see what would happen next.

The sails filled and lifted up with the wind. The PVC pipe masts of each boat started to bend forward as the sails became tight. We looked to the shore on either side and realized we were moving. We were sailing! We cheered and laughed and just kicked back and let the wind and river take us. We were all so grateful we had thought of making sails. Unfortunately, the tail wind didn't last long and we finally had to admit it was time to get back to work.

We paddled across small lakes and portaged over a few more small dams. Canyon Ferry Lake was the largest, named after a river ferry in the area that transported pioneers and trappers across the river back in the 1880s. That water crossing is now buried underwater, as Canyon Ferry is a long, thin lake following the route of the original river.

There were no waves on the lakes but we kept close to the shoreline anyway. At the first hint of a tail wind we put up the sails, making great progress, just sitting back taking in the scenery.

We saw a number of pelicans and great blue herons patiently fishing along the shore. Each day we would see red tailed hawks circling effortlessly high above us. We spotted a turkey vulture that was even uglier than the hundreds of huge carp we paddled through in the shallow southern section of the lake.

The hills around the lake were sprinkled with trees. At some points, high walls of reddish brown rock jutted out to the water's edge. Beyond the river valley, mountains filled the horizon, somewhat hazy in the hot afternoon sky.

On Canyon Ferry Lake we paddled past an old man fishing from his olive green metal rowboat. He was a scruffy guy in old overalls and a faded tee shirt. He must have noticed all our gear in our boats.

"Where you boys headed?" he asked, as he slowly reeled in his line.

"St Louis, Missouri!" we all chimed back.

He shook his head and didn't hesitate offering his opinion. "You won't make it." He waved his arm at us, as if dismissing the whole idea. We were all in a good mood so the fisherman didn't bother us.

The morning hours were quiet on the lakes with hardly a breeze. We would paddle easily on the smooth, glassy surface of the water, watching the morning light change on the hills and mountains as the sun rose.

The portage around Canyon Ferry Dam was not an easy one, being much larger than the previous ones. Its huge concrete wall spanned across a narrow valley. With a continuous roar, water rushed through certain sections, dropping perhaps two hundred feet to the river below. Our route around the dam would be up an earthen embankment, then about a quarter mile walk down a rocky gravel road, over another embankment, then over a four foot chain link fence.

We made a long, hot, dusty trip with the boats, the light gear inside, and then went back for the larger, heavier bags. We were sweaty and out of breath, when after about an hour and a half, we were back in the boats, enjoying a clear, cold and fast current rushing downstream.

Hauser Lake was an even narrower lake. The barren hills were gradually being replaced by pine-covered, rock strewn mountains and steep banks. We all agreed it was some of the prettiest country we had seen so far.

By midday we paddled into Upper Holter Lake, where it widened and we couldn't tell where the river continued. High rolling hills surrounded us with a massive rock mountain to our northeast. We had reached the place Captain Lewis from the Corps of Discovery Expedition had called the Gates of the Mountains. As we paddled closer to what appeared to be a dead end, we could finally see where the river seemed to push its way right through the mountain. The opening was maybe one hundred feet across with steep rock walls that rose almost straight up hundreds of feet. Captain Lewis commented in his journal that the canyon was dark and gloomy with towering and projecting rock walls ready to tumble down on them. Those same rocks still appear ready to tumble but on this gorgeous day with the sun shining, it was far from gloomy.

As we made our way into the narrow canyon, we marveled at all the rock formations and the natural caves that appeared hundreds of feet above the river. We saw birds of all kinds, including a bald eagle. Pine trees grew in rocky crags and crevices, in some places clinging to rocks where there didn't even appear to be any dirt at all. The beautiful canyon was the site of one of Lewis and Clark's campsites on July 19, 1805. Though historians don't know the exact location, they have a pretty good idea since there are very few flat places through that stretch of river.

The canyon continued for about six miles till we came out the other end, the opening here being as narrow as where we had first entered. The river stayed narrow and we seemed to make good time with no wind. We eventually came up onto Holter Lake, so we knew the dam was not far off. We stayed close to the western shore and reached the dam as the sun was getting low in the sky.

Within a few days we were all thoroughly sunburned, especially our faces. My lips were sore most of the time and I tried to not to chew or pick at them, which only made them hurt worse. My nose peeled so many layers, I began to wonder if it would permanently scar.

Our one main objective was to reach Great Falls by the sixth day and on Day 5 it seemed we were less than thirty miles away. Ron Shade, a fellow worker at Yellowstone, had graciously agreed to drive up to meet us at Great Falls to help us around the five dams in the town. We all had agreed we could make it in six days, meeting him somewhere before the first dam. It looked like we had planned well.

The Great Falls of the Missouri was a spectacular sight for Lewis and Clark and their men as they came upon them. They could hear the unmistakable sound of the water and the white mist rising over the prairie from miles away. Today the falls compete with five dams that have somewhat tamed them and the town of Great Falls now surrounds the river on both sides.

It took the Corps of Discovery a month in the summer of 1805 to portage over twenty miles around the falls. Their work was grueling and torturous, carrying gear and pulling canoes up hill through ground covered with prickly pear cactus. Our portage would be a whole lot easier with Ron's red Chevy Blazer carrying us around in no time at all.

Since we were so close we decided to just kick back and enjoy the afternoon. The river was flowing well enough to just float for awhile. We played word games as we sat on our soft gear, lounging in the sun. We tried some fishing now and then and each of us dozed off once or twice over the next few hours.

The dramatic hills and mountains had changed to somewhat flat prairie with brush and short trees here and there along the river banks. The river was quite narrow now and awfully shallow with sandbars appearing suddenly, forcing us to steer the boats now and then to avoid bottoming out and going aground.

The sun was going down and there was only an hour of light left. A three quarter moon would be coming up soon, which would provide enough light. It was a gorgeous night and once the sun had dropped behind the horizon and the moon was up, we started paddling again. It was peaceful and provided such a feeling of calm as we paddled by the moonlight. It seemed even quieter than during the day, if that was even possible. We enjoyed the scene for about an hour but in the shadows the sandbars were almost impossible to see until we ran up on them.

We decided to find a campsite and relax. Steve and Tim wanted to sleep under the stars. I had felt enough bugs around my ears to convince me to put up our tent. We could hear beavers somewhere in the dark, smacking their flat tails in the water, protesting our presence.

At some point after midnight, the wind picked up and blew hard, sounding like a roaring freight train. Our tent shook and flapped so loudly we were sure it would be flattened or ripped in two at any moment. We spent the night waking up to the noise of the tent and the wind, wondering when it would subside. Amazingly, by morning everything was still and calm.

The next day was our big rendezvous with Ron so we got on the river early. We paddled and played more word games all morning, reaching the little town of Ulm around noon.

The approach of a town is quite different from a river then on a road. There are no signs to announce your arrival. We noticed the first sign is almost always the town's water tower peaking up over the horizon, sometimes a mile or so before the rest of the town appears. While main street gives you the view of town we all are familiar with and expect to see, the river enters usually from behind, often intruding on backyards or even the town dump, creating a very different view and perspective. As quickly as they appear, another bend in the river and the town is gone and we're all alone again with our river.

At one turn in the river, the road came close by with a sign that read, "Great Falls- II miles." We decided to paddle hard, hoping to do those miles in two hours or so. We did have a slow current to work with and we seemed to make good progress the first hour. The river seemed to turn into a snake with one switchback after another. Many times we would paddle east for less than one hundred yards then turn and paddle due west the same distance, only to turn east yet again. At one point we stood up in the boats to see over the bank, only to see the river just fifty feet away, heading in the opposite direction. We even considered carrying the boats in a straight line overland rather than staying on the river! After well over two hours and no sign of Great Falls, we were becoming tired and frustrated. As we paddled through yet another switchback, we came upon a fishing boat.

It was just the size of a typical rowboat, with an outboard motor hanging on the back. There was one lone fisherman casting his line, wearing a large straw hat.

"Howdy!" I said as we paddled up to him, but not too close to interfere with his lines. "How far is it to Great Falls?"

He was a muscular guy in a dark blue tee shirt and jeans. His deep tan suggested he'd spent a lot of time on the river. "Well, you gentlemen have about five or six more miles till you get to town."

We all moaned at the prospect of paddling six more miles.

"Oh man, how can that be? We saw a sign on the road hours ago that said Great Falls was only eleven miles away!"

"Yup, I'm sure you did. That's by road miles. You gentlemen are on river miles. Those eleven miles by road are prob'ly about 45 river miles! Didn't ya notice all those switchbacks?"

"Yeah, we noticed them all right," John said as he leaned back, stretching his back and arms.

"We're meeting someone in town and we thought we'd be there by now."

"Well, if you'd like, I can give you gentlemen a tow. I was planning on head'n in anyway."

There was no hesitation from anyone. "Sure!" we all said together.

Our new friend had enough rope to tie both canoes to the back of his boat, giving enough clearance for the engine churning up the water. As the motorboat started forward, the rope slowly tightened and we felt the tug as we started moving. He gave it enough throttle till we felt we were going as fast as we could, the water rushing by, the front of our boats cutting through the water. It was a strange sensation moving so fast after almost a week of slow paddling. The engine noise was loud enough that it was difficult to talk. We grinned at each other and laughed as we went through the switchbacks effortlessly, our escort looking back now and then to see if we were still there.

LIFE'S SWITCHBACKS

As I think back to what that fisherman had said that day, it's funny how we can look at life the same way. Our roads are built to be nice and smooth, as straight as possible, simply to get us from where we are to where we want to be. Unless there is a terrible mishap, traveling a road like that is simple and uneventful and you get to your destination as quickly as possible. A four lane super highway is probably the best example of that.

But river miles are very different. A river route takes the long way around, following contours of the land, the flow taking you in one direction one minute, then the opposite direction a moment later.

Isn't life like that? Don't we all want our journey through life to be nice and smooth, simple and uneventful, except for the events we prefer and enjoy? River miles are slow and every bend in the river offers another opportunity to experience life in all forms—joy and sorrow, triumph and failure, fulfillment and discouragement. If our eyes are set on the final destination, every change in direction will seem like lost time, a waste of effort, creating a sense of frustration, not realizing there is a purpose in each bend and change of direction.

Peter tells us in 1 Peter 4:12 that we should not be bewildered or surprised when we go through the fiery trials we suffer as though something strange were happening to us. Though most of us will not suffer from the persecution Peter and Paul wrote of in their letters, we all live in a fallen world and will suffer in many ways. Peter didn't say "if" we go through trials but "when." Even as His children, we will suffer, but He promises to always be with us.

God is not the outfitter that provides the canoe for the journey. Sometimes we forget that He created us…and created the river too, with every bend and every twist! When you paddle through deep, still waters through a wide peaceful valley, He is there with you. When you are carried through swift rocky rapids with thundering waves crashing all around you, He is there with you. When you're paddling due east but know you're supposed to be heading west, He is still there. And when you're facing a strong headwind pounding your boat and your body and every stroke of the paddle is slow and draining your energy and you seem to be standing still in the water, the Creator of you and the river is always there.

He has given us His assurance that He causes all things to work together for good. Romans 8:28 is a verse that only truly has meaning when you are in a state of helplessness, deep in the valley of suffering.

> And we know that all things work together for good to those who love the LORD, to those who are called according to His purpose.

As much as we might not prefer it, the Bible tells us clearly that we will face trials in our lives that will test our faith, teach us in ways no other means can, help us to be conformed to His Son, and give us opportunity to help and minister to others.

That's the purpose of river miles.

For years I didn't realize the power of Romans 8:28 is that through fellowship with other believers, opening up and sharing our experiences, both good and bad, is how God works all things for good. Others benefit by being encouraged, taught, or even warned. No wonder Paul said we are members of one another.

In our human condition, it would not take us long on a nice smooth highway to forget our dependence on God and each other. It's only on those river miles that we can be reminded He is in control of all things and our dependence is day by day, even moment by moment. Though we have all been tempted to pull our canoe up to shore and climb up the bank onto the road and take the shortcut, that would be out of God's will for us.

For reasons perhaps only He can truly understand, God has chosen to send each of us down a path of river miles, perhaps leaving the super highway for the angels to travel on. Perhaps the most important thing to remember is that the river will get you to your destination but it will take much longer, and the actual journey becomes just as significant as the destination. How blessed is the Christian that recognizes God is with him as he travels those river miles, understanding God has a purpose for every bend in the river and whatever is found there.

Within no time we were spotting houses on the hillsides indicating we had finally reached the outskirts of Great Falls. Amazingly we spotted Ron on the north side of the river, our left, just sitting there watching us. As we were towed closer, he was smiling, shaking his head in a condescending way. I suppose we did look a bit silly being towed in. Thankfully, Ron didn't have a camera to capture the moment.

It was dinner time so we loaded the boats easily on Ron's huge Blazer and found a place to fill up on cheeseburgers. It was quite a distance to the other side of town. I don't know how we would have done it without Ron's help.

We set up camp on the downstream side of Maroni Dam, the last one of five. As we sat around the fire telling Ron about our first six days on the river, we could look down on the river by moonlight. The current was extremely fast and turbulent. We hadn't paddled in water like that yet and there was a sense of anxiety among us. We all agreed we would tie everything down extremely well in the morning.

We had definitely re-entered the 20th century that day. We were towed by a motorboat, cruised around town in a Blazer, and shopped at a grocery store, all in and among the sights and sounds of civilization. Much had changed since Lewis and Clark explored there.

Captain Lewis wrote several pages in his journal about the beauty of the "great falls." He watched a herd of bison that he estimated were over 1,000 in number roaming east of the Sun River, what is now the west side of the town. It was in this area that Lewis was hiking alone, ahead of the main party, and was chased by a grizzly bear…all the way into the river!

Though the grizzly has moved north and the herds of bison have moved south, the landscape is still the same. Even though a busy town has replaced the wilderness, the grand size of the land and the immense sky above seemed to swallow it up and we could sense we were still in the frontier.

The morning found us securing our boats for the fast water ahead of us. As soon as we launched we enjoyed a speed we hadn't achieved so far on the trip. The river was still quite wide and shallow but a rocky bottom made the swift current churn and choppy waves jumped and crashed around us. The waves were noisy, making it difficult to talk between boats, never mind the front and the back of the boat. Whatever anxiety we had the night before was replaced by sheer excitement.

Tim and John were in the front of the boats, responsible for spotting any rocks or boulders just below the surface. At such a speed, any obstacle would flip us for sure.

Our adrenaline was pumping as the shore seemed to fly by. We yelled and cheered as the waves bounced the canoes around, while we struggled to keep them straight. The excitement lasted for quite a while as we quickly traveled a number of miles. Gradually the waves subsided and the current diminished. We all started to hear the distinct sound of flowing water.

"Whoa, what is that?" Tim and John carefully stood and could see a distinct thin break on the water all the way across the river, just ahead about fifty yards. We each took turns standing up and peering at it, what appeared to be a manmade shelf of rocks and boulders, creating a ledge across the length of the river. As we paddled closer, we could see sections where the water had chosen to flow through, tumbling down from two to four feet in about a short distance of ten feet or less, each narrow channel strewn with rocks.

"What do we do?"

"Can we go through it?"

"We gotta decide fast, guys!"

If there had been time to paddle to shore, the opportunity had passed. The current had picked up, the water choosing one of the four or five chutes through the rocks. Tim and Steve's boat was in the lead so they got to choose which narrow chute to take. I decided we'd follow them. We'd all make it together or we'd all go over together! I hoped they had a better vantage point as they hit the brink of the chute to aim correctly.

John and I were about twenty feet behind their boat when they went over the brink and disappeared. Their yells were washed out by the roar of the water. A moment later our boat went over the top, slid through a series of boulders and out onto flat water, Steve and Tim still laughing and yelling in front of us.

We now had a full view of the manmade waterfall and we realized we had chosen well. Most of the other chutes would have spelled disaster for sure. We would have hung up or gone for an unwanted swim.

In less than ten minutes, we heard the now familiar sound and spotted our next shelf of rocks up ahead. As we paddled closer I let Tim and Steve take the lead again.

"Go ahead, guys! It's all yours!" I shouted. They'd chosen well once. They could do it again. "We're right behind ya!"

We used the same routine, noticing most of the flow of the water was in the center of the river. I made sure we were right behind their boat, now expecting that anxious moment when their boat would disappear out of view for a brief moment.

As Tim and Steve went over the brink I steered for the same exact spot. As we followed their boat over, I immediately saw their canoe had hung up right in the middle of the rocky shelf, the front nose down, at least three or four feet lower than Steve in the back. In a blur, with no steering on my part, our canoe bounced off theirs, slid on by, and was out onto flat water before we knew what happened.

John and I watched helplessly as Steve and Tim sat motionless, the water thundering by them on either side but miraculously never coming in the boat. We could hear them yelling to each other over the roar of the rushing water but couldn't make out what they were saying. They must have agreed on a strategy because at one point they both carefully put one foot on the slippery wet rocks and nudged the canoe free. In one moment, the force of the water thrust the boat forward with its passengers barely holding on. When they came into the flat water, still in one piece, we all cheered and had a good laugh. The Missouri River Rats still hadn't dumped into the river!

There were no more waterfalls to tackle and we settled into paddling for the next few hours as the sun got hotter. Thankfully there were no switchbacks and the current was steady. In late afternoon we came upon an old steel bridge across the river, letting us know we had reached the town of Fort Benton. On the left bank there was a narrow park that followed the river for about a quarter of a mile so we decided to take a break.

It was a quiet, pleasant town. We all got ice cream at a Tastee Freeze by the park and walked around looking at the statues commemorating Lewis and Clark and the Corps of Discovery. Sitting in the cool shade with cold ice cream was a real treat.

At the far end of the little park was an old brick hotel from the 1800s. We walked in just to see the furnishings inside. It was like stepping back in time. Even the huge wooden bar off the lobby reminded me of the old west. There wasn't even a thought about staying there overnight, but after we met the friendly manager on duty, we negotiated and got showers for two dollars each. The hot water and soap made us feel like a million bucks so we figured it was a good deal. The historical building was the Grand Union Hotel.

Shadows were stretching across the river when we got back to our boats. We had hidden them in an obscure place, in bushes where we hoped no one would see them. We paddled away, all agreeing Fort Benton was a nice place with nice people. As soon as we were away from town we found a place to camp. The bugs were exceptionally annoying so both tents went up in a hurry. Even the smoke from our fire didn't seem to deter them.

By the light of the fire we studied our maps and could tell we had passed our last town for quite a while. We would now be entering an area about 300 miles long with no civilization at all, just one highway that would cross the road at about the 150 mile mark. Our first week on the river had gone well. The weather had been perfect and we were all still healthy and in one piece. We had gotten around the Great Falls and the dams and had paddled about 300 miles. We still had about 2,200 miles more to go but we were enjoying the journey and we knew there were more adventures ahead.

Fatherhood Through God's Eyes

The Boys' First Day

August 19, 2002

"Hey, Dad, could you pass me a drink?" Joshua asked as he leaned back and reached across our gear. I passed a plastic bottle of juice to him. He wouldn't understand, but being out here with a cooler full of ice cold drinks and lots of food was quite a luxury.

"How far to the white cliffs?" he asked.

"They should start showing up in just a few miles according to the map."

I was just as anxious as Josh to see the beautiful white sandstone rocks and cliffs, with all their various shapes and forms. The gently sloping hills were green with prairie grass in some areas and dry and parched in others, where the grass had died off due to lack of rain.

The hills produced coulees and ravines that led up into the countryside, beckoning us to pull over and go exploring. I had promised the boys we would do some hiking and climbing so it wasn't long before they wanted to stop.

Up ahead, Dustin had pulled up on shore, his camera fixed on a few birds that were rummaging near the water's edge. It was a flat piece of land covered in smooth round rocks the size of baseballs. With their long spindly legs, the birds, two sandpipers, kept their distance from him. I quietly slid our boat up beside his and we watched them for a few minutes till Dustin was satisfied he'd gotten his shot.

"Let's go explore up there," Josh suggested, pointing toward a small ravine that narrowed as it led away from the river.

"What do you think, Dustin?" I asked.

"Yeah, I vote we go for it," Dustin replied, placing his camera back in its case. "Let's see if we can find anything."

This section of the river had many old homesteads still standing where the hearty souls of a century ago attempted to scratch out a life in this harsh land. I was hoping we would discover some while we were exploring.

We slid the boats carefully over the smooth rocks till we were sure they were secure.

"Just watch where you're walking and keep an eye out for snakes," I reminded them.

We had been warned numerous times that rattlesnakes were very plentiful along the river and sightings were quite common. I knew this all too well, thinking back to my first encounter with a rattlesnake on Ft. Peck Lake.

As we started down the ravine the wispy, foot high grass got even thicker. There was an open plateau ahead that we decided on as our destination. The walls of our little canyon grew steeper and narrowed as we walked. The sun seemed stronger on land then on the river, with no breeze. The scent of sage brush filled the heavy hot air.

"Oh, Dad, look at your legs!" Dustin shrieked. I glanced down at my legs with rattlesnakes on my mind, but instead saw a strange sight. There had to be no less than fifty tiny bugs of some sort attached to my legs, mostly on my calves, producing tiny spots of blood. I started swiping my legs, my attackers taking flight, the blood smearing on my skin.

"Oh man, they're on me, too!" Josh shouted as he started hopping around.

"Let's get out of here!" I yelled, the boys already running back through the ravine. "Run away, run away!" I laughed as we dashed to the boats.

Once back in the boats we realized the punctures from the bug bites were almost invisible, leaving hardly a mark and no pain at all. The many ravines didn't look as inviting after that!

Within a few miles the first of the white cliffs became visible up ahead, the smooth white rock shining in the bright sun against the green hills. As we paddled closer, the rock face grew larger. The rock wall was about thirty feet high, disappearing into the water.

"Let's go up closer, Dad. I wanna touch it."

I steered the boat over and we ran our hands along the rock. Somehow on the smooth surface swallows had built their clay nests in clusters.

For the next few hours, giant white ledges emerged from under the hills on both sides of the river, only to disappear back under the treeless knolls. When we passed deposits of driftwood, we'd pull up and load some into the boats to be sure we had plenty of wood for a fire.

At one point while we were collecting some nice pieces, two canoes went by. We waved to our fellow paddlers and they waved back. The river was already more crowded than in '79.

At about our fourteenth mile from where we launched we came upon LaBarge Rock, a huge white and grey rock that stood high above the river on the south side. It was the first specific landmark I remembered. The boys were impressed with its height and pleaded to stop and see if we could climb it.

Eagle Creek was directly across from the immense rock, now with a row of campsites, with water and pit toilets. There were a few campers at most of the sites, tents already going up and a few fires burning. We decided we'd try to climb LaBarge Rock, and then find a campsite on the opposite side of the river.

As with all the other rocks and cliffs, this one grew as we approached. The steep rock wall towered over us as we pulled ashore. In front of the sheer wall, there a steep pile of broken rock stacked up at least thirty feet. From there the wall rose a few hundred feet straight up. There was a grassy ravine that seemed to run behind the rock fortress so we headed that way. We almost immediately found a trail that seemed to end at the side of the wall.

"It keeps going inside!" Dustin exclaimed. "Come on!"

I came around a few bushes and could see there was a large opening where the rock had eroded, creating a smooth and very steep opening to climb upward. Joshua and Dustin led the way, with me taking up the rear. Thankfully, there were many places to put hands and feet and climbing was relatively easy. I had to be careful my camera around my shoulder didn't slide off and hit the wall as I climbed.

After climbing about ten feet, the opening narrowed to only three feet. As we each climbed through our path widened suddenly, taking on the shape of a large bowl about thirty feet around and even steeper. I chose my foot and handholds carefully. The boys were already on top when I finally could walk out onto the top of the cliff and take in the incredible view of the river.

"Was that worth the climb, or what?" Josh asked smiling.

"It is awesome," I said, trying to catch my breath from the climb.

The view was spectacular from this height. Far below us on the opposite bank, trees lined the river along with a row of campsites. Beyond those cottonwoods a field a few hundred yards deep sloped up to another outcropping of white cliffs running parallel with the river. Beyond were miles of vast prairie and in the distance the faint image of mountains far off.

Behind us, huge mounds of strange brown volcanic rock rose even higher so the boys half walked, half climbed to the top. As they climbed, I took photos in every direction. I noticed some movement not far from the boys and discovered a large mule deer buck in a thicket. I motioned to the boys but they never noticed. It just didn't seem right to yell to them in the tranquil, silent surroundings.

I took my cell phone from my camera bag and turned it on, hoping I could pick up a signal, realizing how unlikely that would be out here, literally in the middle of nowhere. The tiny LCD screen indicated it was searching but it finally gave up, producing a busy signal type sound. The boys were about fifty feet higher than me so I climbed up to them, the soft but jagged rock crumbling under my feet. Unfortunately, the phone still wouldn't pick up a signal

I hoped Karen, Emma and Dad had made it back to Great Falls safe and sound. In a way, I was glad the phone didn't work. The boys and I were separated from the rest of the world and it felt good. But how I wanted to know they were fine and let Karen know the boys were safe and having a ball.

As I realized we were without a phone, I gazed up river. Though over a hundred miles apart, our family would be sleeping beside the Missouri River, whether in a hotel room in Great Falls or a tent on the riverbank. Instead of modern technology, the river was our link to one another. Lewis and Clark didn't have the benefit of a cell phone and that had not changed in all these years. Neither would we.

The climb back down the smooth rock was slower and more difficult, at least for me. The boys were more like mountain goats climbing around me almost without effort. I was indeed humbled but it was great to see them loving the river I had spoken of so often through the years. We finally made it down to the ground and back to the boats.

"We're going to have to paddle hard to go straight across," I said, watching the strong current that separated us from the other side of the river. "Dust, make sure you keep your nose pointed a bit up river so you can keep control."

"Right," Dustin replied as he turned the boat in the shallow water.

We paddled hard across the current and made it to the other side while drifting down stream less than forty yards. At the water's edge, the river bottom continued for another twenty or thirty feet, mostly hardened mud, till the ground sloped up to a grassy plateau with a variety of trees.

Among the trees, there were about half a dozen campsites occupied by paddlers who were starting fires and preparing dinner. Canoes of various colors sat parked along the river's edge. The place seemed crowded to me, thinking back to my last time here, not a soul in sight. We walked up and found a nice spot for camp but noticed there wasn't a fire ring so I wasn't sure if we could start a fire or not. Not far from us was a campsite with two elderly gentlemen sitting on collapsible chairs around a fire.

"Hey, guys, I'm gonna go check to see if we have to be a designated site or not. We might not be able to stay here." Josh and I walked over and asked them if they knew.

"If you're staying here at the campground I believe you have to be on a site with a fire ring," the man stoking the fire replied.

The man relaxing in his chair, a pipe in his mouth, chimed in, "You're more than welcome to share our fire with us. There's plenty of room!"

There indeed was plenty of space between sites and our small three-man tent would fit anywhere so I was considering it.

"Are you having a good time on the river?" he asked Joshua

"Yeah," was Josh's response without offering any more information, the typical response from an eleven-year-old.

"Have you guys been on the river before?" he questioned further.

"This is our first time together. I came through here in 1979 on my way to St. Louis," I answered.

"Is that so? All the way to St. Louis! How long did that take?

As I started talking about the trip and asking what brought them to the river, I realized I would spend the evening around the fire talking with them and not with my boys. With that in mind, I decided we'd find an open site about fifty yards away, and make camp there.

As we walked back to the boats Joshua asked, "Why didn't you want to stay here with those guys?"

"Well, kiddo, I wanted this trip to be just the three of us. I was afraid I'd spend the night telling them about my trip"

"That's okay. That would've been cool."

After my telling tales of the river trip all these years, he was now interested in hearing about it? Perhaps the river was working on him!

The guys had been nice enough, too. They were friends from New Jersey who had never been west of the Mississippi. They had both read Stephen Ambrose's book, Undaunted Courage, about the Lewis and Clark Expedition, and were inspired to come and see it for themselves. They had spoken with rangers that mentioned the book had made an impact in the number of paddlers heading down the river in recent years.

We unloaded the canoes and carried our gear over the hard mud to the trees. Our tent would fit perfectly under a tree not far from the metal fire ring. Our self-standing tent went together quickly and we piled the drift wood we had collected next to the ring.

"Turn the tent door towards the river, guys. I want to see that view when we wake up in the morning." The view across the river was LaBarge Rock in all its splendor, the bright white and grey rock now softened shades in the light of the setting sun.

The boys weren't ready to settle down for the night so we decided to follow the trail behind our campsite. We grabbed two bottles of water and headed across an open field of brush, sage, and prickly pear cactus. After a few hundred yards, the trail headed into a narrow valley. We could see high sandstone walls ahead. Shadows were forming down on the dirt trail while the light glowed on the rock walls above and ahead of us.

Without any warning, a very large eight-point mule deer buck came running around a bend in the trail, directly at us. We were as startled as he was as he froze in mid stride, then bounded up over the small bank and noisily ran through brush and tall grass to evade us.

A moment later, a group of eight hikers came walking through, heading back to the river.

"Hi there," a young teenaged girl said as she strode by. The group consisted of a few teens and adults, most giving us a greeting or at least a pleasant smile.

"Where does this trail go?" I asked a young man with a bandana on his head and an oversized walking stick.

"It heads through some neat rocks and comes back around," he said, waving his arm in a circle. He looked like a modern day Moses, walking with his wooden staff.

"No wonder that buck was running so fast," Dustin commented after they had passed and were out of sight.

"Man, he was huge!" Josh said softly, yet excitedly, obviously hoping there were others in the area.

We abruptly came upon a wall of sandstone about a hundred feet tall. The trail followed a narrow corridor right through the rock, with no more then a width of five feet.

It was like walking through a rock maze, the narrow passageway turning to the left, then bending back to the right, the smooth rock walls almost straight up and down.

At times the canyon floor was flat and easy walking, at other times steep, with piles of rocks we needed to climb over. We were slowly making our way around to the left. I expected we were making a wide circle that would bring us back to the beginning of the trail.

Unbelievably, the tall rock walls closed in to where my shoulders were almost rubbing both sides. Very little sunlight came into this narrow passage so darkness engulfed us as we continued on. When I looked straight up and out of our rocky labyrinth, the sky still had some light, but dusk was approaching. I was beginning to wonder how far we still had to go and also starting to regret not bringing a flashlight with us.

The walls finally started opening up, letting more light in. Shrubs and small trees were up ahead as we walked out into an area surrounded by steep slopes covered with sage and cactus.

"Where's the trail?" Joshua asked, looking for a route through the knolls.

There was no sign of any trail so we decided to climb up to the top of one of the larger hills to try and get our bearings. We were careful to avoid the low lying cactus as we made our way up.

"Whoa, look at that!" Dustin exclaimed, pointing across from me.

It was a large porcupine lumbering up the side of the neighboring hill, the biggest porcupine I had ever seen. Dustin pulled out his camera and snapped a few shots of it. It didn't seem to mind our presence. In fact it simply ignored us as it rummaged around for food. We left it alone and it left us alone.

When we reached the top the view was incredible. In every direction the horizon was just endless hills and knolls, now shades of gray. The huge sky was deep blue in the east, while the western sky was bright orange, the sun hanging just above the horizon. The scene appeared to be a painting with endless layers of land and sky. As breathtaking as it was, there was no sign of the river. It was down in one of the endless valleys below us, but out of our sight. And speaking of sight, the sun was about to disappear, bringing on dusk.

"Guys, we don't have much light left," I said. "I knew I should have brought a flashlight. I thought of it, but I decided not to bother."

"What happened to the trail heading around and back to the river like the guy said?" Dustin asked.

"Good question. I don't see how we could have lost the trail in that narrow rock canyon."

"So now what do we do?" Josh asked.

I looked around us, trying to get my bearings. "We were walking in a wide counter-clockwise pattern, so the river should be down there somewhere," I said, pointing ahead of me.

Dustin was studying the land, glancing at the setting sun, then back across the barren landscape. "Dad, which way were we headed on the river?" he asked.

"Due west."

"That would mean we headed straight north up the trail and made a wide circle. Right?" he asked, still looking around, figuring things out. "Wouldn't that put the river south of us, in that direction," he said, pointing over my shoulder.

I thought through what Dustin had said and he was right. "That makes sense. We know which way west is thanks to the sun. You're right." I looked in the southern direction and saw only steep hills, which we hoped led down to the river.

The sun was sinking even faster now.

"Guys, we have to decide what we're going to do here. We have a few options. One is to go cross country due south and hope we find the river…and not too far from our campsite. If we're wrong and don't find the river or our campsite we're looking at spending the night out here."

"I'm not spending all night out here," Joshua stated in no uncertain terms.

"Well, once it's dark we're not going to be able to do much traveling.

"What's our other option?" he asked.

"We can take the trail back the way we came. We know where it leads, but it will definitely be dark before we get back."

"It was already getting dark in some of the narrower sections on our way through," Dustin commented.

"Yeah, but we'll have about a half moon in a little while. That will provide some light."

Going cross country over unknown terrain with the sun almost gone seemed like quite a risk. The temperature was dropping and the boys and I were in shorts and t-shirts. It would be a long chilly night without a fire. I had done a few of those in the army but I wasn't featuring pulling an all-nighter tonight with the boys.

"We'll go take a look at how steep it is heading south toward the river," Dustin suggested.

"Okay, but be careful."

Dustin and Joshua headed down the steep slope to the south, only to return within minutes. They reported it was extremely steep and there was still no sign of the river.

"Guys, I think our best bet is to head back the way we came. We know what to expect and though it might get difficult in the dark, we won't get lost in that narrow canyon."

"Man, that's a long way back," Josh commented. It really wasn't a complaint but it was a true statement.

With that as our cue, we all took a swig from Joshua's canteen and started making our way down the slope, back toward our trail that would take us home. The boys were almost running so I told them to slow down. A twisted ankle out here would not be a good thing at all.

We briskly but carefully climbed through in between the rock walls. It was much darker but the light color of the rock made it possible to still see where we were stepping.

Though it was cooler now, we were all sweating, with no need for a sweater or jacket. We took only one short break to catch our breath and have a drink. The familiar landmarks went by quickly. Each one encouraged us as there was comfort in more familiar surroundings, even though it was getting more difficult to see. We made great progress and before we knew it, we were out of the canyon, crossing the open field leading to the tree-lined river and our camp.

"We made it," Josh declared, tired and out of breath.

"Just barely," I chided, as I pulled my sweaty t-shirt over my head. "I need to go for a swim and cool down. Who's up for an evening dip?"

"Now?" Josh asked me.

"Sure! It'll feel great!"

"The water's freezing!" said Dustin. "I'm not going in there. Especially at night."

"Come on, guys! You're only out here for three days. You gotta do it all."

There was no convincing Dustin. He stayed and built a fire while Josh and I changed into our bathing suits and water shoes and walked down to the river's edge by our canoes.

In the moonlight, the current seemed even faster than it appeared during the day. We stepped into ankle deep water and both let out a gasp. The water was freezing and I have to admit I had second thoughts about getting totally into that river.

"Oh man, this is cold!" Joshua shuttered.

We slowly walked in further till the water was up to my thighs, even higher on Josh. The bottom was covered with slippery round rocks, the current almost knocking us over as we tried securing our footing.

"Okay," I said, out of breath from the cold. "On three, we go under together."

"You sure?" Josh asked, holding his arms up above the water. "You better do it if I do!"

"I will. I will," I promised. "Ready? On three. One, two, three!"

We both took a deep breath and plunged under the surface. The cold seemed to strike every inch of my body at once. I lunged forward into the water, my feet sliding over the rocks on the bottom. I tried grabbing on with my hands to the rocks, so the current wouldn't drift me downstream. After what I'm sure was just a few chilly seconds, I planted my feet and stood up, raising myself from the water.

Josh was standing up as well, splashing about, out of breath and gasping from the cold. "I'm freezing!" he yelled, but laughing at the same time.

"Had enough?" I asked, laughing as well, ready to head back to shore.

"Yeah, I've had enough!" We made our way to shore and headed back to our campsite.

The evening air seemed warmer now after the chill of the river and felt wonderfully relaxing. Dustin already had some kindling burning as we dried off and changed into dry clothes.

We had collected a large amount of dry driftwood in both boats throughout the afternoon so we had plenty of wood to burn. The boys piled it high as the flames grew and consumed the wood.

After a few cans of beef stew and bread, the three of us settled down around the fire and talked about how great the day had been. The boys especially enjoyed climbing to the top of LaBarge Rock and of course getting lost on the trail. I was very proud of how well they handled themselves and I told them so.

For me, the climbing was great but paddling down the river through the white cliffs was a thrill after all these years. The first day on the river had been even better than I had imagined.

I put the coffee pot on the fire and heated up some water for hot chocolate. Darkness came quickly but soon a half moon rose over the hills.

"Look, Dad, the mountain looks like a perfect buffalo silhouette," Joshua commented, pointing across the river. Sure enough, just to the left of LaBarge Rock, the horizon was the exact shape of a giant buffalo—the massive head, broad shoulders and tapering back. We wondered if countless campers before us had noticed the same thing. Dustin took a few photos of it.

With stomachs full, and eyelids becoming heavy, the soothing warmth of the fire did us in. After awhile we were all talked out and though I was reluctant for our first day to end, it seemed it was time for bed. I got little protest from Dustin and Joshua. They unzipped our three-man tent and climbed in while I put a few things away and made sure the fire was spent. The glowing coals would undoubtedly burn for hours.

I stood on the river bank, my hands in my pockets, trying to take in the scene before me. Moonlight illuminated the gigantic sandstone rock across the river, the vast starlit sky above. The spot where we had climbed to now seemed even higher. The current of the water reflected light from the half moon as swells created tiny waves and ripples, producing points of light up and down the river.

The cool, clean breeze seemed laden with history as I pictured the men of Lewis and Clark's expedition and the hearty souls that followed them through the years. That old LaBarge Rock had seen it all. That huge chunk of rock was there while every Indian, every trapper and every huge steamboat had come by.

It was standing there while four naïve, know-it-all teenagers paddled through twenty-three years ago. The river had not changed in all those years, yet those four paddlers had indeed. As my sons talked in the tent, I tried to remember who that young man was who now stood in my shoes.

"Okay, Dad! We're all set!" Josh yelled from in the tent

"I'll be right there," I said, still not willing to admit the day was over, still wanting to enjoy the sights and sounds around me, still trying to realize I had finally after so many years gotten back here with my two sons; a dream fulfilled. I was tempted to just pull my sleeping bag out of the tent and sleep under the stars, like we had done so many nights along the river, but I had promised Karen that with all the rattlesnakes in this area we would spend the nights in the tent. With medical attention being days away, way too long for a rattlesnake bite, that seemed wise.

After all, it had been twenty-three years. Now instead of the impulsive, careless nineteen-year-old adventurer, I was the wise, careful forty-two-year-old father. At least that's what I was supposed to be. Yet here on the river, in this place of incredible rugged beauty, you can't help feeling young, impulsive, careless, and so alive. The scene around me made it appear that time had simply stood still, that nothing had changed.

For me, those two boys teasing each other in the tent surely had changed my life. Fatherhood has a way of changing your life perspective, to say the least. These two boys, soon to be young men, had been entrusted by God to me. It had taken me too many years to finally realize the awesome responsibility and privilege that was.

When they were born, all they needed was Mom. She took care of their every need. After awhile they grew into little boys and were great fun to play with and buy all the new boy's toys I couldn't rationalize buying for myself. Things seemed to fall into place rather well.

But there were other responsibilities too. I spent a lot of time getting my career going and teaching at church. Instead of working on relationships, I kept myself busy with the tasks that needed to be done. Of course, for every task finished, there were at least two more that pop up.

It had only been a few years ago that I realized my fatherhood had been very passive. Oh, I was a good, loving father as fathers go, but one day I decided to see what the Holy Scriptures had to say about fatherhood. What I found was astonishing. With all the time and energy I had put into so many pursuits and goals to accomplish in my life, I discovered one of my highest callings was my role as "Dad."

God's Word is full of relationships. After all, relationships are what God is all about. The idea of husband and wife, parent and child, friends, all originated with Him. Our society tries to redefine it all these days, but God's plan is very clear. When I looked to the scriptures to read about fatherhood, there were two things that jumped out at me, two eternal truths that left me both awestruck and with a knot in the pit of my stomach, brought on by sheer humility.

When someone asked Jesus to show us how to pray, Jesus responded in a way that must have astounded all the Jews around Him. The Jews understood the perfect holiness of Jehovah and the sinfulness of man. They knew God's omnipotence and His omniscience. They were well aware of the barrier that separated them from their God. Even the High Priest could only get so close.

Yet Jesus tears down that barrier by saying,

> In this manner, therefore, pray: Our Father in heaven…
> Matthew 6:9

Jesus introduced an amazing concept. We could have a personal relationship with the Father. At that time the world was just beginning to understand that relationship would come through His Son. If that's not enough to overwhelm our human mind, consider what Paul wrote.

> For you have not received a spirit of bondage again to fear, but you received the Spirit of adoption by whom we cry out, "Abba Father." The Spirit Himself bears witness with our spirit that we are children of God.
> Romans 8:15,16

We are all familiar with this passage, aren't we? Most of us know that "abba" is an Aramaic term of endearment, more like "Daddy" than "Father." I had read that passage many times, but on that particular day it struck me in a new way. The creator of all things, the LORD of LORDS, the King of kings, the God of the Bible with a divine nature and essence we can only begin to imagine, chooses to be known by us as "Daddy." Of all the titles He could choose!

Those of us who are dads know how special that word is. The boys are older now and "Dad" is the term they now use, though a "Daddy" does slip out now and then, especially when they're begging and pleading to get their way. But Emma at three years old, she only knows me as "daddy." When she climbs into my lap and wraps her little arms around my neck, and says, "I love you, Daddy," the world is perfect at that moment for both of us. Perhaps that's what God has in mind for His children. With all the deep theology within the pages of scripture that we must never neglect, what better picture of a loving heavenly Father with His loving children than a child on the lap of her daddy?

The image left me feeling content and loved as His chosen adopted child. God has chosen to show Himself to us as "Father."

How important is fatherhood to God, that He would reveal Himself in that way? The scriptures reveal just how important fatherhood is to Him…and that was somewhat intimidating when I realized He has called me to be a father here on earth, to imitate Him…

In Deuteronomy 4:9, Moses writes the fathers of Israel:

> Only take heed to yourself, and diligently keep yourself, lest you forget the things your eyes have seen, and lest they depart from your heart all the days of your life. And teach them to your children and grandchildren.

Moses was not simply warning these men not to forget the amazing miracles they had seen God perform before their very eyes, but even more importantly, not to let their hearts grow cold toward God. What struck me was God's concern not simply for these men, but for their future generations.

I thought about how future generations of young men, my grandsons and beyond, would have their lives impacted by how I lived my life and what example I was to my sons now. That was quite humbling and terrifying.

> ...that you may fear the LORD your God, to keep all His statutes and His commands, which I command you, you and your son and your grandson, all the days of your life...
> Deuteronomy 6:2

My actions now as a father have such far reaching effects. That is why God mentions obedience affecting at least three generations, if not more.

> And these words, which I command you today, shall be in your heart. You shall teach them diligently to your children...
> Deuteronomy 6:6, 7

The idea is not simply knowing and obeying God, but having a deeper relationship at a heart level. Only then can we truly teach our sons about God. I struggled with the word, "diligent." I had to admit to myself I had not been diligent. At least not in the way I had been diligent about the many other roles in my life.

There's a reason we are warned to be diligent. The consequences of ignoring that warning can be devastating.

> So the people served the LORD all the days of Joshua and all the days of the elders who outlived Joshua, who had seen all the great works of the LORD which He had done for Israel.
> Judges 2:7

Scripture tells us that Joshua and his contemporaries, who had seen the amazing miracles of God, served God well. But in vs. 10 we find they all died off.

> When all that generation had been gathered to their fathers, another generation arose after them who did not know the LORD nor the work which He had done for Israel.
> Judges 2:10

I marveled at how this new generation did not know of God and His mighty works for Israel. Were those men so busy serving God in other ways that they ignored what Moses had written in Deuteronomy? The consequences proved to be grave.

> Then the children of Israel did evil in the sight of the LORD, and served the Baals, and they forsook the LORD God of their fathers, who had brought them out of the land of Egypt, and followed other gods from among the gods of the people who were all around them, and they bowed down to them; and they provoked the LORD to anger.
> Judges 2:11, 12

I shudder when I think of all the false gods that could capture my sons' hearts if I should neglect my responsibility of telling them about the one true God of the Bible.

> If you then, being evil, know how to give good gifts to your children, how much more will your Father who is in heaven give good gifts to those who ask Him!
> Matthew 7:11

Here Jesus compares earthly fathers to our heavenly Father. Earthly dads generally want to give good gifts to their kids, and I am no exception. Good gifts come in many forms: a home to live in, good food, a good education, vacations as awesome as this canoe trip, etc. We earthly dads spend so much time on these gifts that we can easily miss the best gift we can give our children. That is a strong spiritual heritage produced by a dad living out his Christian faith. That heritage will never be built by passive fatherhood!

> But seek first the kingdom of God and His righteousness, and all these things shall be added to you.
> Matthew 6:33

Do our sons see us seeking God's kingdom and His righteousness or all the other things of this world?

I know I've been speaking of fathers and sons, mostly due to my life experience with Emma being only three years old, but also because many verses are directed to fathers and sons. I believe the reason for that is God has called men to be the spiritual leaders of the family. That responsibility rests on them. The principles are just as valid with both parents and both boys and girls.

It has also been my experience that a man will not be very effective at leading his family in spiritual leadership without the encouragement and support of a loving wife and the fellowship of other Christian brothers.

The boys had finally settled down in the tent. I took one more look all around me at the river, Labarge Rock, the surrounding hills, the moonlit sky. "Thanks, LORD. It was an awesome day," I said out loud, my voice trailing off into the cool gentle breeze.

Reluctantly I unzipped the tent door and climbed in. We had no padding on the ground, but in no time the three of us were fast asleep.

THE WILD,
WONDERFUL RIVER

DAY 8 THROUGH DAY 22

AUGUST 6 - 20, 1979

We had a few really productive days, paddling up to fifty miles. They were also some of the hottest. The mornings would start warm and just get hotter as the day wore on.

Though we all had peeled and tanned a number of times, our skin seemed to suffer new burns again. There wasn't a cloud in the sky and it seemed all the intensity of the sun was on us. The cold water was a wonderful relief whether you splashed yourself or each other or simply jumped in.

The landscape was low barren hills with few details. In fact, the scenery changed very little mile after mile and could almost be described as monotonous.

What the scenery lacked the wildlife made up for, at least as far as birds. We watched great blue heron fishing along the shore. Most would stay motionless as we paddled by, while others would take to flight, with wingspans of easily four feet. Dozens of pelicans were amusing to watch in flight and in the water. They seemed to be the only fishermen catching any fish because we weren't. Various ducks, Canadian geese, doves, and an occasional red-tailed hawk spent time with us.

If there was any section of the Missouri River that hadn't changed since the Corps of Discovery explored it in 1805, it was here. The rolling hills on both sides of us were shades of golden brown and tan, depending on the low vegetation, or lush shades of green in certain spots, especially closer to the riverbanks. As we floated down the river, every few miles these colors would abruptly be contrasted by huge walls of bright white and grey rock walls jutting out from underneath the hills, often reaching right up to the waters edge, rising sometimes hundreds of feet straight up. Juniper and Douglas fir trees were sprinkled here and there, especially around the rocks. The occasional stand of cottonwood and juniper trees was like an oasis in an otherwise treeless environment of rock, grass, and river

Captain Lewis had described this area as, "scenes of visionary enchantment, and a most romantic appearance," and he had not exaggerated. As we paddled on the smooth water, the scene around us was silent and tranquil. The erosion of sandstone and igneous rock formed cliffs and steep ledges that one could imagine were statues or castles or a variety of manmade objects.

We paddled fifteen miles down river from Coal Banks Landing and approached a huge white and grey rock wall on our right that must have stood hundreds of feet high above the river, with a sheer drop to the water below. It was named LaBarge Rock after a steamboat captain well known in his day. On our left was Eagle Creek, a small stream emptying into and becoming part of the Missouri. Lewis and Clark had named the stream Stone Wall Creek, no doubt due to the giant sandstone rock wall on the opposite bank. I don't know when or why the name was changed to Eagle Creek, but it was at the mouth of this little creek that Lewis and Clark and their men camped for the night on May 31, 1805.

The sun beat down on us without mercy. Not getting wet meant you felt like you were baking. In fact, paddling past the tall white walls of rock with the extreme heat did somewhat resemble being in a giant oven. The silent stillness of the place made it feel even hotter. At one point I thought I heard ringing in my ears in all that silence and heat.

Six miles further downstream, the river made a sharp turn to the left, revealing another landmark named Citadel Rock. At the edge of the river, looking very much like a dark brown church building with its tall steeple stretching high into the sky, this immense volcanic rock stood proudly, seemingly watching over the river. As we paddled by, it seemed to take on the shape of a castle or a guard house, a place you might pay a toll to continue on.

As soon as Citadel Rock was out of sight, the next natural feature to catch our eye was Hole in the Wall, high above the river, still about a mile ahead. The mountain on our right was about four hundred feet high, with a narrow light colored rock wall jutting out of it, perpendicular to the river. Close to the top, almost directly above the water's edge, there was a hole in the wall, visible even from where we were. We all guessed how big the hole might be if you could walk, then climb up to it. The map didn't say and we weren't about to go find out.

After traveling over thirty miles, we decided we'd camp at the thirty-five-mile mark, a place called Slaughter River. The curious name for this spot is explained in the Lewis and Clark journals. The explorers reached this spot and found a heap of bison carcasses being devoured by a group of grizzly bears and scavenger birds. The party assumed the bison had broken through the spring ice, drowned, and eventually were deposited here. I suppose to these men the scene appeared like a slaughter, and the name stuck to this day.

The map stated "Slaughter River Campground," but this campground wasn't the type with hot showers and rows of RVs, offering just two old wooden lean-tos with space for about four people each. There were about a dozen cottonwoods so we made our camp right under them. Behind our tents the terrain was flat for a few hundred yards and was covered with what had to be thousands of wild sunflowers. The field of green and orange was quite a sight and didn't seem to fit out here. Hills rose behind the field of sunflowers, creating a horizon with shades of blues and grays as the setting sun cast shadows on them. There wasn't a soul around.

Across the river, the other bank was a sheer sandstone wall about 75 feet tall and running along the river for perhaps a quarter of a mile. With the sun going down, the temperature quickly became cool and comfortable. A slight breeze blew, rustling the leaves above our heads, a sound I have always found pleasant and relaxing.

Later, in the quiet of the night, we guessed how far away the closest human beings might be. It seemed like we were alone in the world. Of course this place was very busy on May 29, 1805, when over forty rugged men of the Lewis and Clark Expedition camped on this very spot. Though the world was very different then, Slaughter River had changed little.

We had passed many hills and bluffs that towered over the river, but one of them had been the high hill that Captain Lewis had climbed and looking around from the summit, beheld the Rocky Mountains for the first time. Since we were headed downstream instead of up, we were now leaving the mountains behind, leaving the mountain river we had enjoyed for the last ten days. Soon we would be entering the prairies of the Midwest and hundreds of miles of lakes.

We could almost judge what time it was by where the sun was, so our one watch we had got put away in our food bag. When we thought about it, all that mattered was whether it was light or dark. Who cared what time it was? In fact, we were starting to forget what day of the week it was since that really didn't matter out here either. Time seemed to be measured more by miles than minutes or hours, or even days. Another way of telling time was simply noticing the faint orange, pink, or purple that would start shading the early evening sky. Almost every night was an evening of color before darkness finally settled in and the stars appeared.

One afternoon we came upon a farmer and his wife on the water's edge working on their irrigation pump. We started talking with them and before long they were insisting we come have lunch with them. Their names were Terry and Sandy. We pulled the boats up on the bank and walked through a large vegetable garden and across a field to their house.

The house was a large wooden two story ranch, stark white with a simple wrap around porch. The screen door screeched as we entered. Though there was no air conditioning, it felt very pleasant to be out of the sun. We made ourselves comfortable while Sandy got cold drinks for everyone. The place was a typical farm house with no fancy frills but solid wood furniture, family pictures on the walls, a gun cabinet in the corner, and a worn, but sound hardwood floor. It had a warm, inviting feel, much like the people that made it their home.

Sandy cooked up hamburgers, steaks, potatoes, home made apple sauce with cinnamon, and fresh beets. Then came fresh banana bread that was still warm and watermelon for dessert. There was just no end to the food and the generosity of these folks. Terry wanted us to stay the night, but his dad called and needed help rounding up some cows so he had to go and we needed to get back on the river anyway.

We thanked Sandy for taking such good care of us, and walked with Terry back down to the boats. As we passed through the vegetable garden, he insisted we pick some of the ripe green beans, squash and cucumbers. It felt like we were leaving good friends as we got back in the canoes and pushed off. It had been a great time but we needed to get a few more hours of paddling in before we could call it a day.

Within a short time the river widened and from the map we could tell we were entering the very beginning of Fort Peck Lake. It would take a few days to hit the main section of the lake but the river had definitely changed character. We instinctively stayed close to shore. None of us were that comfortable being out in the middle of all that open water.

We camped under some trees at dusk, getting in about thirty miles for the day. As our fire grew in the early evening light, no one noticed there were leaves on the ground, something we hadn't seen before. Without warning, leaves ignited and caught fire quickly, spreading across the ground. Our campsite filled up with flickering light as we all started stomping leaves, trying to smother the flames. For a long twenty or thirty seconds it looked like we would have an uncontrollable brush fire on our hands until Steve grabbed his sleeping bag and used it to stamp most of the fire out. The excitement ended as quickly as it had started. Needless to say, we cleared the leaves that were left around the fire and finished our evening chores.

We had our first rain shower on Day 13. It never dropped below 70 degrees so we decided to just get wet and not bother with rain gear. The ground was so dry that it seemed to absorb every drop of water as soon as it landed. It rained for about twenty minutes or so and it was over.

We awoke one morning to a steady wind blowing across the hills, causing our tents to noisily flap back and forth. I guess we all knew paddling would be hard because we all slept late, no one eager to get out on the water. Even Steve, who was the early riser, didn't budge. When we finally got on the water, we realized it was worse than we thought. The strong wind was heading straight north, slamming us in the face. The water was choppy and it seemed every few strokes of the paddle I would accidentally hit the surface of the water, splashing John. It felt like we were dragging an anchor behind us as we dug into the water with each stroke. Over the next few hours the spray of our paddles on the tiny choppy waves had soaked our arms and legs and more than a few times I had to wipe my face with my shirt.

When our arms and shoulders were starting to wear out and our stomachs were growling, we went ashore. We lounged on the beach for awhile, each of us taking a short walk among the hills and prairies either exploring the landscape or taking care of bathroom activities.

We really had no idea how strong and persistent the wind could be along these lakes.

One day we were only able to paddle three miles before we had to give up for the day. We paddled as hard as we could in the waves, realizing we were hardly moving forward. Gusts would blow so hard the boats would stop even in mid stride. Out in the middle of the river that now looked more like a large lake, we could see the tips of white caps crashing in the wind. It became obvious we needed to stop wasting our energy.

Though we thought we would be stranded for hours, it turned into days. We spent the time reading and writing in our journals, sitting against a large weather smoothed log or taking cat naps on our sleeping bags. The wind was incredibly loud and strong, coming off the lake and over the golden prairie grass on the hills behind us. There was nothing in all this empty space of water and prairie to slow it down. It was almost impossible to hold onto a magazine without the pages ripping out of your hand. As the hours passed it seemed amazing that it could continue for so long.

Though it didn't seem like rain, the sky became overcast and seemed to drain color from the landscape. The sky was gray, the distant shore across the lake seemed a darker gray, the water looked gray with the waves tipped in white and the wind continued to blow.

We set up our tents, not so much to get away from bugs...since none could handle this wind...but just to get out of the wind ourselves! When I napped I wrapped a towel around my head to muffle the endless noise of the wind.

One day while I was collecting firewood from a large tangle of driftwood, I heard a sound I had never heard before but somehow knew exactly what it was. My whole body instinctually froze and I think I even held my breath. Though I couldn't see anything, the rattling sound I heard was extremely close and even as seconds went by, seconds that seemed like minutes, the rattling sound continued.

"Rattlesnake," I whispered, still not seeing a snake, but knowing it was there.

"Guys, rattlesnake," I said just a bit louder, as if the snake would strike if he heard he'd been discovered.

"Huh?" John was the first to look over.

"Rattlesnake!" There really were no other words for me to say as I stood there frozen, with a few pieces of wood under one arm, my other hand still on the branch stuck in the pile. The guys dropped everything and started walking slowly towards me.

"Where?" John asked in an excited whisper.

"I don't know. I just hear it and it sounds like he's not happy we're here," I said.

"Hold on, hold on!" Steve shouted as he ran to the canoe to get his gun, as if I was going to even move a muscle!

Tim and John carefully lifted a few pieces of wood to reveal what looked like an extremely large rattlesnake. He was all curled up with his head up, his tongue quickly darting back and forth, and his tail standing straight up and twitching wildly.

Steve approached with the gun, getting as close as he dared.

"Shoot for the head," Tim whispered.

The shot was perfect and the rattling stopped. Tim reached in and picked it up, the snake's body unraveling to a length of about four feet, about as thick as a baseball bat. The rattle had seven sections on it.

If we couldn't paddle, at least now we could eat! Tim skinned the snake, letting me keep the rattle as a souvenir. None of us had cooked or eaten rattlesnake before, but we decided to simply wrap the cleaned snake in aluminum foil and bury it in the hot coals of the fire. The method worked great for baked potatoes so it was worth a try. After only about twenty minutes in the coals we unwrapped our meal and found the white meat along the back bone was easily removed and yes…it tasted just like chicken!

As we ate we realized that rattlesnake had been only five feet from where we had been sitting all day! We no sooner got done eating, when Steve came back from a quick hunt with a dead prairie dog. It wasn't very large and even smaller when it was cleaned and cooked, but we spent the evening feasting on it. The meat was a bit greasier than chicken, but it still tasted great. Any other time I would have been grossed out sitting around a fire, picking meat off the carcass of a prairie dog, but this night I had no problem!

The small two man tents shook and flapped in the wind for the next three days. Each morning we would awake to gray skies and menacing waves.

Since we were stranded we spent more time hunting for food, mainly snakes and prairie dogs. Those prairie dogs must be smarter than they look. They seem to have their own defense network to alert the group. A squeal from the lookout and they're gone! We did find a huge bull snake though that became our lunch. He measured five feet and had much more meat than the rattler from the day before.

Finally, I awoke one morning to Steve's voice shouting to get up. I realized there was no flapping of the tent or howling of the wind. It was time to get back on the water. It would take us three more days of good weather and good paddling to finally see the dam miles ahead. Once we could make it out in the distance, it still took hours to reach it.

As we approached the dam there were numerous signs warning us to not get close and then eventually a barrier across the water preventing us from doing just that! The dam consisted of concrete arches at water level with a second story of arches; just a massive structure. One could only imagine the strength of a structure that could hold back all the water we had paddled through in the last week!

The marina consisted of slips and docks with a few rows of smaller motorboats tied up. Being a weekday, it was pretty quiet. There was a small restaurant/ bar that even though the sign on the door said, "OPEN," was closed. Thankfully there was a store and it was in fact open! We tied our canoes to the dock beside a shiny new white and blue boat with an immense outboard motor. Our canoes did appear somewhat out of place. There weren't any other canoes around, though we weren't surprised.

We met a nice elderly gentleman tinkering with his engine who asked us what we were up to. He was actually very helpful and gave us the telephone number of the administration building of the Army Corps of Engineers, the guys in charge of the dam. We found a pay phone and I called them to explain our situation and they sent a ranger down to meet us within about fifteen minutes!

Allen was a tall, thin man, probably in his thirties. He had a wide smile with a friendly face and seemed genuinely excited about our trip. He offered to drive our canoes over to the campground for the night, and then in the morning would have another ranger bring them down to the access ramp on the other side of the dam. Now that's service!

One canoe at a time, Allen drove us over to the campground, the canoe sticking out of the back of his white government pick up. After a week of seclusion on the lake, we again felt out of place in such a civilized campground. Our boats sat beside our picnic table and our metal fire ring, amongst children riding bikes, senior citizens playing cards in front of their RVs, and bored teenagers hanging out by the Coke machines in front of the store.

We grabbed a change of clothes, or at least underwear, and headed for the showers. Our last hot showers had been in Fort Benton at the old Grand Union Hotel. Though the shower stalls didn't have the atmosphere of the fabulous old hotel, the hot stream of water felt just as wonderful. We must have drained the campground's hot water heater we stayed in so long!

Walking back to our site, we all felt like a million bucks; a cold drink, a hot shower, and now a good meal and munchies all night! We all felt a sense of accomplishment having completed Fort Peck Lake. I suppose it gave us the confidence to face the four hundred miles of lake water we would paddle in North and South Dakota.

As dusk was approaching, we cooked ham and potatoes, sitting at our picnic table, just watching our neighbors.

We all had to chuckle as it got dark and we sat around the fire. Instead of the solitude we had enjoyed for so many nights, tonight we could hear a radio playing Big Band hits from the '40's with some senior citizens playing a card game. We couldn't see it, but a dog would bark now and then for no apparent reason.

After almost three weeks on the river we decided to make a change in our daily routine. As it turned out, taking turns cooking dinner wasn't really working out. It was great for the three exhausted River Rats who got to relax after a long day of paddling, but pretty miserable for the one designated cook. I know it didn't put any of us in a very good mood when it was our turn. We decided to all pitch in cooking the meal and would take turns doing the dishes.

In the morning, Allen drove us to the downstream side of the dam, next to the huge concrete spillway. It didn't seem like there was much water being released, but the narrow river had a strong, crystal clear current. The temperature was so cold my feet ached as we stood in the shallow water, pushing the canoes past the muddy shore.

The swift flow carried us quickly downstream and within minutes we were alone again to enjoy the Montana landscape. After spending over a week on the lake with its wide open expanse of water, the narrow river was a welcomed change. There were more trees and greenery along the shore now. Large cottonwoods and willow grew on both sides. And now we had a wonderful current!

Overcast skies continued for a few more days though it never did rain. Nonetheless, nothing could diminish the beauty of the land around us. Paddling was steady and easy. We camped just downstream of the town of Wolf Point. In the darkness of the cloudy night, without any moon or stars, the seemingly endless rolling hills were still and empty, but on May 4, 1805, Captain Lewis wrote that there were hundreds of buffalo along the river here, some so tame that they would hardly look up from grazing when the men passed. Sadly, even if there had been stars and a moon to light the prairie this night, there would be no buffalo for us to see one hundred and seventy four years later.

A Soldier's Battle

In a nice soft bed I would usually wake up a few times during a night, but that first night on the river with the boys, lying on the hard river bottom, I didn't even stir once.

As the boys and I slept, the partial moon slowly made its way across the clear night sky, softly illuminating LaBarge Rock in its light. The campsites along the river were dark and silent, just a few fire rings still glowing with hot coals slowly dying in the cool night air.

At first light I was staring out the tent screen door at the picturesque view. I gently nudged Joshua next to me. "Hey, guys, its morning. Time to get up."

Dustin slowly woke up, still wearing the pants and shirt he had on the night before. Just like at home, it took more coaxing to get Josh out of his bag.

I unzipped the tent door and stepped out into the fresh morning air. Other campers were emerging from their tents, fires getting restarted, and the smell of fresh coffee in the air.

"Dad, why don't we skip breakfast and get on the river before everybody else," Dustin suggested, looking up and down the river. "I don't wanna have a bunch of people around all day."

I couldn't help but think the same way, anxious to be alone with the boys, much like the way it was back in '79. "Well, we could eat break-fast bars or pop tarts in the boats if you guys want. That's fine with me. What do you think, Josh?"

Joshua crawled out of the tent, still looking half asleep. "I don't care. That's fine."

We rolled up our bags, packed everything away, and carried our plastic bins of supplies to the canoes. Much of the ice in the cooler had melted but everything was still nice and cold.

Dustin took the supply boat again, getting no complaints from Josh that early in the morning. When Dustin was settled I pushed his boat out into the current. If I wasn't fully awake yet, the cold water on my feet and ankles surely woke me up. Josh and I pushed off next, breaking free of the mud, the river current grabbing hold and leading us downriver.

I couldn't help but remember those many early mornings so long ago, getting back on the river to start yet another day of paddling. All my senses again took in the river and the surroundings, bringing back not only memories but the very feelings I felt those many weeks as the river became home for us.

The morning was beautiful and still, just as I had always imagined it would be. The only thing that could have made it more perfect was a hot cup of coffee. I munched on my pop tarts in between strokes of the paddle, washing it down with cold Gatorade.

We paddled along, prairie grass laden hills on both sides of the river, with rock formations appearing every mile or so, some small and flat, others at least a hundred feet above the water, sheer walls of white and gray rock.

The sun was warming up, but it was still very pleasant. The sky was blue and cloudless. In all my years of imagining the trip, I couldn't have imagined a prettier day.

After a few miles, I pulled out the map to see where landmarks would be. "We'll be coming up on Kipp's Rapids soon," I said, shoving the waterproof map back under a strap across our gear.

Josh twisted his body around to look at me with a stern expression. "I thought there weren't any rapids on this river!"

"Relax, kiddo. It doesn't mean white water. The sections along here called rapids were shallow spots during the 1800s when the steamboats would sometimes run aground and even be destroyed. You won't even notice a difference in the current."

Joshua and Dustin couldn't be more different when it came to their preferences about canoeing. For Joshua, the canoe was just a way to get out to a good fishing spot, put down the paddles, and fish…simply a form of transportation. For Dustin, with the heart of a snowboarder and the need for speed, the only canoeing worth doing was in fast water with rapids, or at least enough obstacles to make it exciting. He and I had explored a few of the streams and creeks around our home in central upstate New York and had a few real adventures. We even prided ourselves on doing one run down a creek that the canoeing books said was "not navigable."

So with the fisherman and the speedster, I was somewhere in the middle, happy and content to paddle along a meandering stream or river, taking in the sights and sounds and looking forward to what lies around the next bend. The gentle way a canoe carries you along and how it so easily responds to every movement of the paddle or your body is a feeling like no other.

As I had said, the "rapids" turned out to be just a notation on the map and totally indiscernible as we paddled along.

After another mile or so one of the familiar sights I was looking forward to came into view. On the right side of the river, just up ahead, the unique shape stood as it had the last time I paddled through. Citadel Rock looked even taller than I remembered, still resembling either a fortress or a church with a massive steeple.

"Oh, cool! Let's climb it, Dad! Can we?" Josh asked excitedly.

I looked at the steep walls, bare dark brown rock that looked rugged and crumbly, like the other brownish grey hills around it. "There's a place coming up in a few miles where we can do some climbing."

"Where?" he asked impatiently.

"It's just a few miles ahead. It's called "Hole in the Wall." You'll love it," I said. "For now, how about a swim?"

I steered our boat up beside Dustin's and grabbed hold of it. "Let's tie the boats together and take a dip."

"It's freezing!" Dustin protested.

"C'mon," I pleaded. "You guys have to experience the whole river! You only have three days to do it all. Put on your life vest and just float along with the current!"

It was obvious the boys weren't going in if I didn't go in first. I pulled on my vest and slid onto the very tip of the back of the canoe. "Here I go!" I said as I dropped into the chilly water.

I was surprised by how cold the water actually was. It stung my skin all over and seemed to suck the air right out of my lungs. I was also surprised when my feet scraped the bottom as the current took me along. The water was about five feet deep.

The boys just grinned as they watched me.

"Let's go! C'mon in!" I shouted, grabbing the rope attached to the back of the boat. "Who's coming in next?"

Josh got up on the tip of the canoe and slid his legs over the side. As his feet and legs touched the water he yelled, "It's cold!"

"It feels great!" I replied, not totally telling the truth. It felt great to be floating in the Mighty Missouri again but it was awfully cold, realizing I wasn't warming up after the first few minutes.

Josh finally slid in, gasping for air much like the night before, but with a big smile on his face. The bright red life vest rode high on both sides of his head as he moaned and groaned and laughed.

Dustin was not to be outdone, and eventually came in, if even for just a few minutes.

The depth of the water got shallower to maybe three feet. We walked along with the canoes, feeling the rocky bottom under our feet. In the shallow water, we easily climbed back into the boats.

As we drifted along, soaking wet, somewhat numb but thawing in the sun, Citadel Rock slowly passed us, its immense size and detailed features of wear and erosion silencing us for a few still moments.

It was just over a mile before Hole In The Wall came into view. The right side of the river consisted of gray rocky slopes that towered over the river at least three or four hundred feet into the air. On top the rock formations resembled ruins of an ancient fortress long gone, yet its remnants still standing. This narrow yet massive rock wall ran perpendicular to the river.

I didn't see it at first but as we got closer I could make out the distinct hole at the extreme top corner of the wall, high above the rivers edge. I pointed it out to the boys and it took them some time to find it. Within a few minutes, the hole became obvious, the bright blue sky appearing through the rock.

"How big is the hole, Dad?" Dustin asked

"I don't know," I replied, thinking back to the first time the guys and I had seen it in '79.

"Can we climb to it?" Joshua asked. "That would be so cool!"

"Yeah, let's do it, Dad," Dustin chimed in.

"That's the plan. Last time I came through here we were too much in a rush. We wondered how big the hole was then, too."

A ranger at the small visitor's center back in Fort Benton had marked on my waterproof topographical map where the trailhead was. We pulled up under a clump of cottonwoods in a large field of tall prairie grass. We secured the canoes on shore and immediately found the trail, a worn path through the grassy field.

The trail took us across the field, actually heading away from our destination, toward the rocky hills and buttes to our right. After about a quarter of a mile, the trail turned back toward our left and we started heading uphill.

The hillside revealed a thin path of switchbacks. Within just minutes, I was breathing harder and feeling sweat on my forehead, but before long we were looking down on the river and the vast expanse of barren land, shades of tan, brown, and gray, with the contrast of the bright blue sky.

I snapped pictures in every direction, knowing they wouldn't capture the essence of what we saw all around us.

While I believe the view was just as inspiring for Dustin and Joshua, they had other things on their minds. The trail passed through rock crevices and outcroppings that just had to be explored and climbed. Half the time, I couldn't even see them or know exactly where they were. "Be careful!" I yelled out. "Take your time! Make sure you have a sure hand and foothold!" I tried not to sound like a doting mother, but I knew any help was a long way off.

Nonetheless, I could hear Joshua excitedly calling Dustin to come look at this or that and Dustin calling Joshua to come through this way or that. They had played in many playgrounds as boys but never one like this—not man-made, but carved out by the very hand of God.

I walked along feeling very content, surely with a smile on my face. If back in '79, Tim, Steve, John and I had taken the time to climb up to the Hole In The Wall, it would have been quite an adventure, but to do it now with my two boys was so much more, something that maybe only a dad could understand. To watch them climb and leap among the rocks like nimble mountain goats or Rocky Mountain bighorn sheep was a thrill and a blessing.

The last turn of the trail brought us up onto the highest point. We realized we were walking on top of the gigantic wall, gazing down at the river hundreds of feet below us. The actual hole was now just beneath us, the wall we were standing on being probably less than ten feet wide! The boys of course wanted to walk all the way out to the edge, but I cleverly suggested we'd try and find a way into the hole for pictures.

We found a path that led down and around to where the hole came back into view. It seemed to end at a rock face with just a narrow ledge to walk across.

"Is that the only way?" I asked, hesitating.

"Relax," Dustin said confidently, walking around me and taking the lead.

He easily walked across and Joshua followed without even a word. They both were truly in their element! Once on the other side, they both scrambled up a smooth rock gully that went up about fifteen feet to the gaping hole in the rock.

"I've got to sit up in that hole," I told myself under my breath. I'd come too far to not do it now! I leaned my body against the smooth rock and deliberately placed each foot one at a time along the ledge, being careful not to look down. Once on the other side, I was delighted to find the smooth narrow rock gully was very easy to climb and within seconds I was sitting with the boys. There we were, sitting right inside the Hole In The Wall, hundreds of feet above the river. It was time to pose for pictures!

It was obvious we weren't the first to reach this spot. Carved into the smooth white rock were dozens of names and dates, some as far back as the late 1800s.

"Hey, Dad, too bad you didn't carve your name in here on your river trip," Joshua mentioned, running his hands over a name carved back in 1979.

Far below us, a string of canoes came down the river. We waved our arms back and forth till many of the paddlers waved up at us.

"Hello!" one of the paddlers yelled, his voice echoing up and all around the river valley.

"Hello!" I shouted back.

We relaxed and enjoyed the view but I reminded the boys we still had about fifteen miles or so to paddle for the day, so it was time to head back down.

Unfortunately, that was easier said than done. The smooth rock was easy to climb up but as I started to slide back down the narrow gully, it was difficult to keep from slipping. I struggled to find a good foothold or a handhold around me. After only a few feet I found it almost impossible to go any further. To make matters worse, if someone slid down the smooth, rocky chute, there would be nothing to stop them from going right over the cliff and down a few hundred feet to the rocks below.

I could feel my heart rate increasing and my breathing getting deeper. Anyone who is afraid of heights knows the feeling all too well. I just froze where I was.

I hadn't always had issues with heights. I had no problem climbing ladders as a kid, loving the opportunity to get on the roof of our house to help my dad do anything up there. But as I got older, I wasn't as comfortable...

My fear of heights didn't stop me from enlisting in the US Army when I was twenty-one, joining the elite 82nd Airborne Division, and becoming a proud paratrooper. I made nineteen jumps in my two years with the unit, never losing my fear but more importantly learning how to control it.

My dad had taught me a lot of military history growing up and I had developed a deep respect for veterans and the sacrifice they have made for our country. Though I was pretty sure I wouldn't make the military a career, I knew I would regret it if I didn't serve my country. The famous 82nd Airborne Division seemed like the place for me.

Jump school had been at Fort Benning, GA. After four grueling weeks, the five qualifying jumps to earn my "silver wings" weren't so bad. Each of us jumped one at a time out the door at a nice safe altitude of 1,500 feet; safe meaning you had time to react if your chute didn't open. We jumped in broad daylight except for one night jump. And we had no extra weapons and equipment.

When I arrived at Fort Bragg, NC, I quickly found that real paratroopers don't jump that way! The 82nd, the only airborne unit left in the army, ready to ship out at virtually a moment's notice to any "hot spot" in the world, had their own way of doing things.

I learned the term "mass exit" on my first jump. That's when a full airplane of paratroopers exits the plane one right after the other in a steady stream, out of two rear doors on each side of the fuselage. Within literally seconds, anywhere from 60 to 120 soldiers are in the air, quickly falling to earth.

What you worry about is tangling with another jumper, especially before your chute is totally deployed. It is a heart-stopping experience that I lived through twice in my short career.

Then add the fact that it is pitch black night and you are jumping from an altitude of only 800 feet! Then add about 65 to 100 lbs. of weapons and equipment strapped to your body and you have a mass exit, 82nd Airborne style!

In the two years I served with them, a total of twelve paratroopers lost their lives in parachute jumps. Though some might say the training we went through was too severe, it would be such training that would equip and sustain the unit years later when our nation would call on them to fight in more than one war in the Middle East.

For me, at the moment, the battle was getting off that rock! As I got my breathing under control I still could find no good handholds. Dustin was patient with me. I'm sure he could sense my anxiety.

"How do I stop myself from just slipping all the way down?" I asked, somewhat rhetorically. "I'm gonna go right off the edge at the bottom."

"Do you want me to get in front of you?" he offered.

"No!" I said with obvious frustration. "I don't want to take you with me if I fall!"

"Use your arms to wedge yourself so you won't slip." Dustin slid down to me almost effortlessly, his arms stretched out, holding him in place.

I did the same thing and found it much easier to hold on and move down the gully under control. I slowly made my way to the ledge, Dustin and Joshua right behind me, but wisely giving me plenty of space.

Once I got to the ledge, I hugged the rock wall and stepped along, trying to take my time, even though I was anxious to get to the other side. When I finally stepped off the ledge, I felt an incredible sense of relief. The breeze felt extremely cool as I realized I was covered in sweat.

"That was awesome!" Josh exclaimed. "Let's do some more climbing!" He scrambled across the ledge and started up another rock crevice.

"I'll take pictures of you guys, okay?" I said, still enjoying the cool breeze and feeling my heart rate settling back down.

As we made our way back down the mountain, the boys again

made their own paths, up and over rocks and down through crevices, sometimes going ways I wouldn't even dream of. But they were having a fabulous time.

They joined up with me on the last few switchbacks and we crossed the field gazing back up at Hole In The Wall.

"I can't believe we were up in there!" Joshua said proudly, his hand raised up in the air to shade his eyes from the sun as he looked up the mountain.

I sighed. "I can't believe it either."

Dustin just laughed.

It felt good to get back in the canoes and back on the river again. As we started to paddle downriver I turned and took one final look back at Hole In The Wall. It was distant and tiny again, as I had always remembered it.

I had accomplished one of the goals of the trip; to climb up and sit in the hole. In the process, the boys had experienced an adventure they would never forget. I couldn't help but wonder if either of them might one day return here with their own sons and perhaps start a family tradition. I imagined bringing little Emma on this same trip when she was old enough, not really wanting to think about how old I would be.

The next few hours were spent enjoying the river. Josh got to paddle solo for awhile. Dustin got more pictures of scenery and wildlife. I went for another short swim. We pulled over now and then just to get out and stretch our legs, collecting firewood as we went.

"How far to our campsite?" Josh asked as we got back into the boats after taking a short break on land.

I had just spent some time looking at the map but had a hard time identifying exactly where we were. "I'm not sure." Over the last ten miles or so there had been few distinguishing landmarks and I had lost track of the twists and turns.

The boys were quiet as we paddled along. As time went on even I grew tired, feeling the muscles in my shoulders and arms starting to burn. How long before we hit Slaughter River, our next campsite?

We could camp anywhere we wanted along the river, but Slaughter River was a designated campsite and it was where we River Rats had camped back in 1979. The other reason to camp there was it would give us only ten or twelve miles the next day to meet up with Karen and Dad at noon. I didn't want them waiting out in the middle of nowhere for us.

Joshua asked a few more times where we were on the map. Though he never complained once, I knew he had to be getting awfully tired. I studied the current and admitted to the boys it was a bit slower than I had remembered it.

We paddled on.

"So how would you like to do this for three months, Josh?" I asked, trying to start some conversation.

He laughed and turned around to look at me. "You guys were crazy!"

I laughed as well. After a day and a half on the river, what we had done back in 1979 did seem a bit crazy even to me.

It was then I made a decision to try and help things along. I steered us up alongside Dustin's boat. I figured there would be some resistance but I thought it was the best thing to do.

"Hey, kiddo," I said to Dustin, "I'm going to put Josh in your boat and tie it behind this one so you and I can pull him for awhile. He needs a break."

Dustin was a typical teenager. A good kid, but like most teenagers somewhat self-absorbed, or at least self-centered. And after all, this was his little brother. I expected and was ready for a fight or at least some resistance from him. Why should Josh get to rest when all three of us were tired? Why should we have to pull him along? I was ready for the argument, but it didn't come.

"Okay, Dad," he said matter-of-factly, grabbing our boat as we came up beside his.

Joshua carefully climbed into Dustin's seat as Dustin stepped around him into the front of my boat. I tied the front of Joshua's boat to the rear of ours.

Josh immediately curled up in a ball to sleep as Dustin and I started paddling. I was still amazed there had been no fight, not even a comment made. As the rope became taut, I could feel the drag of the other boat as we paddled, but once we were moving, I didn't notice the weight of Joshua's boat.

I looked at the young man in front of me, paddling without a complaint, working as hard as he had in his own boat, now pulling his brother along. I was surprised, but even more than that, I was keenly impressed. My oldest son was growing up…

I learned something that day that has stayed with me, something I didn't expect to learn on my long-awaited canoe trip on the Missouri River. It was simple enough; young men need a mission. Actually, that's not totally accurate. Whether young or old, all men need a mission.

Some people might call it "purpose" or "a cause." Something to live for. Something to strive for. Something that gives your life meaning. Something that makes it worth getting out of bed in the morning.

Any Christian would tell you that they live to follow Jesus. They strive to live a life that glorifies God. They will tell you their meaning in life is found in a relationship with Jesus and knowing Him personally makes life worth living.

That is all well and good, and also sound theology, but at the risk of sounding heretical, it can leave a man wanting more. I believe that has to do with the way God made us, the way we men are wired.

We look at Adam, the first man, and see God gave him a mission. Tend to the garden, take responsibility over the animals and of course, his mate, Eve. If there was any fault in Adam, it was passivity. Because of it, Adam failed miserably in his mission and the Apostle Paul tells us in the first chapter of the Book of Romans that the whole world has suffered and all creation has groaned from the effect of sin ever since.

Among all the things this world is, the Bible tells us it is a spiritual battlefield. Good verses evil. Light verses darkness. Life verses death. Perhaps that is why the Apostle Paul spoke of spiritual warfare and being a good soldier of Christ. Though he also uses examples of farmers and athletes, he says much about the soldier.

There is no passivity with soldiers. They are men of action, brutal and deadly against any enemy, yet compassionate and nurturing to the innocent and those in need. They are the epitome of allegiance and obedience.

Some of the great men in the scriptures showed such attributes. Moses, though at first reluctant, went and boldly stood before Pharaoh, demanding the release of his people. Joshua bravely declared, "We can take on those giants!" while others cowered in fear. It was the same with a young shepherd boy named David when he stood in front of the towering Goliath.

Though these men were men of faith and prayer, when the time came they stepped out in faith and got into the fight. They were indeed soldiers.

War is a terrible reality of this fallen world, never to be glorified or glamorized, but it has an incredible effect on the soldiers that fight it. It is through war that steadfast leaders are made. It is through war the very best qualities of a man can be demonstrated. It is in war that a soldier's sense of mission enables him go far beyond the call of duty. It is where perseverance in the mission outweighs preservation of one's own self.

Peace is a wonderful thing, but it is the time soldiers struggle with. They train long and hard, day and night, never knowing when they might be called on to fight, while the civilian world safely sleeps. The fact is a soldier performs best when on a mission with a real objective, against a real enemy.

I saw that in Dustin that day. He was the typical teenaged big brother at home. Very rarely did he offer to help Joshua with anything and I was amazed at how easily they could start arguing over really nothing. All the trappings of home and routine seemed to bring out the worst in the boys, yet out here on the river, actually spending more time together than ever, they had not fought once. And now here was Joshua, exhausted but not complaining, and Dustin stepping up and going the extra mile because he knew it was necessary. I hadn't realized it, but he had shown the same attitude when he talked me off that steep cliff just hours before.

The river had a profound effect on the boys that I surely wouldn't have expected. They were acting like young men. They were on a mission. And loving it, too!

THE WAR AT HOME

Any Christian dad wants his sons to grow up to be good soldiers for Christ. We want to be good soldiers ourselves. If there is one weakness in the modern church in America, I believe it is that we are not raising the next generation of soldiers and not doing a very good job with the present generation. We have forgotten we are at war…and by doing so we lose most of the battles we face. We have forgotten we have an enemy. Ask any veteran who has faced combat if he ever forgot about the enemy. Nothing could be more deadly. Yet I sometimes wonder if that is true for most Christian men.

I recently heard a story about a young couple in California. They had a little child they brought to the park to play on the swings and go for a walk. What the young mom and dad didn't know was that all the recent forest fires in California had driven some of the wildlife out of the wilderness and into areas they normally wouldn't go…areas where there were people.

Well, these young parents took pictures of their little child and had them developed. When they got the pictures back, they were shocked by whet they saw. The photos revealed something they had been totally unaware of. Just inside the wood line, almost hidden in the bushes, was a mountain lion. It was crouched down, muscles tense, no doubt waiting to pounce on its prey at the right moment when the father might step just a few feet away from the child.

The image of a little child and an unsuspecting parent being stalked by a mountain lion is an alarming image. There is no father I know that would not defend his wife and child any way he needed to, even with his own life. Yet, as Christian men, so often we forget we have such an enemy.

> Be sober, be vigilant, because your adversary, the devil, walks
> about like a roaring lion, seeking whom he may devour
> 1 Peter 5:8

This enemy wants to destroy us, our wives, and especially our children. Since God has a heart for future generations, it makes sense that Satan hates them as much as us.

How differently would we act as Christian men, as the spiritual leaders of our families that we are called to be, if we acknowledged we have an enemy and are at war?

Mankind has seen many wars in its six thousand year history. There has been incredible suffering and unimaginable loss through those many tragic wars. And we now find ourselves in a war on terrorism, a war that started with a "sneak attack" by terrorists on our own soil.

War for Americans has always been fought "over there," in far away lands like Europe or Asia. With the attack on the World Trade Center, war came to our homeland for the very first time. With it, a new attitude toward terrorism, self-defense, and a willingness to fight has emerged.

As Christians, I wonder if we have the same attitude about spiritual warfare. We are all familiar with missions trips to foreign lands to help various people groups in different ways, sharing the gospel with them. We all consider missions and full time missionaries as being the ultimate in spiritual warfare, the front lines, the combat zone. In other words, the war is "over there."

But the reality is that spiritual warfare is fought everywhere, especially in our own homes. I was once a member of a church that had a unique sign above the door as you left the building. It read, "You are now entering the mission field." It was a reminder for all of us that the mission field is not overseas somewhere, thousands of miles away. Our mission field is where God plants us—with our friends, our work colleagues, our family. While that is so true, we forget Satan does not play by the rules. We return home after a hard day of perhaps being all things to all people, our physical and mental energy spent, now to spend time with the most important people in our lives…and we have nothing left for them. We let down our guard, quit fighting the spiritual fight, and our families suffer for it.

If a dad thinks about it, his first mission field is to his kids. Perhaps each of us should put a sign above the doors of our homes that reads, "You are now entering your own mission field." From reading the scriptures, I can't help but believe a Christian man's highest calling is that of "Father." Who will stand as the spiritual warrior for the family if not the dad? Sadly, in many homes, it's the mom that does her best to fill in the gap left by a husband not fulfilling his calling.

How much more responsive would young men be to spiritual things if instead of telling them to be "good boys" and "behave" we brought them up preparing them for the battles ahead? How would they respond to the challenge to be "warriors" instead of being "well behaved"? How would older men respond?

That boys are designed to be warriors is so evident in my opinion. I know Christian parents that decide to not let their young boys play with toy guns, believing that it glorifies violence and is not very "Christ-like." To the parents' dismay, they find their little boys waging war with broom handles and sticks as rifles. Don't give toy guns to your little boys and they will come up with their own!

There is a John Wayne in every little boy. And I thank God for it.

For those who are called to be Christian men one day, they will need that fighting spirit for the battles that lay ahead.

In Paul's letter to the Philippians, he speaks of Epaphroditus as his brother, his fellow worker, and as his fellow soldier (Phil 2:25). In his letter to Timothy, Paul says to "fight the good fight." In his second letter to his younger protégé, Paul deals with the reality of such a fight by encouraging Timothy to "suffer hardship as a good soldier of Christ Jesus" (2 Tim 2:3). In that second letter, realizing his death was imminent, Paul wrote, "I have fought the good fight, I have finished the course, I have kept the faith." To Paul, living a godly life, keeping the faith and fighting the good fight were synonymous. They should be with us as well.

Dustin had always been a good kid and I had always been proud of him, but I saw that fighting spirit in him for the first time that day. The fighting spirit of a young man. I have to admit, it meant far more to me as his dad than his obedience to my rules or even good grades in school. After all, what better obedience to God then stepping up and getting in the fight?

In 1 Timothy 6:12 Paul again tells Timothy to "fight the good fight, the good fight of faith; to take hold of the eternal life to which you were called." Fighting the good fight is really just another way of saying obeying God, but it helps us remember it is a battle we are in. The very verse before says the man of God should pursue righteousness, godliness, faith, love, perseverance, and gentleness. The chapter speaks of the dangers of the love of money and how it can destroy lives. It speaks of giving and good works, storing up treasures in heaven rather than in this world. Though we hear sermons all the time exhorting us about such things, it is usually not in the context of spiritual warfare the way Paul saw it through the inspiration of the Holy Spirit.

Paul was well aware of the enemy.

> For we do not wrestle against flesh and blood, but against principalities, against powers, against the rulers of the darkness of this age, against spiritual hosts of wickedness in the heavenly places.
> Ephesians 6:12

Though Paul recognized that Satan and his legions of demons were very real, he also knew that for most of us, our spiritual battles would be against our flesh, that part of us still bent on rebelling against God. Paul knew the struggle personally.

> For we know that the law is spiritual; but I am carnal, sold under sin. For what I am doing, I do not understand; for what I will to do, that I do not practice but what I hate, that I do.

> For I know that in me(that is in my flesh) nothing good dwells; for to will is present with me, but how to perform what is good I cannot find.

> For the good that I will to do, I do not do; but the evil I will not to do, that I practice.

> For I delight in the law of God according to the inner man. But I see another law in my members, warring against the law of my mind, and bringing me into captivity to the law of sin which is in my members.

> Oh wretched man that I am! Who will deliver me from this body of death? I thank God through Jesus Christ our LORD!
> Romans 7:14, 15, 18, 19, 22–25

The Apostle Peter understood the warfare that rages both around us and within us.

> Beloved, I beg you as sojourners and pilgrims, abstain from fleshly lusts which war against the soul.
> 1 Peter 2:11

James, the half-brother of Jesus, in his very practical letter to believers in Jerusalem, said the same thing about the flesh.

Where do wars and fights come from among you? Do they not come from your desires for pleasure that war in your members? You lust and do not have. You murder and covet and cannot obtain. You fight and war. Yet you do not have because you do not ask. You ask and do not receive, because you ask amiss, that you may spend it on your pleasures. Adulterers and adulteresses! Do you not know that friendship with the world is enmity with God? Whoever therefore wants to be a friend of the world makes himself an enemy of God.
James 4:1–4

The battle is against Satan, the world system that opposes God, against our own flesh and the false idols and false religion that so easily enslave us. It takes a spiritual warrior, a soldier of Jesus Christ to fight and be victorious through God's power. And it's what every Christian man wants for his sons...and himself.

Some might think that seeing our time here on earth as a lifelong battle is an awful way to look at life. They might prefer more flowery speech. Some might ask, "Where is the joy in the Christian life with such a view?" The fact is the Apostle Paul taught much about spiritual warfare, yet he also spoke the words, "Rejoice, rejoice, again I say rejoice." Paul learned to rely on God through the battles he faced. He found joy in knowing Christ, being in God's will and fulfilling his purpose. If victory came easy we would quickly begin relying on ourselves, fighting in our own strength, and would soon forget God. So in a very real way, it's a blessing life is sometimes hard, to keep us relying on Him. It has taken me years to realize sometimes the blessing is in the battle.

The sun was starting to drop lower in the western sky as Dustin and I paddled. The river took a sharp turn to the right, heading south. With that distinct turn, I was pretty certain I had found our location on the map. We had less than four miles till we reached Slaughter River where we had planned on spending the night.

We had just passed where Lewis and Clark had camped on the left side of the river on May 30, 1805. Though it was exciting to see the actual places the Corps had camped, I was even more excited to see the very spot the River Rats had camped just a bit more recently, only twenty-three years before.

Joshua woke up and without me asking started paddling. He was thrilled to hear we had only a few miles to go. We passed a grove of cottonwoods that didn't appear on the map. A young couple had set up camp under them. A brand new campfire gave off more smoke than flame, and a tiny dome tent stood near their canoe parked on the bank. We exchanged waves as we floated by.

There was a discussion among the boys about where to stop for the night. Dustin wanted to camp somewhere all alone like that young couple. If there were any people at Slaughter River, he wanted to push on and find another site. Josh was pretty adamant about calling it a day at Slaughter River. Though part of me couldn't help but agree with Dustin, I also knew we were beat. Slaughter River would be fine.

We passed the area known as Pablo Rapids. Just as I had told Joshua, there were no rapids for us to worry about. That surely wasn't the case back in the 1800s when steamboats had to deal with a much more wild and dangerous river. In that very spot back in 1864, Captain Abe Wolf ran the steamboat Marian aground. The Luella, a vessel from Fort Benton, Montana came down and rescued passengers and freight before the current and the rocks finally destroyed the Marian. The peacefulness of the surroundings made it hard for me to imagine all the drama that took place there.

It came up rather abruptly on the left bank of the river, a tiny hand-written sign that read Slaughter River Campground.

"We made it," Dustin declared as we headed for shore.

"Yes!" Josh exclaimed.

I noticed right away that our campsite of twenty-three years ago had changed. Just beyond the small muddy beach was a rustic wire fence with wooden posts made of large tree limbs. A simple wood and wire gate allowed entrance to the handful of campsites, distinguishable only by the metal fire rings on the ground. Out in the middle of nowhere, I had to question the purpose of the fence—was it to keep someone or something in or to keep them out?

The first site just inside the gate was occupied by three college students from Missoula, two guys and a girl. They were very friendly and thankfully didn't have any loud radio with them. We exchanged some small talk as we started unloading our canoes.

About fifty yards away, a large group of paddlers were having a good time laughing and talking. We figured they were the canoes we had waved and yelled to from the top of Hole In The Wall earlier in the day.

The thousands of wild sunflowers that had carpeted the fields around us in 1979 were sadly absent. We had camped here on Aug 7th in 1979. Now it was August 20th , the same time of year, yet there were no sign of sunflowers. The mostly barren fields and hills had only brush here and there and some prairie tall grass growing in spots. The horizon had the same rugged hills in the distance, just as I remembered them.

The opposite side of the river had no shore at all but a tall rock wall at least seventy-five feet high that must have extended over half a mile up and downstream. Clusters of swallow nests clung to the smooth rock face. The swallows looked like tiny bats as they darted through the sky and seemed to play and dance over the surface of the water.

Dustin noticed how the western sky was turning different shades of purple and pink so he grabbed his camera and tripod and went to find the right place to take a few shots. Josh and I got wood together for the fire. We were starving. Dinner would be simple enough. Just pick which canned soup or stew you wanted, open it and heat it up in the fire. We had plenty of food and the cooler still was cold with some ice in the bottom. We were all set for a relaxing evening around the campfire. Maybe I could even talk Josh into another evening dip in the river.

But it was not meant to be a relaxing evening. The colors in the sky had faded as dusk set in, but we really hadn't noticed the dark threatening clouds that had been gathering. As I started heating up water for hot chocolate, the first drops of rain fell. Flashes of light lit up the distant hills and we knew the night would be getting interesting. The drops started coming just a bit steadier as we started to hear the rumbling of thunder far off.

"Close everything up and get something heavy on the lids of the bins," I instructed the boys. We zippered up the windows to the tent and put the waterproof fly on. The heavens let loose just as we were ready to climb into the tent. Rain suddenly pounded the fabric of the tent and the thunder grew louder. The flashes were now more frequent, lighting up the prairie like daylight for just an instant, then back to almost pitch black.

Dustin insisted on keeping the door flap open so he could watch, but the wind gusts were blowing water into the tent so I made him close it.

"Can I go outside and watch for a little while?" he asked with pleading eyes. I had seen that same look years before when we were in a Denver hotel. Funnel clouds and twisters had been reported just east of the city and Dustin pleaded with me to take him storm chasing with the Ford Explorer we had rented. We had just driven about ten hours that day and I was awfully tired. Karen wasn't thrilled with the idea but she agreed to stay with Joshua, so off we went.

Dustin and I spent the next few hours driving through downpours of rain and hail, listening to the local radio station tracking the storm and twister sightings. We never did see a tornado but we had a ball. Again he had that same look on his face.

"When the lightning gets close, you come in!" I had to shout over the rain battering the tent. Dustin put on the jacket of his rain gear and quickly slid out the tent door.

Even with the rain and thunder I could hear him yelling, "Oh man, this is so cool!"

Our self-standing dome tent shuddered with the steady wind, the walls bending one way then suddenly twisting the other. By the time Dustin finally unzipped the tent door to get in, water was already seeping through the tent, pooling in the corners of the floor. Unless the storm passed over quickly, we were in for a long, wet night.

As if the thunder and the driving rain were not loud enough, the wind took on the sound of a train bearing down on us, yet never reaching us. As the three of us laid there, the sides of the tent were bent all the way down on top of us, just to then snap back up for a few moments, then back down again. The deafening noise of the wind was somewhat disturbing, even though I knew we were far enough from any trees and perfectly safe. We agreed the incredible sound must be the wind rushing by the massive rock wall on the other side of the river. How else could wind make such a sound?

I tried sopping up water with our dirty clothes but I could see it was a futile attempt. Our sleeping bags were wet even before we got in them. Thankfully, it was a warm night. I had learned in the army that it's much better to spend the night wet and warm than wet and cold. I started to wonder how much sleep we would be able to get through the night. It wasn't even ten o'clock and morning was a long way off.

Wind and Waves

AUGUST 21–SEPTEMBER 5, 1979

With the swift current of the dam, we paddled about eighty miles over the next two days. We knew if things went well, we would run into the Yellowstone River perhaps the next day. The Yellowstone seemed like a link to home, Yellowstone National Park, now hundreds of miles to the southwest. It was probably the first time I thought of Montana as home, wondering how long before I would be back. I don't know how the other guys felt, but I think we all had a sense of accomplishment. We really were on our way!

We slept on sand bars the last two nights. We learned the soft sand was great for sleeping and you didn't lose small objects like we did in grassy campsites. There seemed to be fewer mosquitoes on the sand bars as well, but there were flies that seemed to come from nowhere to harass and pest us.

We were getting quicker and quicker at breaking down camp and getting the boats packed. The organization of supplies had been modified over the weeks as we learned the best way to pack things. Routines and procedures had been established and seemed to be working quite well, from setting up camp, to packing the boats, to bathing, to cooking, to dish washing. We were growing accustomed to life on the river

On the morning of August 23rd, we ran into a few fishermen in a John boat. They assured us we were now in North Dakota waters and the Yellowstone was just up ahead on the right. One of the fishermen, named Wade, was a thin, tall fellow, probably in his thirties. He gave us his telephone number and told us to give him a call when we reached Williston, a town we would hit sometime tomorrow. He offered to give us a ride into town to get supplies. It seemed like quite a nice gesture, though we each probably wondered if it would really happen.

After another hour of paddling, John asked, "So where's the Yellowstone?" laying his paddle across the front of the boat. Our canoes were side by side, just a few feet apart.

"Well, according to those guys, we should have run into her by now," Steve said, adjusting his blue baseball cap on his head. He had started adding bird feathers we found along the river and it was starting to look like an Indian headdress.

It was when I stopped paddling that Tim was the first to notice it. We were drifting, but not forward. The current started taking us the other way...upstream? "Oh man," Tim moaned, "we're paddling upstream! This is the Yellowstone!"

"Naw!" Steve shouted with a laugh. "It can't be!"

"Look at the current," I had to admit. "We'll be back in Yaccland if we keep going this way!"

"Man, this is embarrassing!" Steve cried as we turned the boats around and headed down river. Within a few hundred yards we were at the mouth of the Yellowstone, rejoining the Missouri. The Yellowstone had entered from our right, and seemed to just be a bend in the river. We didn't notice the Missouri had continued on the left.

John turned around as he paddled and gave me a smirk. "Let's try not to do that again. I don't need to do any extra paddling."

Lewis and Clark both agreed that this place would be an excellent location for a trading post. In fact, Fort Union would be built on the north bank of the Yellowstone River, a busy fur trading post from 1828 through the 1860s.

In 1866, Fort Buford would be built in the same area. This military post would hold both Chief Joseph in 1877 and Chief Sitting Bull in 1881, after they had finally surrendered to the U.S. Army. As we paddled by, the thick brush and scattered trees gently rustling in the warm breeze, we had no idea of the history and the human drama that had played out here so long ago.

Soon the river started to widen and the current slowed, indicating we were entering the beginning of Lake Sacajawea. As the river valley widened, the river's bottomlands became full of dead trees, many still standing, others strewn along the river bank, all remnants of a forest flooded when the lake waters rose.

As the sun got hotter and with no breeze at all, we paddled through a forest of dead trees. There was hardly any bark left on the tattered, worn trunks that jutted out of the water, bare branches stretching out over the water. There was a strange silence as we made our way through them. It had an eerie feel to it and I was glad we hadn't gone through there at night.

The next day the water tower of Williston came into view in the distance. We pulled up the boats next to a concrete building that turned out to be a water treatment plant. We found a pay phone and called our new friend, Wade. Surprisingly, he was home, knew where we were and promised to be there in twenty minutes.

Wade drove us a few miles into town He took us to a small grocery store, waited while we shopped, then gave us a ride back to the river. It was great fun sailing down the highway at seventy miles an hour, the radio blasting, drinking ice cold drinks; the simple pleasures in life! When Wade dropped us off, we said our grateful good byes and packed our new supplies.

We put in a few more miles, the lake becoming wider and the dead trees becoming a common sight. There would be no shortage of firewood tonight! We stayed close to the northern shore of the lake, which consisted of about thirty yards of flat muddy clay, then logs and twigs of every size piled in a tangled mess. A few trees and green brush grew in the ravines of the barren bluffs that towered above the river.

As the sun was hanging low, we decided to find a campsite. We found a clearing in the scattered logs, about 30 feet from the water, just at the foot of the bluffs. We started a huge fire, the first thing we did every night, and started cooking up another version of River Rat Stew with all the ingredients we bought that day.

The sky remained overcast and it was the first night in quite a while that we saw no stars. A huge fire and a cold breeze blowing from the west seemed to keep the mosquitoes and flies away. We put both tents up, not sure whether it might rain or not.

The next morning we all decided after twenty seven days on the river, we deserved a day off. We spent the day eating fresh fruit we had purchased the day before. We read, slept again in the afternoon, and took a few short hikes through the grassy hills that surrounded us.

When it was a bit cooler in late afternoon, I climbed the bluffs behind our campsite to get a view of the lake. The opposite bank was at least a mile away, the shore just a thin grayish stretch of land. The wide expanse of open prairie and rolling hills had its own beauty and was an awesome contrast to the immense sky that seemed as endless above us.

That evening, sitting around the fire, we all agreed we would need to take another "day off" again. The real question was when. In another four weeks? Where would we be in another four weeks…and how would we all be doing?

The first day on our new lake was a pleasant one. A steady tailwind allowed us to sail for most of the day, letting the wind do all the work. The second day started out much the same way. We would pick out a distant point to aim for and keep the boats headed in that direction. Slowly that point would grow closer and the landscape would become more defined. Once we finally reached the high ground jutting out above the water, it was time to pick another prominent point ahead and keep on going. Thankfully the barren shoreline and the steady wind kept going in the same direction!

It was late afternoon when the weather started to change on us. The gray sky was becoming darker and darker to the south of us. At first we weren't too concerned, but as time went on, the large puffy clouds on the horizon increased in size, filled almost half the sky, and took on a threatening appearance. A gusty wind was starting to whip up some small waves and making paddling difficult.

"Hey, guys!" I shouted over to Tim and Steve's boat. "We need to take it in!"

"Let's do it!" Steve yelled back.

The timing was perfect. Up ahead there was a break in the shore line that led into a small circular cove. We paddled in, finding a small bay about two hundred yards in diameter almost surrounded by hills with low green shrubs and tall grass, producing a nice shelter from the oncoming wind.

Once the boats were on shore, we got on our rain gear and carefully turned the boats over with all the gear tied in. We had only had one short sprinkle in our first four weeks on the river but it was obvious that was about to change any moment. Flashes were appearing on the horizon well before we heard the thunder. As the storm grew closer, streaks of lightening cut through the black sky, some branching out into a dozen dancing lines of electricity. Suddenly those clouds opened up and dumped everything they had. The raindrops pelted our backs as we hid our faces. I pulled the hood of my raingear tightly around my face, sitting with my back to the wind.

"It's cold!" Tim yelled, sitting beside me. I wasn't sure if he meant the rain or if he had noticed the storm had dropped the temperature quite dramatically within just a few minutes. It was really too loud for the four of us to talk so we just sat down and waited it out, watching the show. The downpour only lasted about twenty minutes, though the light show in the sky continued for about an hour. The sky lightened but there was still a thick layer of clouds hovering over us.

We noticed there were quite a few fish jumping in the small bay so we decided to try fishing I don't know if it was the rain or the temperature or just the location, but the fish were biting. I caught six large Golden Eye and Steve caught two. Our little red and white lures worked like magic. With dinner already caught and a cloudy sky above us, we decided to stay there for the night.

Our easy days on Lake Sacajawea abruptly came to an end the next morning. Winds were blowing across the waters, creating white capped waves as far as we could see. We soon gave up and made camp on a beach of pebbles and small rocks. We laid out our sleeping bags for a comfortable place to sit or lay down. The flies seemed to find us almost immediately. We started a fire but fires seemed to only work with mosquitoes, not flies. We'd had pretty good luck lately so we decided to try catching some fish for lunch. . Besides, standing knee deep in the water was one way to stay away from the flies on shore. Tim caught a large Walleye and we also came up with seven Golden Eye. We spent the afternoon cooking and eating fish and baked potatoes. The Walleye was a big hit. We all decided it was the fish to catch for eating.

We spent the afternoon reading, going for short hikes, and taking naps, waiting for the wind to cease. I tried napping, throwing a shirt over my head to keep the flies away, but they would always find an exposed part of my arm or leg to land on right before I dozed off. We were all just too lazy to put up the tents, figuring it would get too hot in them anyway.

Thankfully we paddled about twenty five miles the next day, our fifth day on Sacajawea. We were reaching the widest part of the lake, almost six miles across.

That evening I had dishwashing duty. As I washed the dishes by the riverbank, I couldn't help but be taken in by the beauty all around me. The lake was unusually choppy and the prairie grass on the treeless rolling hills was blowing in the wind, resembling waves on the ocean rather than land. The only sound was the water hitting the gravel shore and the rustling of the tall grass beside me.

It had been a month now on the river and the stark beauty of it all still awed me at times, especially in the early evening when the lighting and the colors created inspiring scenes around us. The serenity of it all was not missed by any of us. We spent many an hour around the fire talking of the incredible sunsets, sun rises, our first storm, the sky and the stars. Somehow it meant more to us because there was nothing else to distract us from it. We didn't simply see it but experienced it. In a sense we were part of it.

Waking up to the sound of wind had grown to be a very depressing sound and it's what I heard the next morning, even before my eyes were open. It was another day on shore. This 178 mile long lake seemed to be getting the best of us. We realized the wind could possibly be the only thing that could prevent us from making it to St. Louis.

It was another windy day but than another gorgeous sunset. We went to bed with the wind still strong and feeling just a bit frustrated. None of us were in the mood to spend another day in this same spot. To discourage us even further, lightning started flashing sometime before dawn. As I looked out through the tent screen, the flashes came every few seconds, so bright that it was temporarily blinding. Bolts of lightning started streaking through the sky, followed by crackling sounds and deafening booms. A huge dark cloud had come over us but there was no rain. As quickly as it all started, it was over and we could sleep.

In the morning we spotted a few motor boats in the distance. None came very close to us but we took it as a sign that the marina at the dam was not that far off. Of course distance is different in a motor boat compared to a canoe.

In the afternoon we could sense a wind starting up. Fortunately it was a perfect tail wind so the sails went up, filled with air, taking us downstream. We got comfortable, figuring we'd be sailing all day. We were finally making progress and the dam up ahead was on our minds.

We sailed into the late afternoon, enjoying the warm sun and the cool wind. We estimated we were traveling over five miles an hour with no effort. What a change from the day before!

We thought about stopping for dinner, then getting back out on the lake, but we couldn't bring ourselves to stop. The wind seemed to increase and our speed got faster and faster…and louder. I could hear Steve giving a joyful howl as we flew over the water. Swells would come along side the boat and lift us for a moment, then drop us while pushing us forward. It felt like the water was moving us as much as the wind.

The masts of the sails were bent forward, straining further than they ever had. The swells now were riding higher on each side of the boat, the boat rising even higher and dropping even lower with each swell. At times, the other boat would disappear from sight, then reappear on top of another wave. I started to have a gut feeling that things were getting just a little out of control, but who could complain with the speed we were going. John and I yelling to each other guessed we were doing about twelve or thirteen miles an hour!

Without any warning the mast in our boat suddenly snapped in two with a loud crack. The blue sail, now freed from its foundation, flew off the side of the boat, falling into the waves. John and I instantly grabbed the ropes and pulled it back in the boat. With no forward motion now, the boat rocked and dipped in the waves and it was hard to keep our balance. A wave hit the left side of the canoe and to my horror the water rolled right over the rim and over the gear, crashing onto the floor at my feet.

Once our beleaguered sail was saved, John and I grabbed our paddles and headed for the safety of the shore. We were only about thirty yards away but the wind and the waves made it difficult to head in that direction. As I paddled, my stroke would either miss the water completely or my whole forearm would be submerged as the waves swirled up and down. Waves were crashing onto the beach in such a way that I thought the boat would be flipped over before we could get on land. When we were within fifteen feet, in shallow water, John and I clumsily jumped or fell out of the canoe and guided it to dry land. I was out of breath and my heart was pounding, but the boat was finally safe. I noticed Steve and Tim made it to shore not far from us, further down the beach.

"Whoa, that was incredible!" Steve shouted, running over to us. "I thought you guys were gonna lose it!"

"You and me both," John replied with a sigh of relief, sitting down in the sand.

"Next time we stop before it gets that bad. That was nuts," I said, holding the broken mast in my hands. It had snapped right above where it fit into the larger pipe that was fastened to the frame of the canoe. It would have been impossible to repair but we found the shorter mast would still fit, just being about a foot shorter.

"We had waves coming over the sides!" Tim exclaimed, checking out the rest of the sail.

"I had one land right in my lap!" I laughed.

We made camp, cooking up spaghetti and baked potatoes, relaxing by the fire. It was about dusk when the wind suddenly died and we decided to get back on the water. We were tired but we were really anxious to get to the dam and we knew we were close. We paddled for about two hours in the peaceful light of a ¾ moon. It had a very calming effect after the ordeal earlier in the day. It was late when we finally got into our bags.

DAY 34 LAKE SACAGAWEA, N.D. SEPTEMBER 1ST, 1979

The first day of September brought beautiful weather. It was sunny and clear and thankfully not a hint of wind. We paddled hard, following the southern shoreline from one point to the next. We saw more boats, a few coming closer, probably wondering what nuts would be out here in canoes!

Finally, after over a week on the lake, with a slight headwind to keep our muscles straining and our pace slower, we finally could see the flat horizon of Garrison Dam, the fifth largest earthen dam in the world.

As we paddled the last few miles the marina became more visible. It was much busier than Fort Peck, with dozens of boats and even a few craft I would call yachts, streaming in and out. We stayed close to the shoreline to avoid getting run over or overturning in someone's wake. If we looked out of place at the marina at Fort Peck, here our little loaded down canoes must have looked ridiculous. At least we felt that way from the stares we got. People were still amazed when they learned we were planning on paddling all the way to St. Louis.

We called the Army Corps of Engineers and arranged to be picked up and taken around the dam. The gentleman that came wasn't very friendly and didn't even offer his name. We figured he must be very busy with all the tourists around and wasn't really in the mood to help transport canoes, but he did take us to a grocery store, than drop us off at the campground on the river side of the dam.

Pick City, the little town on the map that had the grocery store, was hardly a town. It consisted of the store, two bars, a gas station, and a few other miscellaneous buildings. The grocery store had a very limited inventory with incredibly high prices. We bought a few things but decided to hold out till the next town.

The campground was along the river. It was full of RVs, pop ups, and tents. It was the busiest place on the river so far. We put our boats in the narrow river and let the new current take us downstream for about one hundred yards, then made camp under a small canopy of trees. After all the solitude in the past weeks, we didn't feel like staying in the campground, but we stopped to take showers. What is it that makes hot water feel so good? We washed some of our clothes in the showers with us. We hadn't realized how fowl they had gotten.

It was a pleasure to be off the lake and paddling down a narrow river with a current. Trees lined both banks of the river with the prairie grass hills beyond. From the map, we knew we would have a few days of current before the water would start backing up with the start of Lake Oahe. That day I didn't want to think about another lake; just enjoy the river.

As much as any area of the Missouri River, this section was extremely rich in history. It was in this area that the Corps of Discovery decided to spend the winter of 1804–1805 on their way upriver. Five Indian villages lined both sides of the river, two Mandan villages and three Hidatsa. After a few cautious days of counsel, Lewis and Clark were able to begin a friendly relationship with these people. The shelter they built to survive the winter was aptly named, "Fort Mandan" in honor of their new neighbors.

Fort Mandan was a crude fort made from cottonwood logs. It consisted of four rooms, each 14 feet square. A person might have to spend some time in North Dakota in the winter to appreciate the severe cold the men would endure in their crude shelter.

It was here that Sacajawea, the young Shoshone girl, comes into the picture. A Frenchman named Toussaint Charbonneau showed up at the fort about a month after the men had moved in, and joined the expedition as an interpreter. This man had two "wives," both Shoshone. The captains recognized the value of having someone who could speak to the Shoshone tribe when it was time to try and trade with them for horses to travel over the Rocky Mountains. For whatever reason, it was Sacajawea who was chosen to accompany the expedition. What is so interesting about that choice is that she was quite pregnant and in fact Lewis helped deliver her baby boy there at the fort on February 11, 1805. His formal name was Jean Baptiste Charbonneau, but in time the men would call him, "Pomp." In the spring, Pomp would be by far the youngest member on the amazing journey. As a dad of three children and the time and effort that goes into newborns still somewhat fresh in my mind, I can't begin to fathom how Sacajawea could care for him under the conditions they faced. She was barely fifteen or sixteen herself!

Tim came back from a walk one day swearing he had seen an albino heron but since no one else got to see it, it made for a few jokes around the fire. There were many white tail deer along the river, coming down for a drink and to enjoy the corn growing in fields nearby. We couldn't resist climbing the bank to grab a few ears ourselves.

On September 5th, our thirty eighth day, we reached Bismarck, N.D., the state capital. It was bright sunshine without a trace of wind when we glided under the interstate Rt 94 Bridge high above us, listening to the roar of the traffic. With smaller bridges we usually sent at least a few pigeons flying out from between rows of steel, but this bridge towered high above the water.

Bismarck appeared on our left, much larger than we expected, with tall buildings, crowded streets, even a good size airport on the far side of town. We paddled past the downtown area. The whole riverfront length of the town had to be at least four or five miles. On the outskirts of town to the south, we found a park and a grocery store not far away. We couldn't find a secure place for the boats so John volunteered to stay with them while the rest of us sought out supplies.

We decided since this was our last "real" town for the next two or three hundred miles, we should get just a little more food, but also celebrate our half way point of the trip here. We bought cold drinks, pretzels with mustard, and some homemade cookies we couldn't resist.

We all sent out some postcards to family and friends, and especially one to Yaccland. We were proud of the fact we hadn't returned to Yellowstone a week later with our tails between our legs...and we were actually still alive into week five!

We found bathrooms, of course, never passing up the opportunity for what most people take for granted. It was always fun to stand in front of the mirror and see how grungy we looked! Our faces were getting darker and darker, we always needed a shave since we never bothered on the river, and our hair started to take on a new look, since we hardly ever brushed it. My nose and lips were finally starting to clear up from the August sunburn.

We loaded up the boats with the groceries and traveled down the river just for a few miles till we were alone again on our river. There was a huge sandbar that split the river in two, probably over one hundred feet long and thirty feet wide, made of nice soft sand, perfect for our campsite.

It was a clear night with a full moon. It was so bright out we could almost read our maps without a flashlight. Lake Oahe was just a day away and looked formidable. It wasn't as wide as Fort Peck or Sacagawea, often just two miles wide, but extremely long. We would have 230 miles of it to paddle!

It was a cool night and the bugs weren't bothering us so we all just slept under the stars in the sand, staying up late, talking and admiring the full moon as it made its way across the night sky.

This whole area was rich with the memory of Lewis and Clark and the tribes they met and made peace with. Decades later, a military installation would be built not far from our campsite for a very different mission; Fort Abraham Lincoln would be the last post of Lieutenant Colonel George Armstrong Custer of the 7th Cavalry Division.

A Soldier's Training

I had planned on waterproofing the tent before the trip but never found the time. Needless to say, that night I really wished I had. It was almost as if the tent had simply given up holding back the rain, letting the water invade from all directions. The light from our flashlights darting across the tent walls and ceiling revealed the end of any idea of staying dry through the night.

Josh climbed into his bag and curled up, burying his head. Dustin and I tried to talk over the crashing and crackling of thunder and the incredible sound of the relentless wind as it swept over the hills and down along the river. The driving rain pounded the nylon tent. As we shouted at each other in order to hear, the lightning flashes lit up the tent for an instant, only to leave us in total darkness again.

It seemed like hours went by as we tried to stay as comfortable as possible. At one point, having not seen Joshua move a muscle, I mentioned to Dustin that he must be asleep. With that, Josh rolled over and with the next flash of lightning I could see he was wide awake, looking at me. He had obviously decided to ride out the storm curled up in his now soaking wet sleeping bag.

The boys were taking it all rather well. I had not heard a complaint from either one of them and I must admit, at the moment there was plenty to complain about. I had learned long ago that adventure usually brings with it a certain amount of physical discomfort, but I wasn't sure the boys were ready to accept that. In only two days and two nights on the river, we had experienced quite a variety of weather. As I crawled into my wet sleeping bag I reminded myself that was the whole point of the trip. Adventure for all it was worth!

I lay awake, my body warm though most of it wet. I could still see the flashes of lightning with my eyes closed and all the sounds bombarding me made it almost impossible to relax. Each of us tried to fall asleep but I knew it would take some time, even after such a grueling day of climbing and paddling.

It was good training for the boys, I thought. Life, after all, comes with a certain amount of trials and adversity, especially a full and active life. If we as Christians are to consider ourselves as spiritual soldiers as the scriptures tell us, we must consider the training we must go through. Training is something we are all familiar with in our lives, from potty training, to training for a new job, to training as an athlete. But no training is more critical than the training a soldier receives. His training can mean the difference between accomplishing the mission and failing, between freedom and tyranny, between life and death, his own and others.

Paul told Timothy how important spiritual training was.

> For bodily exercise profits a little, but godliness is profitable for all things, having promise for the life that now is and of that which is to come.
> 1 Timothy 4:8

Living in a physical world, it's not surprising we tend to focus on the physical. Our five senses seem to constantly compete for our attention. Unfortunately most of us end up neglecting the spiritual. We forget our physical bodies are perishing and it is our spiritual selves that will last forever.

When it comes to spiritual exercise, most Christian parents are familiar with passages that discuss training our children.

> Train up a child in the way he should go; And when he is old he will not depart from it.
> Proverbs 22:6

Though many parents hold on to this verse as a promise, we must remember proverbs are principles, not direct promises from God. We cannot claim this verse as a guarantee. We all know godly parents who raised their children well, yet not all walked with the LORD. To me, as a parent, this verse is simply a reminder of a command from God, that I have the responsibility to train my children. The results are and always will be in the hands of our sovereign God and His purposes.

> And you, fathers, do not provoke your children to wrath, but bring them up in the training and admonition of the LORD.
> Ephesians 6:4

I had a friend who grounded his teenaged son for an act of open rebellion. His son, who attended a good Christian school, responded by stating the Bible says fathers shouldn't provoke their children to anger. Grounding him was definitely angering him. We all can be guilty at times of taking scripture out of context but perhaps no one does it better than young people in Christian school!

That young man needed to keep reading to see his dad had a responsibility to discipline him and instruct him. He also should have gone back a few verses.

> Children, obey your parents in the LORD, for this is right.
> Ephesians 6:1

The original word for "obey" denotes a sense of listening as if your life depended on it. How true that is as our early development can set the course of our lives for years to come.

The key phrase in these verses is "in the LORD," again the burden falling on the parents. Fathers throughout the ages have raised their children based on either how they were raised or on what the culture told them at the time. The parent that is trying to train up or raise his/her child outside the authority of scripture is simply disobeying God. No matter how successful certain methods of parenting may be in worldly terms, the best way is God's way. It is sad how we who are Christian parents can so easily fall for the latest fads of our society and conform to fallen men's and women's theories concerning our kids, rather than trusting in the authority of the God who made both us and our children!

If our highest calling as men is to be fathers of our children, and God's direct command is to train them up in the discipline and instruction of the LORD, we all need to constantly ask ourselves how we are doing. For most men, I believe that can be too humbling and awfully convicting. For that reason, we simply avoid the topic. We just rely on the belief that our kids aren't as good as some, but are much better than most, whatever that means. We get comfortable with passive fathering rather than approach our parenting as the "training" we are commanded to provide to our children.

As I recall the different types of training I have been through in my life, I think back to football practice when I played high school football. My coach was from the old school, believing in the motto, "No Pain, No Gain." Though always fair, his ways were sometimes somewhat harsh, methods that would never be allowed in high schools today. But Coach was respected by all of his players and he somehow inspired us to go beyond our physical limits and give all we had. He expected nothing less. Though we ended up on the short end of the scoreboard more often than not, I learned many life lessons on that football field, many that prepared me for the challenges to come.

Perhaps the most effective, life-transforming training a person can go through is in the military. It was there that my physical and mental limits were stretched even beyond what I could imagine. Though I didn't want to make the military a lifelong career, I learned much about myself and the realities of life as a soldier.

Think about the mission of the US Army, my chosen branch of service. They have to take in young men from all over the country, different backgrounds, beliefs, and abilities and transform them into a disciplined army, ready and willing to take on any enemy, anywhere in the world, at any time. When I think back on how they accomplished that, at least in the early 80s when I went through it, I can break it down to three simple principles.

A Soldier's Training
  - One Step At A Time
  - Continuous
  - Real Life

As I consider the training for a spiritual soldier, I believe those principles are worth applying. Since it is fathers who are commanded to provide this training to their sons, I asked myself how well I was following these principles in my own fathering.

SPIRITUAL TRAINING - ONE STEP AT A TIME

After completing Basic Training at Fort Leonard Wood, MO, and medic training at Fort Sam Houston, TX, I was shipped to Fort Benning, GA for Parachute Training, affectionately known as Jump School.

The Black Hats, Airborne drill sergeants with black hats and equally dark dispositions, welcomed us with screaming, declaring we were all "Legs." Paratroopers call any soldier who isn't Airborne "Legs," clearly a derogatory term. We had three weeks of training before we could get the coveted "silver wings" pinned on our chest and head out to our permanent unit.

The army has the concept of "one step at a time" down to a science. They don't just take fresh recruits up in a plane, open the door and yell, "Jump!"

The first week of training is called "Ground Week." Ground Week consists mostly of learning how to land correctly, something you want to learn to do well! The PLF (Practiced Landing Fall) is mastered by jumping off a five foot platform into sand, then by suspended harnesses to learn how to land drifting forward, backward, and from left and right. The harness came to be known as "suspended agony" by the troops, a great motivation to get it right and get out of the thing! We also used mock airplanes to learn movements in the plane, the hand signals and sequence of the equipment check and jump, and finally how to jump out of the mock fuselage door.

All the basics were learned and mastered before you could go on to "Tower Week"

Tower Week got even more exciting. We started the week on the 35 Foot Tower. This tower is basically a large box with a mock door on top of a simple wooden frame with a staircase winding up to the top. The idea is to teach recruits how to exit the plane correctly. Though only 35 feet high, jumping out that door in a parachute harness connected to a pulley system that grabs you after you fall about eight feet is just a bit unnerving, especially if you're not comfortable with heights. Black Hats watch you from the ground to make sure you don't close your eyes as you exit and maintain correct tight body position. To increase the stress, as you climb the stairway and enter the small enclosed area on top, Black Hats are screaming at you and you're hoping and praying the Black Hat hooking your harness to the line as you step into the doorway is doing it correctly as he's yelling at you. I would learn only later that all the noise and creating the stress all had a purpose.

The second tower we experienced was the 250-foot tower. There were two of them, resembling high tension wire towers, easily seen from anywhere on the fort. The top of each tower had four arms that stuck out on each side, with each arm having a cone-shaped frame underneath. The four frames would drop down on cables and a parachute would be connected. The cable would then slowly pull the open chute and the paratrooper candidate all the way up to the top. A loud speaker would then direct you to unhook your safety belt and prepare yourself. Suddenly the frame would release the chute and you would glide down freely, steering the chute away from the tower and hopefully performing a perfect PLF when you hit the ground. It is hard to describe the feeling as you are hoisted 250 feet into the air, your feet dangling, and then the amazing feeling gliding back down to earth with the massive canopy above you.

The third and final week of training was Jump Week. It was a cold, clear February morning when we suited up and boarded a camouflaged C-130 transport. At 1,500 feet, at about 150 miles per hour, I shuffled into position, grabbing both sides of the door. The prop engines and the rushing wind were deafening. The jumpmaster let me stand in the door for what seemed like an eternity, staring out at the distant horizon and the tree lined sandy drop zone below. When the green light illuminated and the jumpmaster yelled, "Go!" I jumped. And I must admit my eyes were tightly closed!

"One thousand, two thousand, three thousand, four thousand," I counted out loud. It felt as if I had been shot out of a cannon rather than actually falling. The first thing I noticed was the roar of the engines as I exited the plane quickly disappeared, replaced by a wonderful silence except for the breeze. I looked up in relief to see a big round green canopy over my head. My heart was frantically pounding as I glided down toward earth, trying to comprehend all the space around me. As the ground came closer I resisted the temptation to look down but instead looked at the horizon. Looking down causes you to reach with your legs, usually resulting in leg injuries. I watched the horizon, my knees slightly bent, my feet together, concentrating on the five points of contact of a good PLF.

The impact hitting the frozen ground was harder than I had expected. I had been drifting backwards and had forgotten to tuck my head down toward my chest. With the sudden impact, my head flew back, smacking the ground. It was the last time I ever forgot to tuck in my head!

By the end of the week, after all the training, all the endless push ups, the constant running, and head games from the Black Hats, and five successful jumps, those who endured had sliver wings pinned on their chests during a ceremony on the parade field. Those of us heading onto the 82nd Airborne Division could finally wear our coveted red berets, those going to Special Forces had their green, and the Rangers had their black berets. It was a glorious day for all of us. None of us knew the toughest training would come later with our units.

The point was we were different soldiers in just three short weeks. We arrived as "Legs" and left as paratroopers. We started with the basics, learned what we needed to know, and advanced on.

I believe there is a lesson in that for parents, especially dads. Our goal is to see our sons become fine Christian men and demonstrate the qualities we admire, the qualities that please God. But how much time and energy do we put into considering the training necessary to achieving that goal?

My little Emma at three years old is just entering Ground Week of her training. For now, her mom and I control her world, isolate her from what she is not ready to see or experience, and teach her the very basics of who God is, right and wrong, the most basic of truths of life.

Joshua, at eleven, is still isolated from some things, but he is at the point of understanding more, having his own opinions, seeing and being around things that as his parents we can no longer isolate him from. You could say he's in Tower Week. It would be wrong of us as parents to keep him in Ground Week when there is more for him to learn.

Dustin, at sixteen, is into Jump Week. At this point there is less and less isolation from the world, but you hope and pray all the training has helped insolate him from all the world will throw at him. He is at that delicate stage of somewhere between a boy and a young man.

The challenge for every parent is putting the time into evaluating where your child is and, more importantly, the training they're receiving from you to get through that stage. I believe that is accomplished only when both parents work together as a team to be proactive in that training.

Every parent will discover each child is different. From individual personality to birth order, they each will train differently. I can see Josh already, having the influence of a big brother, will enter Jump Week much earlier than his brother. His mom and I will need to be ready for that.

Though it might seem like a subtle difference, I believe a dad who sees his responsibility of proactively training his children for life will have a different attitude, thus different behavior than the passive dad. It is so easy to simply expect our sixteen-year-old sons to have the wisdom we dads have acquired, sometimes the hard way, over our forty-plus years on this earth. It's like taking the recruit to Jump Week, skipping Ground and Tower Week. It won't work. Perhaps it's a matter of forgetting what it was like to be that age, but I believe more importantly, it's a matter of forgetting our God-given purpose is to shape and mold and guide them through all the stages of living and learning, till they are on their own. That, of course, is the ultimate test of the training they received.

> When I was a child, I speak as a child, I thought as a child,
> I understood as a child; but when I became a man, I put
> away childish things.
> 1 Corinthians 13:11

As we go through life experiences with our children, do we see it all as opportunities to train them? Do we decide on giving permission or taking away privileges based on what they will learn from such actions on our part, or do we simply react out of our own convenience or just to avoid the conflict?

SPIRITUAL TRAINING - CONTINUOUS

The army never seemed to be done training us when I was a para-trooper. Once I got to Fort Bragg, our training continued through the next two years with everything from jungle training in Panama to SEER (Survival, Escape, Evasion and Resistance) training in the middle of nowhere, somewhere in the desert of Texas. The army understood training needed to be continuous and consistent to be effective.

As parents, we often hear, "look for those teachable moments," and "spend quality time with your kids." It has been my experience that both quality time and teachable moments are allusive and come at unexpected, if not inconvenient times. You can try to plan a special time to sit down and talk with your kids only to find they have no intention of sharing anything with you. Yet on the way driving home from a basketball game or while sitting in the waiting room at the doctor's office, they will decide to share what's on their mind or heart. You can decide to set and enforce rules but it won't be as God intended if there is no close relationship.

Dustin is one of those kids that always has something to say. His favorite time to open up and share things is right at bed time, just about the time his mom and dad are exhausted and ready for bed as well. Hardly convenient, but quality time that we can't schedule.

Joshua isn't as talkative as his brother so his rare times of sharing what's on his mind can come at any moment, at any place. Again, not scheduled.

The problem with looking for those "teachable moments" is it seems to assume other moments aren't teachable. The fact is, as parents, we are teaching our children much more in those moments we are unaware of than during those times we decide are "teachable." They are constantly observing how we respond to and react to people and events in our own lives, not simply when and where we decide to give them a lecture of virtue or morality.

If the army soldier needs continuous training, such is true for the spiritual soldier. Everything the military does in training has been thought out and has a purpose. I understood why the Black Hats yelled and screamed as we climbed the stairs of the 35-foot tower, creating noise and increasing the stress level as we approached the mock door, ready to jump. Once I was jumping with the 82nd, I realized it was to help prepare us for performing our task with the deafening sound of the wind when that door opened and all the stress we would be under. It all had a purpose.

Everything our kids experience can have a purpose if we as parents help guide them through it. What can they learn from that experience and how can I help them grow from it? Where are they in their development in that area and what's the next step. Again, it's all step by step, and also continuous.

SPIRITUAL TRAINING–REAL LIFE

The soldier is trained diligently to be prepared to perform under pressure, to be effective under fire, to endure and survive in a combat situation, to destroy the enemy, to accomplish the mission. The same can be said for the spiritual soldier. The Christian, if he is living for the LORD, will know the pressure and will at times be under fire in this world. If he recognizes he is in a spiritual battle, he can endure and be victorious.

The training of a paratrooper is only effective if it is as close to real life as possible.

We jumped out of airplanes on pitch black moonless nights from only 800 feet above the ground because that's what we would need to do in combat if called upon. At times we would go without food or sleep, sometimes exposed to the damp cold, sometimes sloshing through hot, humid swamps. I had the privilege of watching men around me in some miserable conditions, sleep deprived, food deprived, yet carrying out their orders and accomplishing their mission. If they were ever deployed, they would be ready.

As parents, we must keep in mind we are preparing our kids for the real thing, the spiritual combat they will face as Christians in this world. We can't lose sight of that fact. It's ironic to me that parenthood is much like being a soldier. The soldier must stay on mission no matter what the circumstances, no matter how tired or hungry. The parent must stay on mission no matter what the circumstances, no matter how tired or hungry. If we want to be honest with ourselves as men, our fathering is really put to the test when we are tired, hungry, frustrated or depressed. The army somehow can discipline a soldier to carry out his mission and ignore all that, yet as fathers we too often fail.

I often wonder if the failure of fathers to train their sons effectively to do spiritual battle in this world is because dads are simply too busy fighting those battles themselves. Our responsibilities with work, with church, things that have to get done, all become priority over training our kids sometimes, especially when the kids are "behaving" and have no "serious problems." We easily slip into "passive fathering," more interested in the urgent things of life rather than the most important things. If we're honest, sometimes it's simply a matter of affirmation.

Fellow Christians applaud our service to the church. I have received numerous thank you notes over the years from those I have taught and ministered to, thanking me and praising my efforts. And they meant a lot to me. Our companies recognize and applaud our achievements at work. I have more than a few wooden, glass, and metal trophies from my company, recognizing my achievements over the years, all of them in a box somewhere in my closet. Yet the heart of a Christian man is to see his son grow up and acknowledge God and follow Him. Compared to that, nothing else really matters. Yet, we must accept the world in general does not give out honors to great fathering. Sadly, even in Christian churches that cater to every need and every special interest group from singles to divorce recovery, there is little concerted effort put out toward helping men be effective fathers.

You will find youth groups in most churches. You will find men's groups meeting on the very same nights in many churches. Though the idea of small groups getting together is wonderful and biblical, the problem is those young men in youth group should be in those men's groups with the men. I believe the best way to show a young man that there is a spiritual battle out there is to let him see the older men ahead of him fighting those same battles. They would discover that forty-year-old men at a heart level are not much different than young men at seventeen. Someone once said the only difference between men and boys is the price of their toys. As a man I must admit that's pretty accurate. Probably most wives would agree. But I believe if you treat a sixteen-year-old boy as a "teen" you will get the attitude of a teenager, and if you treat him like a young man you will get the attitude of a young man. I believe when Christian men of all ages come together and spend time together there is a mentoring process, a maturing process that God performs. It is where true spiritual training occurs. Without that fellowship, I believe young men have a distorted view of the older men in the church that can affect their view of the Christian life and even of God. Of course, the tragedy is this process is nonexistent in most churches. Perhaps it is because men would have to take the risk of becoming a bit more genuine, perhaps even vulnerable, letting down our guard and that wall of separation we are all comfortable hiding behind.

Risk is unavoidable if training is to be close to real life. The army is ready and willing to take calculated risks. We need to do the same as fathers. Jumping out of an airplane in total darkness at only 800 feet comes with a certain amount of risk. The army realizes and accepts that. Most parents would rather avoid risk, which really prevents their child from growing. It's risky when you take the training wheels off their bike. It's risky the first time you let them go around the block without you. It's risky when you hand your child the car keys.

As parents, we can minimize the risk by preparing our kids for the freedoms we give them, helping them to see their own responsibility and the consequences involved with abusing that freedom. What freedoms your own child is ready for cannot be found in a book. Every child is different and the parents have the final responsibility to decide what the child is ready for. That ever-present risk is what brings most Christian parents to their knees, praying for their children, which perhaps reduces the risk more than we even realize.

With Dustin in that "Jump Week" phase of his training, we accept a certain amount of risk, those tests that we as his parents believe he is ready to face. For Josh in "Tower Week" we are much more careful with what risks we expose him to. For my little Emma just starting "Ground Week" of her training, her risks are quite minimal. As her father it does pain me to know that won't last for long.

Ultimately, for the Christian parent, real life means God's perspective. If we take the time we will realize all the events that occur around us all can be explained by man's perspective or by God's perspective. We can use all the sciences of geology and paleontology to teach evolution and the theories of men or to confirm what the scriptures tell us of God and His creation. We can use the awful actions of man to confirm how the world fell into and still suffers under the curse of sin and why the world needed a Savior. We can offer forgiveness to show the forgiveness God has for His children. We can speak of virtues like sacrifice and faithfulness. We can teach them to be discerning, recognizing error from Biblical truth and that people can be sincere, yet sincerely wrong with worldviews or theology that oppose the Bible. Real life means trusting in the authority of the Bible, the inerrant Word of God, rather than the ideas of mortal men.

Most of all, they will see their parents are not perfect and that we need the same forgiveness from our sin as they do. At six years old, a child doesn't know what a hypocrite is. At sixteen, they can spot one a mile away. If we allow them to see our own walk with God, our stumbling and our victories, they will be getting good real life training.

If you think you don't want to talk about your spiritual failures with your children, try to realize they already know most of them. The question is whether you are willing to use yourself and your dependence on God to point them to Jesus.

It is the Apostle Paul who gives us a great example of this, while writing his first epistle to the Thessalonians believers.

> So, affectionately longing for you, we were well pleased to impart to you not only the Gospel of God but our own lives, because you had become dear to us.
> 1 Thessalonians 2:8

If we are to effectively share God's Word with our children we must share our lives as well. As parents, dads especially, we can live under the same roof with our kids for years and never let them really get to know us. Though none of us are even close to perfect, our kids can learn what genuine Christianity is if we're willing to be genuine with them, especially as they get into the later teen years.

If you are getting any idea that training our sons for spiritual warfare should be like boot camp and we as fathers are to be tough like drill sergeants and Black Hats, a few words from Paul in that same chapter of Thessalonians should clear up any misconceptions.

> As you know how we exhorted and comforted, and charged
> every one of you, as a father does his own children.
> 1 Thessalonians 2:11

Paul saw himself as the spiritual father of the believers in Thessalonica, instructing them, encouraging them, and comforting them. As I think about my own fathering, I must ask myself how much comforting and encouraging I do among all the instructing. Instructing seems to come naturally to most fathers I know. Comforting and encouraging seems to take more effort for some reason. If you are guilty of passive fathering, most likely encouraging and comforting seldom occur.

If phrases like, "Suck it up," or "No pain, no gain," or "Be a man," have entered into your vocabulary, especially with your sons, you might want to think again. Paul may have written more about spiritual warfare and being a good soldier for Christ than any other Bible writer, but he also showed incredible love and compassion.

> But we were gentle among you, just as a nursing mother
> cherishes her own children.
> 1 Thessalonians 2:7

You might say it takes a very secure man to describe himself as a nursing mother, but the toughest, perhaps boldest missionary the church has ever known had genuine love and compassion. There is perhaps no better picture of dedicated love and sacrifice than that of a mother with her child. Yet Paul knew that love is not just a feminine virtue, but also very masculine as well.

Watch, stand firm in your faith, be brave, be strong. Let all
that you do be done in love.
1 Corinthians 16:13,14

This passage really says it all. You will be on your guard if and when
you actually realize you are in a real spiritual battle. To stand firm in
the faith means to hold onto the sound doctrines of the church and to
rely on the authority of the scriptures. Being strong and courageous
is what God asks of men, but with a strength and courage that come
from Him and not from ourselves.

Perhaps the most important phrase is that we do it all in love.
Genuine, sacrificial love. There may not be a passage that describes the
Christian man better than that.

After all, what motivates soldiers to risk their lives in combat?
Is it hatred for the enemy or love for country, freedom, the security
of their families?

It may sound strange to think of a soldier's motivation being love.
I remember back at Fort Bragg, NC, when we had spare time to go to
the movie theater on post. The seats would be full of young paratroopers, most dressed in camouflaged fatigues.

Before the previews would start, a video would play the National
Anthem. Every seat would empty as soldiers stood at attention, salut-
ing the American flag. As the anthem played, scenes of America would
appear on the screen; winter scenes of a small New England town,
gentle green hills in Appalachia, the surf hitting the California coast,
the golden wheat fields of the Midwest. There would also be scenes of
people; children playing in a playground, young sweethearts walking
in a park, an elderly couple rocking on a porch swing, moms and dads
hugging their kids, a family saying grace at the dinner table.

As a young, patriotic paratrooper, it was a very proud feeling to
watch those images, to listen to the anthem, and know we were those
called on to not simply defend our constitution, but to defend our
country and our way of life, and especially those who we love. It was
an emotional event for me every time I went to a movie on post, and I
know I wasn't alone. It reminded all of us why we trained so hard and
why we were willing to sacrifice so much.

For the Christian, love should always be our motivation. The scriptures tell us God is love and all love comes from Him. God demonstrates that love to us every day but never more than when God became a man, willing to die for us on a cross so that we could have our separation from Him through sin destroyed and we could have fellowship with Him.

Paul, the spiritual warrior, said nothing could separate believers from that wonderful love of God. He knew that through the Holy Spirit living in us, we can be controlled by God's love. To the believers in Corinth struggling with conflict, Paul told them love that comes from God is patient and kind, casting out fear. God's love helps us speak the truth and to serve one another.

> Though I speak with tongues of men and of angels, but have not love, I have become sounding brass or a clanging cymbal.
> 1 Corinthians 13:1

With all the authority Paul had as an apostle, with all the boldness he had to fight spiritual battles, with all the doctrine he declared through the inspiration of the Holy Spirit, he never lost sight of God's love and he was motivated by it.

Jesus said to abide in God's love. He told the crowd on the Mount of Olives that the world would know we were His disciples by the love we have for one another. And when we love and live out that love with good works, Jesus said the world will notice and we will have the privilege of bringing glory to the Father.

Hatred can be a strong motivator in this world, but it cannot defeat the power of God's love. A spiritual soldier should hate the things that oppose God, but his capacity to be motivated by God's love will ultimately determine how effective he is for God. I suppose each of us enlisted in God's army should evaluate our own motivation now and then to see where we are. It is too easy to become motivated by other things besides God.

The relentless rain pelted the top and sides of the tent as gusts of wind bent the nylon walls down on top of us. The crashing thunder and bright flashes of lightning continued, the deafening wind rolling over the prairie behind us, then colliding into the tall limestone wall across the river. Where before it sounded like a train going by, it now sounded like a continuous train wreck!

I kept telling myself a storm this fierce couldn't last very long, but the long minutes turned into hours. I don't really know when Joshua and Dustin finally drifted off to sleep among all the clamor, but at some point during the long night, we all three fell asleep in our soggy sleeping bags while the sound and light show played on.

Large Lakes and Lots of Patience

Day 39 through Day 56

September 6 - 23, 1979

The river remained narrow with numerous switchbacks every mile or so. According to the map, we would reach Lake Oahe by the following day. Our campsite that night was in a clearing surrounded by thick woods. It was dark in among the trees even well before the sun went down. Some areas were so thick we couldn't walk through to collect wood. How different from our days without hardly seeing any trees at all!

On September 8th, we paddled past the town of Cannonball, N.D. The town got its name from the rocks in the area. Captain Lewis commented that they resembled cannon balls.

That day there was a bright warm sun in a cloudless sky with just a slight breeze blowing, but you could sense something in the air. Something was different. It was just a subtle thing, perhaps easily missed by others who hadn't spent over a month on the river. The air had a crispness to it that I couldn't really feel due to the strength of the sun, but I could almost smell it. The seasons were changing on the Missouri River. We knew eventually it would happen and the time had finally come. Summer was slowly giving way to autumn.

Trees were becoming scarce again now that we were on the lake, but the few growing along the banks and in the ravines nearby were starting to show colors of yellow and orange around the edges. Though these subtle differences brought no changes to our routine or behavior, we still all felt a sense of urgency. If we were to make it to St. Louis we would be battling the clock, the coming of autumn and colder weather.

Somewhat ironically, Captain Clark mentioned in his journal on October 17, 1804, near this very spot, that the leaves were falling fast off the trees as winter approached. Unlike the Corps of Discovery, we weren't going to be building a fort to wait out the winter months. We had over 1,000 river miles to go and now could count on being on the river till October.

The next few days the miles came slowly with headwinds and hard paddling. We passed the widest part of Oahe, an incredible five or six miles across. We stayed close to the western shore and kept a keen eye out for any sudden storm clouds.

The prairie grass was getting thicker and taller on the rolling hills around us, a deep golden color like wheat. It was amazing how it just seemed to go on forever. We were back to almost no trees, just golden hills and deep blue sky wherever we looked. And the only sound in this vast space of gold and blue was the wind. There were many days that the only reminder we were in the twentieth century was the white vapor of a jet plane high above us.

After one particularly exhausting day, we pulled the canoes into a recreation area at Fort Yates. There was a boat ramp, some picnic tables and a public bathroom. The place was empty and we were in the mood to stop for the night.

We had just started unpacking the boats when a young Indian man, probably in his late twenties, came walking up to us. His name was Gary, a Hunkpapa Sioux. He was easily 250 pounds, a large man, with jeans and a t-shirt, his long straight black hair parted in the center and braided past both shoulders.

He strongly suggested we not stay in that spot for the night. We politely asked why, sensing he was sincere in his concern. He explained that there was a large Indian Pow-Wow that night in Bismarck and when it was over, a large crowd would be coming back here to continue the party. With all the drinking going on, it wouldn't be the best place for four white guys in tents!

He explained we were on the Standing Rock Indian Reservation, home of the Lakota, Blackfoot, Hunkpapa, and Lower and Upper Yanktonai Sioux tribes. We would travel along side the reservation for a few days, well into South Dakota. He knew a nice campsite just a few miles down river and we humbly took his advice. Gary agreed to drive his old pickup there by the river and wait for us so we wouldn't miss it.

We repacked what we had unloaded and got back on the river. In less than twenty minutes we came around a slight bend and found Gary sitting on the hood of his truck, his cowboy boots up on the old rusty chrome bumper. He gave a slight wave as we paddled over to him.

The spot was much more secluded, with a few trees, in between two hills but flat enough for our tents. Gary assured us no one would bother us there. We invited him to stay for dinner once we got it cooked, but he suggested he take one of us into town and bring back burgers so we wouldn't have to bother cooking. The offer sounded great and I volunteered.

We took a dirt road about a mile till we hit the small town. It was late and it was getting dark. Most places were closed that time of night, but Gary knew of one place that would be open. He drove to a home for the elderly that was run by the reservation.

It was a large, one-story building and looked quite new. Gary informed me it was only a few years old. He knew to go right to the cafeteria entrance where we walked in. A very friendly woman sold us ten cheeseburgers and five cokes with extra ice.

Twenty minutes later we were sitting around a nice fire, enjoying our cheeseburgers and getting to know our friend, Gary. He had a warm, jovial spirit and was one of the nicest folks we had met so far on the trip. He told us the great Sioux chief, Sitting Bull, was buried there at Fort Yates. The great chief had actually died near there in 1890 but wasn't buried there until 1953. Gary blamed it on "politics!" He spoke of the difficulties on the reservation, especially unemployment and alcohol abuse, but he was on the right track and was going to make it.

It was well after midnight when we said good bye to Gary and waved as his pickup drove down the dusty dirt road, his headlights lighting up the empty prairie around us. Today I wonder what might have happened if Gary hadn't come along. We were young men living for ourselves and this was just one of the many times the good LORD had protected us, though we were totally unaware at the time.

The next day we woke up to rain and the rain continued the entire day. We didn't even attempt starting a fire. It was a dreary, damp, depressing day.

We all got together in one tent to play cards and then look over our maps. The various flying and crawling bugs seemed to think of our tent as a refuge from the weather. Dozens of flies, moths, beetles and mosquitoes hung on the mesh netting.

Thankfully, the next day brought sunshine and we paddled across the border into our third state, South Dakota, the third out of the seven we would paddle through. We weren't totally sure but knew we were somewhere near the border. Rivers aren't like roads where they say, "Welcome to South Dakota."

With the rain gone the wind returned and we spent two more days stranded on the shore of endless prairie and choppy water. The river had narrowed to about a mile across but there were still white caps to keep us on land.

Perhaps the best part of the days on Lake Oahe was the incredible sunsets. On any given evening, the sky seemed to go through so many changes of color and light that it was like seeing four or five individual sunsets.

On September 13th, after about a week on the lake, I awoke with the fly of our tent flapping wildly. The sky was full of puffy white clouds, but no rain in sight. The water was rough with white caps all across the surface. We knew we weren't going anywhere soon. We sat around the fire eating a relaxed breakfast, trying to stay warm from the chill in the morning air. We had no idea what the temperature was but it seemed to be the coldest morning so far.

What happened next caused me to spill the tea I was just raising to my lips. We were all sitting or lying near the fire when a large jack rabbit came bounding into our camp, tumbling over one of the anchor ropes to our tent. It happened so quickly we all just sat there motionless. In a moment it was gone, leaping across the field and down over the hill.

"What the...." someone started to say, when a large coyote came running at full speed, past our camp, right on the rabbit's trail. We all jumped up to try and watch what was going on, Steve scrambling for the pistol. Tim and John started running in the direction of where we lost sight of the coyote, hoping to see it again.

Steve suddenly yelled, "Look, another one!" pointing back up the hill. I turned and saw another jack rabbit coming toward us, with yet another coyote right behind it in hot pursuit. The rabbit was leaping through the air with incredible speed, the coyote in a full run, gaining on the rabbit as they headed down the hill beside us. The rabbit ran into an area of thick bushes and the coyote followed right behind. It was only a moment or two later when the coyote reappeared and ran back out of the ravine and over the hill, and out of our sight, but without its prey.

The four of us were left just standing there, Tim and John up on the hill, Steve and me over by the ravine, Steve's pistol still in his hand. It had happened so quickly we weren't sure what we had seen! Since the rabbit hadn't come out of the thicket, we walked over, looking through the bushes.

"Here it is!" John exclaimed, walking over to a bush and reaching underneath it. He stood up, his outstretched arm holding the hind legs of one of the biggest rabbits I'd ever seen up close. We examined it and found one small puncture wound in the neck where the coyote must have gotten him, perhaps snapping his neck. We all wondered why the coyote would leave his meal, but all we could figure was that after he killed the rabbit, he spotted us and got scared off. At least that was the best theory we could come up with. No matter how it happened, we were about to eat well!

It was Tim who skinned and cleaned the rabbit. It took a lot of foil, but we wrapped it up and buried it in coals, checking on it now and then. That afternoon we feasted on fresh rabbit and baked potatoes. There was plenty of delicious tender meat and we all ate our fill. When we were done, the bones of the carcass had been picked clean.

The sky remained cloudy and the wind continued to pound us all day. After our rabbit feast, we went for a walk along the lake. About 300 yards from camp we found a gill net strung out into the water. We wondered if gill nets were even legal here but perhaps on a reservation they were. We pulled up the nets to find about three dozen fish caught by their gills, many already decomposing. Its one thing to catch fish to eat but this was just a cruel waste. We made the decision to cut the net down so no more fish would get caught, just to die and rot there. We found three Walleye and two Striped Bass that were fresh and cooked them up later as dusk was approaching. Tim and John made some peanut clusters that turned out pretty well and were a nice treat. It had not been a good day for mileage but had surely been a great day of eating!

We had one particularly chilly morning. As usual, Steve was the first one up getting a fire going. I was extremely thankful when I unzipped my sleeping bag and realized how cold it was. The wind had died down and the waves were gone, but our first couple hours of paddling again proved to be difficult.

Around noon we spotted an old iron bridge and a tall water tower up ahead and arrived at the town of Mobridge. There was no safe place to leave the boats so Tim volunteered to stay with them while Steve, John, and I hitch-hiked into town to get some food. An elderly gentleman in a late model Chevy Impala picked us up and gave us a short ride to a small grocery store. On the way he told us the temperature during the night had almost dropped to freezing. It had felt like it! In a very grandfatherly way, he reminded us we had a long way to go with the weather changing. Reluctantly, we had to agree. We ended up walking back to the boats with our treasures, among them a bag of potatoes and a large jar of peanut butter, a brand I had never heard of. Tim had tried fishing but with no luck. We just put the food in the back of one canoe and shoved off.

About five miles later we came to a campground that had bathrooms and hot showers. We couldn't resist stopping just a bit earlier than usual. There were just a few tents and a pop up, most of the sites empty. We never did see anyone collecting a site fee, so, as usual, we got to enjoy hot water at no charge.

We didn't know it at the time, but on the opposite bank of the river, across from Mobridge, there is a simple stone monument dedicated to Sacajawea. It is believed she died in this area just six years after the expedition, most likely in her early to mid twenties.

One day, while we sat on a rocky beach waiting for the winds to die down, over the noise of the wind, we heard the faint sound of an engine in the distance. As it grew louder, we searched the lake for its source. From the south, a small boat appeared, heading upstream. As it sped by, it made a wide turn and headed toward us. We stood up and walked over to the edge of the water as the boat came toward shore. On board, we could see a family; mom and dad and five young kids. The boat was white with tan trim, open seats in the front and back, separated by a wind shield that separated in the center.

"Hello there!" the dad shouted as he cut the engine, letting the boat drift to us. "You boys need any help?" I suppose two canoes beached in the middle of nowhere during high winds would appear to be in trouble. We explained we were fine, just stranded for the day, not unlike other days lately. Frank introduced himself and his wife, and then rattled off the names of each of his kids. The oldest boy was about ten, then four cute little girls, the youngest just about two years old, all with a different shade of blonde hair. Frank was probably in his fifties, a trim, muscular guy with a short military-like haircut.

He and his wife, Mary, wanted to know all about the trip, asking all kinds of questions. I couldn't help but notice how well behaved and patient his kids were while the adults just talked. When I thought Frank would be shoving off, he asked us if we had ever water skied. Tim and Steve had but John and I had never tried it.

"Well, you boys can't do anything else right now. You wanna do some skiing?" Frank asked with a smile. There was no hesitation from us.

It was a tight squeeze after the four of us climbed in, the children sitting on the sides of the boat, shyly watching us. Frank gunned the engine and we were flying across the water. We all grinned at each other, all thinking the same thing. How amazing it was to glide through the water at such a speed after weeks of slow paddling, one stroke at a time.

We all took our turns skiing and falling into the waves. It was my first time so it took me a few attempts to get up. I was surprised how easy it was on my arms and even going over the wake of the boat went pretty well. Falling was much less dramatic once I remembered to let go of the rope!

We spent the afternoon with Frank and his family, enjoying their company and the cold drinks and snacks from their cooler. After a few hours, we were dropped off back at our boats. We thanked Frank for a great time. The kids, so shy just a few hours ago, were now waving wildly and shouting "Bye!" as their boat headed back down stream.

Within minutes, we were alone again, their boat out of sight, the wind still blowing in our faces, the excitement over. We started a fire for dinner, trying to get back into the routine of the day. It was after dinner, perhaps a few hours before dusk, when the wind finally died down. We looked at the smooth surface of the lake and just couldn't resist. We quickly loaded the boats, not as efficiently as usual, and got back on the water.

It was a pleasant, peaceful paddle as the sun dipped behind the hills. The wonderful spectacle of color filled the western sky, changing ever so dramatically every few minutes, the image reflected on the surface of the lake. The air felt cool and again reminded us that autumn was near.

Again, just like a daily show, the incredible colors would finally fade and dim as the sky darkened and the stars began to appear. Though we witnessed it almost every night, we never got tired of watching it.

If the Missouri River had become like a friend to us, Lake Oahe had become an enemy. Every day for the next week we battled wind and waves. Some days we made some good progress, paying with sore muscles. Other days we sat, feeling helpless and frustrated.

On those days the wind was relentless. It whistled past my head with a sound that was beginning to get somewhat annoying since it represented our being stuck on shore. I sat and daydreamed about being anywhere else. The endless prairie, though beautiful, was getting just a bit monotonous. How could the wind blow so hard and so long without any relief?

To celebrate one particularly successful day battling the wind, Steve burned the old black shoes he had worn all summer (when he wore shoes) and pulled out the pair of brand new sneakers he had purchased in Bozeman back in July. He said it felt like stepping into a Cadillac after being in a beat up army jeep. We had lots of driftwood around us so we built an extra large fire that consumed the shoes within minutes, producing a stench of burning rubber and imitation leather.

On September 22nd, we sang Happy Birthday to Tim around the fire.

I remember one of those mornings waking up to the loud flapping of the tent, the walls shaking side to side, the top fluttering in waves, up and down. I looked over and John was lying there on his stomach, propped up on his elbows, staring out at the river.

"I can't believe it," I moaned, pulling the sleeping bag up around my chin, trying to keep the morning chill out.

John ran his hand through his hair. "I don't think we're going anywhere this morning."

We all got up anyway, refusing to believe we'd be stranded for yet another day. Steve started a small fire as the four of us stood around it. We must have been a pathetic sight, four figures standing together out in the middle of miles of prairie, looking somber with our hands in our pockets, our dirty hair messed, our eyes still half shut from sleep.

But finally, one sunny afternoon, with no wind and no waves, we pulled the boats ashore at the dam and Lake Oahe was finally behind us. It had taken us a total of fifteen long days to cover the 230 miles.

The Army Corps of Engineers again transported us around the dam and we got back on the river and paddled about five miles to the town of Pierre, the state capital of South Dakota. We decided to spend the night. We'd be able to purchase food and hopefully get hot showers.

The current was strong and steady and it wasn't long before the bridges and water tower of the town came into sight. We pulled into the small, half empty marina.

All four of us were anxious to take a walk in town so no one wanted to stay back with the boats. We found a spot under a bridge where they would be hidden, visible only from the river.

The grocery store was our first stop, a large store with a great variety of food. We splurged and bought meat for the first time on the trip to celebrate Tim's birthday. We left with four pounds of bacon and a five pound shoulder roast. We loaded up on cake, fresh fruit and cold drinks. The bill was higher than usual and we were getting a bit concerned about funds. We started to wonder what condition we'd be in financially when we hit St. Louis but that was still weeks away, something to worry about another day.

We went into the lobby of a small hotel and paid eight dollars to use the shower in a room. As each of us showered, the others enjoyed the TV and lying on the soft beds. It was a real treat after eight weeks on the river. Reluctantly, we left our temporary hotel room to head back to the boats with our groceries.

Our boats were safe and sound when we got back. There was a small wooded area just downstream so we decided we'd make camp there, hoping no one would bother us. We noticed a fair amount of bugs in among the trees so we put up the tents and started a fire.

When we had a bed of hot coals, we cooked up the roast, sliced into thick steaks. The sizzle and aroma made our mouths water. We feasted on steak and baked potatoes; finally a night we were all full and could eat no more. John took one of the paper maps of Lake Oahe and ceremonially burned it in the fire.

I don't know who came up with the idea but we decided to take the next day as an official day off and enjoy Pierre some more.

"Don't wake me up with the sun," I kidded to Steve. "I'm sleeping in."

"You and me both!" he laughed, sipping fresh coffee we bought earlier in the day.

The trees kept the morning sun off our tents so they didn't heat up, allowing us to sleep late. As we started a fire in mid morning, it was still cool in the shade, though in the sun it was quite warm for late September.

We scrambled a dozen eggs and cooked up all four pounds of bacon and did our best to toast raisin English Muffins. We even had butter! The joke was that we had probably consumed more calories in our last two meals than in the whole two weeks we were on Lake Oahe!

The YMCA in town was open and we only had to pay one dollar each to get in. There was a beautiful swimming pool, a locker room with showers, and even a sauna.

Steve had never been in a sauna so after spending some time in the pool, we all headed for the tiny wooden room.

"You grew up just outside Chicago," John commented to Steve. "You never used a sauna?"

"I just never had the opportunity."

As we stepped in, the moist heat hit us like a brick wall. With our white YMCA towels wrapped around us, we sat down on the smooth wooden benches.

"Oh man, it's hot!" Steve exclaimed. "It burns the inside of my nose!"

Tim laughed as he shook his head. "What a hick."

"Relax," I said. "Don't breathe so hard through your nose and you'll be fine."

We spent the afternoon alternating between the pool and the sauna and finished up with a long hot shower. There were dispensers of fancy liquid body soap with a strong fruity smell.

"I hope this soap doesn't attract bugs!" John yelled from his shower stall.

"We haven't smelled this sweet in weeks!" I yelled back.

We had another great dinner that night, sitting around the fire. It had been a fun day, much different than most days in these last eight weeks. It was also very different than the experience Lewis and Clark and their men had when they made their way through the area, heading upriver, almost the same time in late September of 1804.

The captains had been warned that the Teton Lakota tribes were not like the more hospitable people along the river. To travel up the river through their lands required gifts from any travelers. If they were refused, the Lakota were known to take those "gifts" by force.

One might think the Indian warriors were outgunned, the soldiers having rifles, muskets and even a swivel gun on the port of the large keelboat, but these were not the automatic weapons of today. A Lakota warrior could release a deadly arrow from his bow and have it ready to fire again in seconds. The soldiers would take much longer. And the Corps had less than fifty men, facing many more warriors.

On September 25th, a council with the captains and three chiefs was held at the mouth of the Teton River, on the opposite bank facing modern day Pierre. Today it is named the Bad River. The meeting was tense and tempers flared, partly due to the fact neither side had a good, reliable interpreter. The Corps spent a week in this area and tensions never did cease. There were a few times guns had been sighted and bows had been drawn.

Fortunately, a week later the corps would get some relief from their tense times with the Lakota, spending a few pleasant days at an Arikara village on the river, the actual site now submerged under the waters of Lake Oahe.

Though much of the land and the river are still the same, and one can picture 1804 in one's mind, it is difficult to sense what those soldiers experienced and felt so long ago As much as we try to imagine and hold on to it, the world as they knew it is long gone, never to return.

In fact, as I think back to that night, feeling so great about finishing Lake Oahe and having such fun in town, I must admit the world for four adventurous River Rats back in 1979 is also gone, never to return. Perhaps that's why the memories are so special.

That evening as we sipped coffee and talked, there were no more Lakota warriors though I'm sure many of their descendants still live peaceably now on these same ancestral lands. Any battles fought now are football and basketball teams battling it out on Pierre fields and school gymnasiums.

The immense herds of buffalo are gone, as well as the wolves, replaced with streets, homes, lights, and all the trappings of civilization. The deer and antelope, along with the coyote have managed to survive and still roam the hills and prairie, though in far fewer numbers.

And today, just over two short decades later, the four Missouri River Rats have grown up and are not so young anymore, living in yet another very different world. Yet people are still people. And thankfully, God is still God and all this human history is simply part of His story, His sovereign will.

Lucky B. Springfield

September 24–October 4, 1979

We left the town of Pierre early in the morning. The water was cold and clear as it was after each dam. The hillsides were taller on both sides of the river and seemed a bit greener with trees and bushes bunched up in the draws and valleys.

"Hey, Glenn, look at those trees," John mentioned, pointing up a steep draw on the right bank.

I looked over and realized there was no mistaking it. The trees were just starting to show shades of yellow and orange in their leaves. The warm sun concealed it but the trees were announcing autumn was upon us. We knew the temperatures would be dropping soon but so far we were comfortable, even at night. The days of hot dry weather in Montana and North Dakota six weeks ago were history. Now the question was whether we would enjoy mild temperatures for awhile or soon be shivering with early winter weather. We all knew we didn't have the clothes for winter.

Lake Sharpe was only eighty miles long, the width only about one to two miles. We stayed close to the west side bank, the opposite bank looking like just a distant band of land, with water below it and a massive blue sky above.

It was one of those days of paddling for hours, zoning out. We spent the day humming songs to ourselves, daydreaming, doing very little talking. I spent time putting more pressure on my left arm, then changing and paddling harder with the right. At times John would forget to switch sides, which is the privilege of the man in the front of the canoe, so we would spend thirty or forty minutes paddling on the same side.

"John, switch," I'd remind him. Then we'd paddle that side till one of us would remember to switch again. There were no distant points to paddle to on this narrow long lake with very few turns.

After the heat of the day passed and the sun was not as strong, we started spotting antelope and deer on both sides of the river. There were all kinds of birds, from pelicans on the water to gulls and hawks in the air.

The Crow Creek Indian Reservation was on the left bank while the Lower Brule Indian Reservation was on the right, where we set up camp. These were descendents of the very people Lewis and Clark had encountered. We saw no one that day or the day before.

There were a few more days of being stranded on shore due to the wind. Some days we took it in stride and other days we would be frustrated and filled with a sense of futility. There were days we would complain to each other and days we knew to just keep it to ourselves.

In one camp we were harassed by wasps for the first time. We never found a nest, but they seemed to be everywhere. We were used to flies and mosquitoes, but these wasps looked mean. Amazingly, no one got stung.

Our last day on Lake Sharpe started with a wonderful tailwind directly at our back. The dam came into view and quickly grew larger. The sight was a familiar one to all of us now; the generator towers, the power plant, the concrete spillway, even the warning signs. It was about three o'clock in the afternoon when we came ashore on the north side.

As with all the other dams, we were blessed with a ride to a store to get some supplies, this time by a friendly retired gentleman who was out for a day of fishing. In no time we had an Army Corps of Engineers truck carrying the boats to the other side of the dam.

Our camp was in the campground, close to where we could shove off in the morning. We still had a few hours of light left, but even though we had sailed most of the day, it felt good to be on land. Food and hot showers were too tempting to pass up.

There were just a few campsites taken so it was quiet and still as if we were out in the wilderness. The evening was again simply gorgeous, another beautiful South Dakota night.

While we were sitting around our fire in the morning, two elderly women came walking by and said hello. They had noticed we didn't have a vehicle and were curious where we were headed and how far we'd come. They were very sweet when we told them our story, congratulating and encouraging us. They wished us well and walked on, but as we were packing the boats, they returned. They gave us a large box of cookies, fresh tomatoes, apples, and a bag of potatoes, not knowing how potatoes had become the main staple of our diet. We thanked them, finished packing the boats, and headed down the river. A few elderly fishermen quietly fishing off a nearby dock glanced at us, one giving a quick wave.

The next town we encountered was Chamberlain, S.D. The town was sprawled out over the open prairie, with two highway bridges going over the wide river. We came across a small campground just before the town itself, so we decided to spend the night there. It had been another day of mostly sailing but we were anxious to get out of the boats. Perhaps just sitting without paddling just makes the day go longer. Whatever the reason, it felt great to be on dry land. We picked a campsite at the end of the campground, away from the few sites that were taken.

We found out it was Friday night. Funny how the day of the week has little meaning on the river and hadn't mattered to us for the last seven weeks. But it was a big night in Chamberlain. It was the homecoming game at the high school and everyone was going. When we were done with our dinner, we decided a football game would be a nice change.

We were told the high school field was only a few miles away so we started walking. Once in town we started hitchhiking and were picked up by two high school girls heading to the game. We had showered before heading out, but I still can't imagine what we looked like out there in the road. Picking up hitch hikers was a bit safer back in the late '70s, but now I have to believe those girls were just picking us up simply because their parents would have forbidden it.

The game was against Mobridge. We recognized the name. We had paddled through Mobridge almost two weeks ago! How different distance is with a seventeen-foot canoe rather than a yellow school bus! Our sense of distance and mileage had become much more similar to Lewis and Clark and their men than people from the twentieth century, the people there in the bleachers.

It had only been a year since I had played high school football. The sights and sounds brought back fond memories. There were families cheering in the stands, little kids running around, cars driving in and out of the parking lot. For a few hours we were back in the real world. Since we were in Chamberlain, we cheered for the home team. Some of the locals were eyeing us, probably wondering who we were, but no one asked.

When the game was over and we headed back to the river, I felt very out of place. Everyone else was heading home. We were heading back to our tents and our boats. I suppose those boats and tents had become home. Maybe I was just starting to wonder for just how long. It seemed like quite a long walk back to the campground.

The day we left Chamberlain we passed through a section of the river with water unlike anything we had seen before. We were paddling close to the left bank when the water took on a different color. It became a strange shade of brown or tan.

"What is it?" John asked, stirring it with his paddle.

"Man, it's like quick sand or something!" Steve exclaimed.

The first four or five inches of the water were perfectly clear, but after that it appeared to be mud or sand. The strange thing was that my paddle went through it like it was water.

"This is eerie," I added. "What would happen if you fell into it?"

"Fish couldn't swim in this," Tim said, leaning over the front of the canoe.

Our tailwind had died so we paddled through the strange water. It wasn't really any threat to us but I have to admit it was a relief when within a short time we were back into normal lake water.

The days continued with perfect sunshine and warm temperatures, as if ignoring the fact it would be October in just a few days. Lewis and Clark enjoyed the same pleasant weather coming through that area heading up river during the same season, mid-September. They spent two days there and even named it "Pleasant Camp."

While there the men saw their first pronghorn antelope, their first coyote, and their first jackrabbit. Captain Lewis, while passing the same area where the town of Chamberlain lies today, wrote that he thought he could look out on the prairie and easily see three thousand bison at one time.

In the evening the men heard what they thought was the howling of different sorts of wolves. They most likely were hearing both wolves and coyotes, a sound that always has stirred strong feelings of wonder in me from the very first time I heard them.

We enjoyed our own Pleasant Camp that night, alone again on our river.

The last day of September found us stranded on the shore of Lake Francis Case.

After sleeping in and sipping tea around the fire, I walked up over the summit of a small hill to get a better look at the lake. Cottontail rabbits were everywhere, standing perfectly still or running across my path. I thought about getting the .22 but decided against it. The view was spectacular on such a clear day. The waves were large out on the lake, the whitecaps rising and crashing all across the open expanse, looking awfully menacing for a canoe. The wind had a bit of a chill to it but was no match for the warmth of the sun on my face and my clothes.

We had pretty much settled in for the night after dinner when the wind seemed to slow, then stop. A peaceful calm came over the prairie and even more amazing, the lake suddenly became still, the water as smooth as glass.

With the moon just rising over the hills, illuminating the night, we decided to pack up and get back on the river. We were rested and fed so why not make some mileage? We didn't pack very well, but got everything in the boats and headed out.

The water was perhaps the most still we had ever seen it. The paddles seemed to grab the water and propel us with hardly any resistance. The canoe felt great as it skimmed across the surface. The reflection of the over 2/3 moon shone across the lake. Tim and Steve were just ahead of us, silhouetted in the glowing light. The hills and bluffs were shades of blue and purple in the moonlight and created a surreal scene all around us.

The only thing that could make the night better would be to sail and after only an hour or so of paddling, a gentle tailwind began hitting our backs. Up ahead of us, I could see Tim and Steve pulling out their sail before Steve yelled back to us. John and I weren't about to protest. We set up our sail and got comfortable. It was my turn to steer the sail with the ropes.

The steady breeze at our backs and the calm water allowed us to travel the fastest we ever had. "I love it!" Steve yelled back to us from about fifty yards ahead.

John agreed this was well worth being stranded all day!

"What do you think we're doing?" I asked John. "About ten or twelve miles per hour?"

The left bank seemed to be flying by. "At least that!" John replied, leaning back against the canoe bags.

There are some events in our lives that we look back on and try to recall how quickly they occurred, since time seems to be altered while we're experiencing those moments. The same was true that night. We were enjoying sailing along, faster than we ever had. Everything was going so well that we hadn't noticed the wind had grown stronger. At some point, instead of the full sails pushing us along, swells were now lifting the boat, carrying us forward, than dropping us down. The motion was wasn't unlike being in the saddle of a galloping horse.

"This is great!" John yelled back to me. The stronger wind was becoming louder as well and I barely heard him.

Tim and Steve were only about thirty yards in front of us but when I yelled to them, it seemed my voice was lost in the wind. I was feeling just a bit uneasy watching the swells coming up along the sides of the boat.

"Hey John, should we head in?" I shouted.

He turned around, and I thought I saw concern on his face, even in the moonlight. "What?" he yelled.

"Should we head in to shore?" I motioned and pointed to the left bank, which now was about forty yards away.

"I don't know!" he shrugged his shoulders and raised his arms. When a swell gripped the boat he quickly grabbed the sides to steady himself.

I noticed Tim and Steve's canoe was getting closer and starting to drift toward shore so I was hoping they were thinking the same thing I was. When they were close enough to hear, I shouted out to them. "Should we head in?" It seemed they still couldn't hear me over the wind.

The waves were now large enough that their boat would disappear for a few seconds before reappearing. If we didn't get close enough to talk soon, I was thinking of heading to shore without them. I was getting very nervous.

Waves began hitting the left side of the canoe, spraying us and splashing into the boat. All I could think of was how poorly we had packed the boats and how much gear we might lose if we went under. The sail turned violently to the left, pulling on the ropes in my hands.

The sound was distinct over the gusts of wind, having heard it before. I thought the guy's boat had disappeared behind a swell, but I realized their sail had snapped in two and was now hanging over the boat, getting wrapped up in waves. I could hear them yelling to each other, though I couldn't make out the words. I knew the waves were tossing them like a toy boat but I also knew there was nothing we could do in those waves.

The wind had shifted suddenly and was pounding us from the side. I reached for the mast of our sail, pulling it out of its anchor, struggling not to have it pulled overboard. John instinctively grabbed his paddle and we tried to turn the boat into the waves, and towards shore.

In the moonlight, the shore was just white with waves crashing on the beach. My heart was pounding as it got even louder as we got closer to shore. As I paddled I looked over my shoulder and saw Tim and Steve now paddling not far behind us, their sail draped over both sides of the boat.

When we were only a few feet from landing on the beach the breaking waves swept right over the sides of the canoe, flooding it. We both jumped out into about two feet of water and grabbing the front of the boat, dragged it through the last of the waves and up onto the beach. Once on dry land, we ran back to help Tim and Steve get their boat in.

Our relief was expressed in laughter and shouting over the waves and the wind that was now deafening.

"I thought we were dead!" Steve laughed, waving his arms in the air.

"Did you see our sail snap right in half?" Tim added.

"I heard it but I couldn't see anything!" I shouted back.

"That was unbelievable!" John said, shaking his head.

"Oh man," Steve moaned, looking at their mast. "It snapped in the same spot yours did!"

At least we knew how to fix theirs the way we had fixed ours. Both masts were now just about a foot shorter.

We had landed on a nice sandy beach. The boats were full of water so we emptied everything out in the sand. Thankfully everyone's sleeping bags hadn't gotten too wet and we could still have a comfortable night's sleep. My life vest had gotten too soaked to use as a pillow so I bundled up one of my shirts. Even while dry and warm, listening to those waves hitting the beach was just a bit disturbing. Though exhausted, it took me quite a while to fall asleep amid the roar of wind and waves.

We had gone about ten miles perhaps in a very short time, but had almost paid dearly for it. If any of us hadn't developed a deep respect for the wind and waves of those lakes yet, we all had now.

The first day of October brought somewhat cooler weather. It was the first time I kept my long sleeve shirt on when it was time to start paddling. It stayed on all day.

Within less than an hour on the water the wind came up and we were able to sail again. As we secured the mast, I kidded to John, "I'm staying close to shore."

He just grinned back at me. "Yeah."

The hills were just beautiful, taller than usual with stands of trees clustered here and there, showing off even more autumn colors. Two deer eyed us cautiously from the bank as we paddled by.

A ¾ moon finally came up over the steep hills as the colors of a serene sunset faded. Compared to the night before, it was wonderfully relaxing. It was one of those nights of enjoying the fire and enjoying where we were.

The Corps of Discovery had spent the night on the opposite side of the river on September 10, 1804. Their evening wasn't nearly as nice with strong winds and a steady rain that had fallen for days.

We reached Fort Randall Dam by the end of the next day. Being mid-week and October, there were very few people around at all. The campground was deserted. There was no store and more importantly, no Army Corps of Engineer folks around.

We walked up the road from the dam and the first vehicle, a small red pickup, came down the road and pulled over beside us. An elderly man stuck his head out the window and asked, "Need a ride?"

Ed was a really nice guy. He lived in Pickstown, the tiny settlement just up the road from the dam. He gave Steve and me a ride into town while Tim and John stayed with the boats. He waited for us while we bought some bread and lunch meat, then gave us a ride back to our campsite. Ed enjoyed hearing all about our adventures on the lake. He laughed when we told him about the wind two nights before, inform-ing us the winds had been ninety miles per hour!

The clerk in the store told us we wouldn't see anyone from the Army Corps till morning so we were stuck on this side of the dam. When we were back at the boats, Ed gave us a box of donuts and eight cans of assorted soups he had in the cab of his truck. We thanked him for all his generosity and he headed back home.

The empty campground had showers in the bathroom but unfor-tunately, with the hot water turned off, it would have been warmer to jump in the river.

"I knew you were getting ugly on the river," I joked to Steve looking in the mirror, "but I didn't realize how ugly I was getting!"

We had a pleasant surprise waiting for us the next morning. When we got up we found a stash of food inside one of the canoes! There were three cans of 7Up, three cube steaks, a half pound of coffee, a half a loaf of bread, some grease, and a Tupperware container with two dozen pre-cooked chicken wings! There was no one around so we had to assume our good friend Ed had come by early before dawn. The food couldn't have been there long since animals hadn't found it yet. Surprisingly, no one had heard his tiny red pickup. We marveled at all the good people we had met so far and their amazing generosity.

That generosity continued. When we finally found a Corpsman and asked for a ride around the dam, he told us the main office in Omaha, NE, had just issued a memo that there are to be no more services offered to canoeists portaging around the dams. Before we could even start to nego-tiate with him, a fisherman walked up and offered to take us around!

It was late morning when we finally got into the water. The current of the narrow river was such a welcomed relief from the lakes. Probably by the next day, we would reach the last lake, only twenty five miles long, and one last dam, than have 810 miles of river with a current all the way to St. Louis.

On the morning of October 4th the chill in the air was noticeable. Even in the sleeping bag I could feel it, wanting to get up and sit by a fire, yet not wanting to get out of the bag at all. Steve wore socks for the very first time on the trip. He hardly ever wore shoes, never mind any socks! Each of us was pulling out clothes we hadn't worn yet, a real sign the season was changing.

The river remained narrow and we encountered sand bars that sometimes we ran aground on. After all the massive bodies of water we had spent the last month on, I didn't mind the shallow water at all. Reed grass and cattails lined the banks, something we hadn't seen before.

In the afternoon we came upon the small town of Springfield, S.D. We were now at the beginning of our last lake, aptly named Lewis and Clark Lake. It was only about twenty five miles long, perhaps five miles wide at its widest point.

As we paddled by Springfield we passed a farm on the left bank. The large farm house was beside the river with a luxuriously green lawn. A large white wooden sign stood in front of the house along a narrow dirt road. "Rabbits For Sale, two dollars."

To be honest, I'm not sure who came up with the suggestion first but we were suddenly talking about rabbit for dinner. We all were remembering the wonderful meal the coyote had given us back on Lake Oahe weeks before, but I kept saying, "This isn't the same as that jackrabbit!" Who's willing to shoot a few rabbits at point blank range? Surely not me! And who was going to clean them?

My vote was "No" but I was outvoted three to one. I had to admit that I would enjoy a rabbit dinner even if I didn't have to do the shooting. Tim volunteered to do the dirty deed and do the cleaning.

We went ashore and found the farmer near the house. He suggested we purchase three to feed all of us, but we decided on two. He brought two rabbits out in a small cardboard box. Steve put it in their boat, which was a relief to me. I knew if I spent too much time looking at them, there'd be no way I could eat them.

We paddled another hour or so as we watched the river widen into the lake. Our camp was on the Nebraska side, our first camp in Nebraska, our 4th state on the trip.

The box with the rabbits was placed on shore while we collected wood. There was definitely a sense of tension about dinner. I think I still didn't believe we were really going to do it. I walked over and looked in the box, two sets of glossy black eyes peering up at me, their bodies motionless white balls of fur.

"Guys, are we sure we want to do this?" I asked, sounding way too much like a wimp.

"Dinnertime," Tim said somewhat matter-of-factly as he reached in the box and picked one up. He had the pistol in his other hand. The unwary rabbit seemed too docile and it bothered me how he didn't even know to put up a fight.

I looked away out on the lake as the shot rang out. With the corner of my eye I could see the rabbit's hind legs pumping feverishly as if trying to escape. It laid there on its side, legs flailing in the air for what was probably only seconds but felt like minutes. When it was still, Tim walked over and picked up the second rabbit.

The mood had changed. I wasn't surprised that shooting that rabbit bothered me, but I was surprised the other guys seemed to be affected by it as well. Perhaps it was just the innocent way it looked up at us. Perhaps it was a sense of its helplessness. Whatever the reason, I could tell no one liked it, not at all.

"Com'on, guys, that was bad. We can't do that again," I pleaded this time.

"What are we gonna do with it then? It can't survive out here on its own," was John's weak reply.

"Well," I said, thinking out loud, "She can be our mascot!"

"A mascot!" Steve laughed.

As silly as the idea sounded, I could tell by the looks on every-one's face that the rabbit wasn't going to die that day. The Corps of Discovery had a dog on their great adventure. The Missouri River Rats would have a rabbit.

"Do rabbits swim?" Steve asked as it looked back at him with a blank stare.

While Tim skinned and cleaned the unfortunate rabbit, the rest of us went about naming the newest member of our crew. "Lucky" seemed like an appropriate name considering what happened to her brother. Since we bought her in Springfield, S.D. we decided on Lucky B. (the B for bunny) Springfield.

We tried feeding her a variety of things that first evening but Lucky seemed to prefer the grasses around camp. We took a blue bandanna and made a small halter for her, attached to a twenty-foot line. She seemed content enough, even when we sat around the fire consuming her sibling. It was a strange meal to say the least. I was grateful I could eat my baked potato guilt-free.

We sipped coffee and watched Lucky enjoy freedom she probably never knew. She scampered around camp, smelling everything and everyone. She seemed to know to avoid the fire.

Away from the warmth of the fire there was a chill in the evening air. Night brought a brilliant full moon climbing up over the hills, the third one for us on the river. I wondered if we would see a fourth. I also wondered how Lucky would do with about 900 miles of river yet to paddle.

A Soldier's Suffering

The Boy's Third Morning

August 21, 2002

I can't imagine how many hours of sleep the boys and I got that night, but at some point we were all sleeping and sometime before dawn the wind, rain, and lightning ceased. At first light I awoke, still soggy in my drenched sleeping bag. It felt awful and I didn't hesitate for a moment getting up. The boys were still asleep. As I unzipped the door to the tent they didn't even stir.

I stepped through a large puddle on the floor of the tent as I climbed out into the morning light. Standing there outside the tent in my wet shorts and drenched socks, it was hard to believe there had even been a storm just hours ago in the dark of night. Though the sun had just peeked over the hills in the east, the air was already warm. The sky was blue and there wasn't even a hint of a breeze.

The ground had been so dry that it had absorbed most of the rain so there were very few puddles. Everything we had left out of the tent had been splashed with mud from the pounding rain but now had dried to a dark brown coating.

I changed into dry clothes and walked down to the bank to check on the canoes. I was glad I had rolled them over the night before. They would have been filled with water this morning. I could sense a slight odor of river mud in the air. It's not a good or a bad smell, something like how earthy the air smells after a rain, but it was familiar and reminded me of our trip back in '79 and made me smile.

I walked back to the tent and woke up the boys.

"Hey, guys, time to get up." I peered inside the tent and found Dustin on his back and Joshua all curled up in a ball. I couldn't believe they could sleep.

"Guys, you'll be more comfortable when you get into some dry clothes." It took more coaxing to get Josh up than it did Dustin, but before long they were both up and dressed.

It was a big day ahead for us. It was our last day on the river but also the day we would rendezvous with Karen at Judith Landing. It was still early morning and we weren't meeting Karen and Dad till around noon, but I felt a bit anxious to get there. I didn't want them getting there first and worrying whether they had missed us or if they were in the right place. Karen would have driven three hours by then through some of the most remote land our country has to offer and I wanted to be there to greet her.

Our wood supply was thoroughly soaked and muddied so we decided to not bother with a morning fire and just eat Pop Tarts. We carried our bins down to the river, loaded the boats, and stepped through fresh Missouri River mud to push the canoes out into the current.

The boys couldn't stop talking about the incredible storm. They both agreed they had never been in such a furious and loud storm in their lives. We compared it to the wild wind storm that suddenly hit us while camping in Monument Valley, Utah, when the boys were younger and the thunderstorm that had come through our campsite up in the woods in Northern Ontario, Canada, just a few years ago. I had to agree it was one of the fiercest in my life. All that of course made it simply awesome to the boys.

I couldn't help but think how ironic it was. I had hoped and prayed for weeks for nice weather for our long-awaited trip. In fact I was quite confident that for just two nights in late August in Montana there was little threat of rain. The odds were indeed in my favor. But God had different plans.

I never would have asked for such a soggy, sleepless night as the one the night before. I would have preferred a peaceful night in front of a soothing fire, watching the sun slip down behind that huge limestone wall across the river, giving way to a sky full of a million stars. Yet, except for maybe the climb up to Hole In the Wall, Dustin and Josh will tell you the night of the storm was one of the highlights of the trip. They had experienced the river in a dramatic and unique way...and I have to say I was grateful. I couldn't have asked for anything more.

As we paddled down the river, again the wonderful feeling of the canoe under me, the fresh warmth of the sun on my face, the sound of the water as we paddled, it all seemed like a wonderful reward after the night before. I'm sure I appreciated that beautiful morning's warmth and brightness so much more after the dark and wet hours during the night. It made me wonder which experience was the real blessing.

The beautiful morning of course was a blessing. I only had to look around at the awesome scenery and feel how comfortable and at ease I felt paddling along. And to make the scene even more perfect, the boys and I spotted a few mule deer by the water's edge, their large ears twitching as we floated by.

Yet in a very real way, it was the clamor of the thunder, the discomfort of everything being wet, the inability to change our surroundings, again those dark and wet hours that now gave me the perspective to appreciate the peace, calm, and comfort of the morning.

If you remember my speaking of "river miles" way back when we got our tow into Great Falls, Montana, back in August of '79, I would consider that storm an example. It was an event that surely wasn't planned. In fact, I prayed against it. Yet like an unexpected bend in the river, it brought with it an experience the boys and I could never have experienced otherwise. A blessing to last a lifetime, and touch two generations, if not more, simply by suffering through a soggy and miserable sleepless night in a tent in the middle of Montana! I wouldn't have missed it for anything!

Those of us who have lived long enough will have to admit though we don't enjoy trials and would almost always choose to avoid suffering through them, it is through those trials of life that we learn, mature, and for the Christian, experience a unique time with God. While saying that, I must also confess that many times, more than I'd like to admit, the learning and the maturing comes sometimes much later. Sadly, too often I will still respond inappropriately to various trials than later when they have passed, I will finally see God's perspective, the big picture, and with a humbled heart, finally see His hand in it all.

Many books have been written on suffering and the Christian faith. I suppose it is one topic that every one of us will write our own chapters in our own life's experience. None of us will escape it. As parents, we must also accept our children won't either. Though it comes in so many ways and forms, each us will be touched by suffering, sometimes even shaping our lives.

I remember when Emma, only three years old, had to learn this sad fact and I had to be reminded of it. A friend from our church was building his own house and on weekends men from the church would pitch in and help. This particular weekend the weather was beautiful and while about a dozen men worked, the ladies prepared an outdoor feast.

While we took time out to eat, a bunch of barn cats came around looking for scraps. They were dirty, flea infested, and really needed some TLC. Well, as you'd expect, Emma fell in love with one, a particularly adorable tiny ball of matted fur. When she walked up to me, cuddling it and giving me a pleading look with her big blue eyes, I was totally defenseless. I looked to Karen for help but from her expression, I knew she would be no help. Needless to say, Emma went home with a brand new kitten.

Emma named her Callie. She and that kitten were inseparable for about a week. We brought it to the vet and started all the shots, the wormings, everything little Callie needed. But one night after Emma had gone to sleep Callie started to have trouble walking. It was as if she had some type of neurological problem. By midnight, Callie was dead.

That night I went in and sat by Emma in her bed, watching her angelic face as she slept so peacefully, breathing ever so slowly and deeply. How could I possibly tell her in the morning that little Callie had suddenly died? I sat there on her bed, praying for both her and me.

The next morning Karen and I sat with Emma and as gently as I could I told her what had happened. Looking into that precious face, watching her eyes as she tried to comprehend what I was saying, all I could see was the face of innocence trying to understand the unfair and sometimes even ugly world we live in. When I had said enough for her to understand she simply wrapped her little arms around me, perhaps tighter than she ever had, buried her face in my shirt, and cried. And her father cried with her.

Oh, I felt bad for little Callie, but the tears I couldn't hold back were for my daughter. Not even so much that she would feel so sad for a time, but for the simple realization that as her father there was nothing I could do to protect her from the harsh realities of this world, try as I might. Suffering is something we can try to shelter our little ones from, at least for a time, and we should, but at some point, even in so-called Ground Week of Spiritual Training, they must start to experience suffering so they can in time learn from it.

> You therefore must endure hardship as a good soldier of
> Christ Jesus.
> 2 Timothy 2:3

In the Apostle Paul's letter to Timothy, a new pastor, he speaks of the Christian life as spiritual warfare and points out there will be hardships to suffer through. In this case it dealt with the conflict between the faith and the persecution of the unbelieving world, but it also includes the war against Satan and even the war against our own sinful natures.

One would think it absurd to enlist in the US Army or Marines and not expect to suffer hardship. Why then should a spiritual soldier expect anything less in such a spiritual war? Paul experienced five whippings, three beatings, and one stoning where he was left for dead. He was shipwrecked three times, one of those times spending a day and a half afloat waiting for rescue. He faced constant dangers in his travels from both man and beast, in cities and in wilderness, dealing often with hunger and thirst, sleeplessness, and being exposed to both blistering heat and numbing cold. Sounds like a combination of US Army Ranger and US Navy Seal to me!

The Apostle Peter wrote of suffering as well. In the Book of 1st Peter, he writes to believers caught up in the terrible persecution of the church throughout the Roman Empire right around the time of the burning of Rome.

> In this you greatly rejoice, though now for a little while, if
> need be, you have been grieved by various trials.
> 1 Peter 1:6

Peter says so much in such a short sentence. "Though now for a little while" reassures me that the trials of this life are indeed very temporary compared to eternity. They all will pass in due time, though admittedly, usually not as quickly as we might like.

Paul says the same thing to the Corinthian Church, speaking of his suffering to proclaim the gospel. "For our light affliction, which is but for a moment, is working for us a far more exceeding and eternal weight of glory." After all these men had been through, they stayed focused on the eternal.

Three little words, "if need be" are also reassuring. It should help remind us that there is a purpose in each trial, even if we don't know necessarily what it is. I am usually somewhat skeptical of those that think they know the exact purpose behind certain events or trials. I hear things like, "It was God judging that person." Or "God wanted to teach them." Or "God wants to build their faith." One of many reasons could be correct, perhaps more than one. I believe asking "Why?" sometimes can send you down the wrong road. The simple answer is to keep trusting God, even through the tough times, even through the river miles, with all the bends and twists they bring.

"You have been grieved" is enough to help me realize its okay to be emotional through those times. God gave us emotions. Sometimes it seems as Christians, we feel guilty if we feel frustrated, saddened, angry, or disappointed through tough times. It's as if we should always have a holy glow with a bright smile because we're so spiritual. I suppose if you're strong enough you can fool most of the people around you, but you're preventing true fellowship...and you're not fooling God. Sometimes this life hurts.

We can all agree that "various trials" do come in all forms. In the same way that a soldier does not get to choose his battles, neither does the spiritual soldier. For someone facing a health crisis, I would imagine they would gladly trade that for a financial crisis. For the person struggling in deep debt, they might feel very differently. For the person suffering through a broken relationship, or even the loss of a loved one, I'm sure they would gladly trade that for anything else. No, we can't choose our battles but we can choose to trust God as we go through them. As I have said before, I have finally realized sometimes the blessing is in the battle. If it helps us see our dependence on Jesus and draws us closer to Him, it is indeed a blessing.

So what does Peter mean by "In this you greatly rejoice"?

> ...that the genuineness of your faith, being much more precious than gold that perishes, though it is tested by fire, may be found to praise, honor, and glory in the revelation of Jesus Christ.
> 1 Peter 1:7

Through trials, we can be assured that our faith is genuine. It is not a test for God to know, since He already knows our hearts, but a test for us. When God gives us the grace to hold on and know He is still there, we can know the power of God and that our salvation is based on Him and not on us. In fact, Peter speaks of that salvation in the preceding verses.

> Blessed be the God and Father of our Lord Jesus Christ, who according to His abundant mercy has begotten us again to a living hope through the resurrection of Jesus Christ from the dead, to an inheritance incorruptible and undefiled and that does not fade away, reserved in heaven for you, who are kept by the power of God through faith for salvation ready to be revealed in the last time.
> 1 Peter 1:3–5

The joy of our salvation is not a superficial emotion like happiness when things are going well for us or unhappiness when trials come. There have been times I didn't feel very Christian. There have been times I was even mad at God. But I have that inner joy of knowing I belong to God because of His love and mercy and not of my own merit or works, and He is always with me. We need to make sure and help our children understand you can have that joy, even while you're grieving through various trials. We need to trust the scriptures, not our feelings. Feelings may be real, but very often they are not accurate. They fluctuate in ways we sometimes can't even understand.

A few years ago I experienced a vivid example of how fickle feelings can be. Joshua and I had just arrived at Father/Son Camp, three fun days out in the woods with sons and dads from all the area churches. We had been doing it for years since Josh was only six. We arrived Friday afternoon and after a short snack we headed out to do all the activities the camp offered.

Josh was disappointed to find they had not brought horses that year, one of his favorite activities. Without horses, we decided to head down to the archery range, another favorite activity of ours. But as we walked across the field, the sky that had been gray all day finally started to drop rain. The weather forecast had predicted rain all weekend and unfortunately for once it seemed to be accurate so far.

I started to think back to previous years when it rained and I wasn't too excited at the prospect of being wet and muddy for three days. I started thinking about the fact we hadn't brought enough change of clothes as my shoulders were already getting wet and my only pair of sneakers were starting to squeak in the wet, slick grass.

Looking around, I realized Josh had gotten older and many of the boys were now much younger than him. He probably wouldn't have as much fun with all those little kids. Before we reached the range, I started thinking about all the work at home that I wouldn't be able to get done being there at camp. I was thinking about everything negative. I could feel the depression hitting me like a brick wall. I even thought about how I hated that Hillary Clinton had been elected our state senator!

At the range, there were just a few dads and boys so Josh didn't have to wait to shoot. He's really a natural with a bow. He landed three arrows close to bull's eye, the other two only about an inch away. Everyone around seemed impressed. I sat on the picnic table behind Josh, really wishing we were heading home.

The next round I got up and shot with Josh. I hadn't picked up a bow since the previous year's camp. Josh challenged me to a contest. Whoever got more bull's eyes this round bought the candy bars back at the camp store. I told Josh, "You're on."

I guess a few dads overheard us because when Joshua's first shot hit the bull's eye, they all cheered and kidded me. I laughed along with them, but when I strung my bow and released the arrow, I too got a bull's eye. There were more cheers now. Josh just smiled, got ready and released another arrow, again hitting dead center. He gave me a satisfied look over his shoulder.

I answered his shot with my own bull's eye, giving him my own victorious smile. A few more dads and boys had shown up and now everyone was watching our little contest. Joshua and I both took two more shots and to everyone's amazement, including mine, we both hit bull's eyes!

A large crowd had now formed, as Joshua confidently got ready to take his final shot. He drew back the bow, held it for a moment, released, and everyone went wild as we all realized his fifth and final arrow hit dead center! I watched my son as he put down his bow, his face just beaming.

Now all eyes were on me. "No pressure, Dad!" a father called out from somewhere in the crowd behind me. I looked down at the target with the four arrows stuck in the center. I had never gotten four straight, never mind five. As I drew back, the crowd suddenly went silent. I held my breath and let the arrow fly. Before I could see where it landed I could tell just from the crowd's reaction that both Joshua and I had shot a perfect round, something no one at camp had ever done, never mind a father and son together!

As Joshua and I walked down to collect our arrows, everyone was talking about how awesome it had been to watch what we had done. As I walked with my son, I now felt like everything in the world was absolutely perfect. I was now walking on air. I had forgotten all about the horses, Josh getting older, the rain, even Senator Clinton!

The point is that I went from a bout of sudden depression based on a few circumstances to feeling on top of the world in just about five minutes and five arrows. If it taught me anything, it taught me to never trust my emotions. I'm glad I learned the lesson because neither Josh nor I were ever able to duplicate our fantastic feat. And we did have a wonderful three days that year.

> Beloved, do not think it strange concerning the fiery trial which is to try you, as though some strange thing happened to you; but rejoice to the extent that you partake of Christ's sufferings, that when His glory is revealed, you may also be glad with exceeding joy.
> 1 Peter 4:12

Isn't it funny how we sometimes argue with God or at least question Him when things don't go our way, as if it must be a mistake. It's almost comical how Peter says not to think it's a strange thing, yet so often our initial response to trials seems as if we are never to suffer or go through trials.

Again, Peter mentions the exceeding joy that comes later, keeping his focus on what matters the most.

> But let none of you suffer as a murderer, a thief, an evildoer, or as a busybody in other people's matters. Yet if anyone suffers as a Christian, let him not be ashamed, but let him glorify God in this manner.
> 1 Peter 4:15, 16

Too often our suffering is from the poor choices we make, our sinful way of thinking we know better than God's commands that are there to protect us and give our lives meaning and fulfillment. There is a big difference in suffering because of our sins than suffering for Christ and what is good and right.

God is so merciful and loving though, that even the suffering we experience due to our sins still helps bring us to repentance and wonderful reconciliation with Him.

> Therefore, let those who suffer according to the will of God commit their souls to Him in doing good, as to a faithful Creator.
> 1 Peter 4:19

I believe it is significant that Peter mentions God as Creator. It is sometimes easy to forget we were created by God. Committing ourselves to Him is just our way of acknowledging we are His. It is our way of accepting that His perfect will may include our suffering, sometimes for purposes we are not to know in this life.

By remembering God as Creator it should remind us that all creation, including mankind, had been created perfect. The scriptures tell us death and suffering only entered the world after Adam had sinned against God. Instead of blaming God, we need to realize we are to

blame. Suffering is in the world because of sin. Forgiveness and salvation are in the world because of God. Understanding that may not
prevent the pain and anguish of suffering, but I believe it allows that
underlying joy of knowing God to get us through.

I know there are Christians who do not believe the first eleven
chapters of Genesis are literal history and instead trust man's silly ideas
of evolution and the earth being billions of years old. Those Christians
need to ask themselves if sin and death didn't really enter the world
through Adam's sin as the scriptures clearly state, then how can we say
with any assurance that death and sin have been overcome, and the
penalty of our sins has been paid for by the death and resurrection of
Jesus? We seem to live in an age where our assurance of God has been
weakened by our compromising the authority of the scriptures. Peter
speaks of that in his second letter to believers.

> Beloved, I now write to you this second epistle (in both of
> which I stir up your pure minds by way of reminder), that
> you may be mindful of the words which were spoken before
> by the holy prophets, and of the commandment of us, the
> apostles of the LORD and Savior, knowing this first: that
> scoffers will come in the last days, walking according to
> their own lusts, and saying, "Where is the promise of His
> coming? For since the fathers fell asleep, all things continue
> as they were from the beginning of creation.
> 2 Peter 3:1- 4

How we all in this day and age need to have our minds stirred
with knowledge of the scriptures rather than just having our emotions
stirred, sometimes by false doctrine and error. Peter speaks of both the
teachings of the Old Testament prophets and also the new teachings of
the apostles, which would become the New Testament documents.

Peter reminds us as believers that scoffers will come in the last days.
They will be preoccupied with their own lusts and self interests and will
mock our assurance of Jesus returning one day. Every Christian who
wants to be a soldier for Christ should examine how Peter describes
these scoffers. They not only mock our belief in Christ's return, but by

saying all things continue as they were from the beginning of creation, they also mock God's judging the world by a worldwide flood.

> For this they willingly forget, that by the Word of God the heavens were of old, and the earth standing out of the water and in the water; (Genesis 1:7) by which the world that then existed perished, being flooded with water.
> 2 Peter 3: 5, 6

Peter is not talking about the Genesis flood as allegory, but as historical fact, explaining that those same people who make fun of our belief in Christ's return are the same people discounting the Genesis flood. I don't know any Christians who would mock the belief in Jesus' return yet they will turn around and say Noah's flood is just a story. Obviously Peter didn't think so. Neither did Paul or Jesus!

> But the heavens and earth, which are now preserved by the same word, are reserved for fire until the day of judgment and perdition of ungodly men.
> 2 Peter 3: 7

Peter speaks of the earth being judged again, this time by fire. Do Christians believe it? If the world really wasn't judged by water, can we really trust Peter?

Picking and choosing what parts of scripture we will believe will eventually leave us doubting God's Word. With that doubt, when trials hit us, we will be spiritual casualties. We might as well hang a glass angel from our rear view mirror and hope for the best!

No, we can have the assurance by the Word of God that though we live in this world corrupted by sin, where bad things do happen to everyone, including God's people, God will get us through them, and will one day restore all creation to perfection. The Apostle Peter and Paul never wavered on that throughout their lives. We each must do the same.

I have had the privilege of meeting and knowing Christian brothers and sisters who have suffered many various trials. Their lives have been testimonies of how God will work through those who will trust in Him. If you look around, you will find spiritual strength and power, sometimes in unlikely places through unexpected people. If we are discerning enough, we can be blessed by those around us.

One of those unexpected times occurred a few years ago. I had a lunch seminar scheduled at a veterinary clinic at noon and I needed to stop and prepare my PowerPoint slides for the presentation. It was such a warm sunny day I decided I'd park somewhere and get myself organized. Ahead was a parking lot I could pull into, but on my left was a pretty cemetery. You know the type. It had rolling hills with fresh new grass, budding trees and winding carriage lanes that were too pretty to pass up. I drove through the beautiful scene with my windows down and the blaring radio turned off. Toward the back, I found a secluded spot among some trees, parked the car, and got to work.

As I occasionally looked up to take in the scenery, I noticed one section of tombstones stood out among the others. The stones were of various sizes and looked just like the others, except for the bright ribbons, balloons, and various toys scattered throughout them. The tranquility of the scene was lost as I realized this was the children's section.

I walked over and started to read the inscriptions.

Some stones were already 10 or 15 years old while others were very new. The dates revealed some of the children were 2 or 3 years old, a few 8 or 9. The names were familiar first names we hear all the time at church or in playgrounds at school. Some stones announced the birth and death as the very same day. A few truly sad ones just said Baby Boy or Baby Girl.

Maybe you have to be a parent to understand, but the lump in my throat was not so much for these little ones, whom I knew were now with Jesus, but for their parents. I thought about all the heartache and sorrow every one of these stones meant.

The worst part was the toys and trinkets the parents had left. There were old helium balloons, now sitting on the ground, windmill toys slowly turning in the spring breeze, a toy truck, and so many stuffed animals. I could almost feel the parent's aching, wishing their little ones were hugging and kissing those little bears and sheep so lovingly, like my own little Emma at home. Yet these little Teddies were worn and dirtied by the elements. There would be no cuddles, no kisses. I was headed back to the car when I noticed a lengthy inscription on the back of one particular granite stone. I decided to stroll over to read it before I left. As I crouched down and started to read, I heard a voice call out, "Is that your little girl?"

At first I was startled, not realizing someone else was nearby, but hearing someone ask if this beautiful granite grave stone was for my precious Emma tore at my heart. The idea of it, even though it wasn't true, rocked me.

She was an elderly woman, with a very peaceful face and sparkling blue eyes that I noticed right away.

"No, it's not," I said, shocked that my voice cracked with emotion, still reeling from the thought of this grave being Emma's. I told her I had noticed the poem written on the back of the stone. She said she walked by it often and never had noticed it. "May I read it with you?" she asked.

As we both read the stone, we read a poem of a very special little girl who could not walk or talk or play like the other boys and girls, but whom God still saw as precious. This little girl would be a special blessing to those whose life she touched. Then, too soon, she would leave them. The poem was written by her mommy.

As I finished reading I realized we both were sobbing. We couldn't say or do anything but cry together. I suppose I should have felt strange. Here we were, two perfect strangers crying over the grave of a little girl neither of us knew. But I didn't. I just cried.

The woman pulled out some tissues from nowhere, an ability my grandmother had. We wiped our eyes and noses. "She was only five years old," I was just barely able to get out. Her name was Amber, but I didn't attempt to talk more.

The sweet woman looked up at me, her blue eyes still full of tears, and told me she had lost her own child, a son. I tried to say, "I'm sorry," but I don't think it came out audibly. She explained he was grown, in his thirties. Cancer. It had been ten years now, yet her eyes revealed a pain that never went away, and for both of us, more tears came.

She told me of an old saying she had never forgotten. It explained how when a wife dies, the husband is called a widower. When a husband dies, the wife is called a widow. When parents die, the child is called an orphan. But when a child dies there is no name for the parent. There is no name because none could describe the sorrow and pain.

Nonetheless, she told me she was a Christian and that we need to trust in God's plan. I told her I was relieved that Jesus had said that all children were welcomed into His kingdom. I told her we all need to trust in the scriptures, yet I think I was saying it more for me than for this faithful saint.

I shared with her my own wife and my two boys and little girl. They seemed even more precious to me as I spoke. She said, "You love them and remember they truly are a gift from God." I told her I would and I said simply, "God bless you," as she walked away down the tiny, tree-lined lane.

I hadn't even gotten her name, but that sweet woman and I had shared a special moment together and I thank God for it. It was evident that she knew what suffering was. She knew what it was like to grieve. Yet I could see the power and grace of God in those deep blue eyes and that joy that Peter spoke of.

As I remembered all those grave stones from the morning, I thought of the Apostle Paul reminding us of the prophet Isaiah's words, "Where, Oh death, is your victory? Where is your sting?"

I wished I had gotten her name before we had parted ways but thanks to our Savior, I thought of a time we would meet again in the future. She'll be with her son, never to be separated again. And perhaps God will introduce both of us to little Amber, with her perfect, glorified body. Then finally, the last tears will be washed away.

That experience with that woman had been such a blessing and a source of inspiration. Through the months that followed I would occasionally stop by the cemetery to pray and just to rethink my priorities in the peace and quiet of the place. The silly problems of the day seemed so trivial when I went there. Now and then I would read the poem etched on the back of the stone, its words always bringing me to the brink of tears. I left flowers more than once. I always wondered how this little girl's family had survived the tragic loss of their daughter. I always prayed for them there.

One day, in late August, I decided to leave a note at the base of the tombstone about how the poem had so touched the woman and me. I wrote, "To Amber's parents." It seemed like such a strange thing to do and felt like I was intruding on their privacy, so I didn't leave my name. I never knew if they had received it or not.

In mid January, I stopped by Amber's grave again. It was a cold, windy day with a gray sky, but there was a pretty Christmas tree about two feet tall with angels all over it beside the stone. As I looked at the stone, I realized the next day would be the anniversary of Amber's passing away. I knew, as a parent, that Amber's parents would be visiting the cemetery tomorrow, so I decided to leave my business card tucked into the tiny limbs of the tree.

The next day, a woman named Cathy, Amber's mom, called me. It was strange to finally talk with someone I did not know, but had been praying for. She said she wondered if I was the man who had left the letter that past summer. She immediately started sharing her story with me.

Little Amber Lynn had been born extremely handicapped, with very little brain tissue, an extreme cleft palette, and no eyes. The doctors expected her to live only 24 hours.

The little girl did survive her first 24 hours, which turned into days, and then weeks. Her mom realized that a life hooked up to machines was no way to live, so one day she bought a beautiful lacey dress for Amber Lynn, and went to the hospital. Against the hospital's wishes, she unplugged her daughter, lifted her from the incubator, dressed her in the pretty dress, and sat down and rocked her in her arms, expecting her to pass away. To the doctor's amazement, Amber lived.

When Cathy decided to bring her daughter home, her husband refused, feeling she should be institutionalized. When Cathy insisted, he left her, never to return.

Cathy's life became consumed with caring for her daughter. At first, friends and family were there to support her, but over time they all had to get on with their lives.

Well-meaning friends and family urged her to consider putting Amber in a facility. The little girl did not make a sound the first year, so there was no way of knowing if she even knew Cathy was there. There were countless surgeries, countless seizures, each time threatening to take Amber, countless hours in the hospital. Cathy stayed by Amber's side always, not even leaving the house to get milk. She could never forgive herself if Amber died while she was away.

In her second year, Amber Lynn started crying and responding to her mom. It became obvious that she knew when her mom touched her and talked to her. She seemed to enjoy music. She would even shake a rattle ever so slightly with her one hand.

Cathy wrote a poem to her daughter that year, the very poem that had touched me so deeply that day in the cemetery.

As Cathy told her story, I marveled at her courage and strength. I asked her how she got through it. She said she was very angry with God in the beginning. Why her? Why her daughter? Though she had no church and knew little of the Bible, she came to realize she had to trust God. It was in His plan that all this was happening and she would accept it. Instead of feeling cursed by God, in time she realized she had been given a precious gift in Amber Lynn. Even through the toughest times, she accepted God's will. But even in her acceptance, she still yearned for her daughter to hug her and say, "I love you, mommy."

Cathy tried to do the normal things parents do with their kids. When her daughter turned four, she had a birthday party for Amber at Chucky Cheese, inviting all the cousins of the family. The other children had fun, but the spirit was dampened when the adults asked Cathy why she was doing it. "After all, Amber doesn't even know she's here," they said.

Cathy told me her favorite times with Amber Lynn were during Christmas. Unlike other families caught up in the hustle and bustle and the presents, for the two of them, it was simply remembering Christ's birth and cherishing the time they had together. She had a little tree that she would decorate with mauve ornaments and little angels each year, every year adding a special ornament for Amber.

She told me she would spend nights lying with her daughter, pleading with her and with God that she would never leave her. Amber Lynn was her whole life. Cathy then told me of a cold, snowy night in January that changed all that.

She watched a movie on TV called "A Heart for Olivia." It was a story of a young couple whose little daughter was dying and needed a heart transplant. As the story unfolded, they finally found a heart, but the little girl died in the operation. Cathy said she watched the funeral scene, imagining how awful that would be. But when the movie was over, she went to Amber's bed and slid in beside her. That night she told her little daughter it was okay. If she was tired of fighting, tired of the seizures, weary of the surgeries, mommy understood and was releasing her. She would not plead with her or God any longer. The very next morning when Cathy awoke, little Amber Lynn was gone, now with her Lord.

At the funeral, the church was standing room only. Cathy said she saw so many doctors and nurses, friends and family and many people she didn't even know. Even her ex-husband, Amber's dad, was there. She hadn't planned it, but she read the poem she had written for Amber, adding a few lines at the end. She is still amazed she had the strength to get through it.

The one thing Cathy knew she had to do was to put her poem to her daughter on the stone. Though it cost an incredible amount of money that she didn't have, the whole poem was engraved.

Cathy said it was hard to let go. She would bring things to the cemetery, even Easter outfits and toys. Amber had been everything to her. She considered suicide but knew that was not the answer. She fought extreme depression. But time went on, and she got through it. Each year, she would bring the little Christmas tree and place it beside Amber's stone, adding a new ornament; the same tree I saw the last time I was there.

As Cathy shared her story, I shared verses from scripture that reflected what she was saying. I was sharing the Word of God and she was sharing those words lived out in her life. I so wanted to share the gospel with her, and didn't know how to ask until she asked me, "What's your religion?"

She said her ex-husband's family was members of a particular church but she didn't like it at all. But she had remembered going to a Baptist Church for a short time as a nine year old girl.

I explained the difference between receiving God's gift of salvation and trying to earn it through good works of religion. I used Amber's total dependency as an example of how helpless and dependent we are without God's grace. I told her how God wants to be not only our Father but even our daddy, as Paul tells us in Romans. I shared His unconditional love, like the love she has for her daughter. I told Cathy I knew I would see Amber one day in heaven and how God promises that.

It was then that she mentioned she had remembered praying a prayer at nine years old in that Baptist church, accepting Jesus as her Savior. I told her I believed that is why God was with her through all that suffering she had been through. She agreed, saying her life was not better because of accepting Him, but He was with her through it all. I told her God loved her so much and now she could see how He was working in her life even back then. We talked about the deeper meaning of Romans 8:28 in all our lives.

Even God's grace on the evening before Amber passed away was so evident. Cathy had felt guilty telling her daughter she could go, believing somehow she had killed her. I pointed out to her that perhaps God, in His patience and mercy, was waiting for her to reach the point of being ready, that point of acceptance, and then He took Amber home to be with Him; all in His timing, not ours. She had been faithful with what He had given her; faithful indeed.

I asked her what God was doing in her life now. She told me she remarried and had a healthy baby boy who was now five years old, and just four months ago, she had a healthy baby girl.

She was dealing with the guilty feelings, having a healthy baby girl. Even family and friends suggested she stop going to the cemetery, now that she had a healthy daughter. I told her I disagreed. She has two daughters now. She had done such a wonderful job taking care of the first, now God was entrusting her with another. He was honoring her faithfulness and she should enjoy the blessing!

I confessed to Cathy that I would walk the lane of the cemetery in prayer, thinking about all the blessings God has given me, but I could still go home and when the kids misbehaved or something went wrong, lose control and get upset. How could that be?

She shared with me the fact that she gets upset sometimes when her son is out of control and misbehaving. If anyone should know better, it's her! She would have given anything to see Amber Lynn running and playing with such reckless abandon. We agreed to stay focused; remembering what are truly the precious things God has given us.

When Cathy's phone started beeping, she told me it was a cordless phone and it meant the battery was running out. We hadn't even realized we'd been on the phone over two hours! We had to say our good byes quickly. I told her that she was a true hero and an inspiration to me. She thanked me that at least she knew two people who had been touched by the poem she had written for Amber Lynn.

When I hung up, I realized I felt drained of energy, yet so encouraged and excited over it all. I was so grateful to God I had made the effort to find out about this little girl and the story behind that wonderful poem. I had been so blessed by the old woman in the cemetery that day the year before, now blessed by this faithful young mother. And blessed to see how God had worked through it all.

I thought of the heroes of faith we read of in Hebrews 11. This young mother had a faith as great as theirs, a wonderful gift given to her as a young nine year old girl, to take her safely through the valley of the shadow of death and despair that would come.

I thought of the faithful saint from that little church who had shared the gospel with that nine year old girl, never knowing how God was working. It comforted me to know one day the LORD in glory will show him or her the results of their faithful service.

In 2 Corinthians chapter 12, Paul speaks of the thorn in the flesh that he endured after asking God three times to take it away.

And He said to me, "My grace is sufficient for you, for my strength is made perfect in weakness." Therefore most gladly I will rather boast in my infirmities, that the power of Christ may rest upon me. Therefore I take pleasure in infirmities, in reproaches, in needs, in persecutions, in distresses, for Christ's sake. For when I am weak I am strong.
2 Corinthians 12:9

Christian men are aware of our culture's war on man's masculinity, but we must also be aware of the opposite extreme. Both secular and spiritual men suffer many of the same vulnerabilities. We strive for success. We respect power. We savor the victories we achieve. We enjoy acceptance and recognition. We have a nature that says we can do it on our own. Humility and humbleness do not come naturally to us.

It makes no sense to this world when Paul speaks of strength being found in becoming weak, but scripture tells us God will resist the proud, but gives grace to the humble. The simple fact is that the spiritual soldier will only have victory in battle by learning how to surrender. Not surrendering to the enemy but to his ultimate commander-in-chief, the LORD Jesus Christ.

I have found the strong spiritual soldier does not fit any mold. He is not necessarily the man with the strongest physique, the most athletic, the best looks, or the most powerful job. In fact, very often he is the man ignored by the world, or even made fun of. He is the man who knows his relationship with his God and seeks to live by God's will and not his own.

The same is true for women, as that young mother, Cathy, demonstrated so well. It seems to me that this strength through weakness seems to come more naturally to women than men. We seem to struggle with the concept.

Perhaps the best illustration of strength through weakness that I have ever seen occurred at a very unlikely place where I least expected it, not from a brother while I was in the army, where physical and mental toughness abounded, but at an elementary school dance recital.

The girls ranged from PreK to 5th grade, the first dance recital for our five-year-old daughter, Emma, and the first for me, since Karen and I had raised two boys. I was sitting up front with the rest of our family and friends, anxiously awaiting the lights to go down and the curtain to open, my video camera ready at a moment's notice. You might think an hour and a half of watching little girls performing ballet and creative dance would be dull, but from the first little angels that glided out onto the stage, we were all enchanted by their enthusiasm and their innocence. They each seemed to have their own way of performing the same dance step and at times the choreography seemed to dissolve right there on stage, only to reappear as the little ballerinas continued. To every daddy there, his little girl was the prettiest and the most graceful in the show and I was no exception. Emma tiptoed out in her flowing blue dress, with a sparkling bodice and spaghetti straps. Her long blond hair was pulled back, still wavy from the curlers Mom had put in that morning. She performed each step with confidence and the biggest smile.

Cameras clicked and movie cameras rolled as each group performed. It was truly a blessing for all the families there, but a second, unexpected blessing came later in the show, when the 4th grade girls came out. They were older and had more experience than the little ones. Their number was more intricate with more difficult moves and more complicated choreography. It was a larger group of about twenty girls and they moved across the stage as one, all except one young girl. I didn't even catch it at first as the dance began, but I noticed someone now and then would be out of step here and there. After a whole evening of little girls being out of step I had grown used to it, but I finally realized this girl was different. Her right hand was not fully formed as neither was her right foot. Her movements, though correct, were sometimes erratic and unsteady, struggling to keep up with the other girls. I found myself cheering her on as she performed, falling out of step, then a moment later back in position with the rest of the dancers. Though you could tell she was concentrating as hard as she could, her face beamed with delight and a bright smile never left her face. Tonight she was a ballerina.

Even during my years as a paratrooper I had not seen such toughness, resilience, and bravery, but somehow in her sometimes awkward moments and her shining smile, I witnessed a sense of strength and courage along with a vision of grace.

I thought of her dad somewhere in the dark audience, a daddy who would do anything to heal his little girl. He probably held his breath through the whole dance, probably not praying so much that she do as well as the other dancers but that she would simply enjoy being there. Talk about courage. How much easier it would have been to tell her she simply couldn't do it, trying to avoid any more pain or disappointment in her life. I prayed for her parents, hoping God had somehow reassured them of His love and His purpose in all things, while honestly being thankful that though Emma had been a so-called "high risk" pregnancy, she was born physically healthy. I thought of the wisdom and compassion of the dance teacher. Again, it would have been easy to say she couldn't participate with the other girls. One could only wonder what lessons those girls and that teacher learned from watching this brave dancer each week.

She was right on queue when the music ended. She had finished well, out of breath, but her smile even brighter than ever.

After the show, I spotted the little girl seated against the wall with her friends. On impulse I walked over and crouched down to be eye to eye with her. She was even prettier close up, her face with glittery makeup, her hair intricately braided, still beaming from the magic of the night. "You were beautiful out there," I said.

She looked at me, sat up even straighter and simply said, "Thank you," and smiled.

I was thankful to her for the wonderful reminder of being grateful for what we have been given and having courage and grace under those tough circumstances that come in our lives. Aren't we just like that little girl when it comes to our Christian lives? We get out of step at times. We stumble, sometimes falling flat on our faces, but just like the loving dad that was somewhere out there in that audience, our Heavenly Father, in all His mercy and grace, sees us as His perfect children. He is not interested in us being the best, just doing our best, even with all the limitations we think we have in our lives. And my thanks to those courageous parents who reminded me I need to be just as courageous as a dad. And to a compassionate teacher, who taught me I must never lose my compassion for those He brings into my life. And to a little ballerina, who had a dream to dance, who proved you can face any obstacle in your life, and even do it with a smile.

> Resist him, steadfast in the faith, knowing that the same sufferings are experienced by your brotherhood in the world.
> 1 Peter 5:9

It is through genuine fellowship that we realize we are not alone is our suffering and there are others facing many of the same trials that we face. As I have said before, there should be no Rambo's in God's Army. We are a brotherhood; a band of brothers. A band that will not be broken, sealed for eternity.

> But may the God of all grace, who called us to His eternal glory by Christ Jesus, after you have suffered a while, perfect, establish, strengthen, and settle you.
> 1 Peter 5: 10

Peter understood God would use his suffering for his own good in this world and the next. Peter was strengthened in his suffering and we can be, too.

The Apostle Paul, after all his suffering, even while languishing in a Roman prison, not long before his death, was able to keep his suffering in this world in perspective, focusing rather on eternity.

Therefore do not be ashamed of the testimony of our LORD, nor of me, His prisoner, but share with me in the sufferings for the gospel according to the power of God, who has saved us and called us with a holy calling, not according to our works, but according to His own purpose and grace which was given to us in Christ Jesus before time began, but has now been revealed by the appearing of our Savior Jesus Christ, who has abolished death and brought life and immortality to light through the gospel, to which I was appointed a preacher, an apostle, and a teacher to the Gentiles. For this reason I also suffer these things; nevertheless I am not ashamed, for I know whom I have believed and am persuaded that He is able to keep what I have committed to Him until that day.
2 Timothy 1:8–12

We all have "river miles" to travel in this life, full of unexpected blessings and unplanned trials. There will be twists and turns and the next unknown bend is always just up ahead. We may always yearn for the smooth, peaceful path that goes straight ahead, but rivers don't flow that way and neither does life.

Yet with all the suffering we might see around us or have to go through ourselves, God has given His children a great gift. He has given us His Spirit, so that we can know Him as Creator and Savior, know His love and forgiveness, and know He is with us every mile of the way.

Band of Brothers
vs Rambo

October 5 - 8, 1979

On the morning of October 5th, the warmth of the camp fire felt wonderful after climbing out of my cozy sleeping bag to dress in the cold morning air. I made a mental note to myself that it was time to keep my clothes in the bag with me so they wouldn't get so cold by morning! There was the thinnest of frost on the ground and branches of the trees. While we huddled around the fire, Lucky was content browsing the grass on her leash. It appeared she had spent the night in her little cardboard box.

We started out the next day paddling but a westward tailwind slowly picked up and we put up the sails. The sun was strong and felt warm on my face but the brisk air forced me to keep a few layers of clothes on. We were all feeling a bit grimy, but it was way too chilly to think about a bath in the lake.

The next two days were a combination of paddling and sailing close to the northern shore, the hills dotted with large old trees. Immense cottonwoods, oaks, and other types of trees I couldn't identify were now showing autumn's colors, splashing the hills with yellows and oranges. The southern shore, about two miles across the lake, seemed to be covered in trees, with even more color.

Lucky turned out to be a great mascot. In camp, I would take her off her leash and she wouldn't run off, though I couldn't get her to come to me on demand. She was content adjusting to life as a River Rat.

After a day of being stranded on shore, one day Steve climbed a giant oak near camp. He must have been fifty feet in the air, almost at the top, swaying with the thin branches in the wind, hooting and howling with each gust. He tried to spot the dam to the east but it still wasn't visible.

A slight tailwind the next day made it easy to reach Gavins Point Dam, tying up in the small marina. If the Army Corps of Engineers had really made it official that they were not to help paddlers around the dams, they sure weren't interested in enforcing it. We found a familiar white Corps pick-up near the boat docks and the friendly corpsman was happy to give us a ride. One boat at a time, he drove slowly down the road to a campground on the other side of the dam. As we backed into a parking space and unloaded the second boat, people in RVs eyed us curiously. When Bill, our Army Corps chauffeur, drove off, the folks in the large RV next to us walked over.

"How are you boys doin?" a white-haired older gentlemen asked, as he gazed at the boats full of gear. "Where you all comin' in from?"

We all enjoyed having people asking that question now. Steve smiled and said, "Well, we left Three Forks, Montana about two months ago. We're headed to St. Louis."

"Is that so? That's quite a trip!" he exclaimed.

"And who is this?" asked the woman beside him, as I lifted Lucky out of the boat.

"This is Lucky," I said. I walked over to her so she and the other woman with her could see our mascot.

"Isn't he adorable," she said as she stroked Lucky's head and ears. "You brought a rabbit on a canoe trip?" she asked.

"Well," Tim said with a sheepish grin, "We actually had two, but we ate the other one the other day."

The two men laughed heartily but the women looked horrified and somewhat annoyed.

"Oh, you're not serious!"

"Yeah, it's true," I said sadly. I was about to reassure her that we had no intentions of eating Lucky but before I could she interrupted me.

"Oh, you just can't hurt this adorable little thing!"

Her friend then spoke up. "Oh dear, there's hardly even any meat on that little thing!"

"We have plenty of food! If you boys promise not to eat little Lucky, we'll let you have some of ours. How's that?"

Both men remained quiet, with looks of amusement on their faces. Their women folk were saving a rabbit's life.

"That sounds great!" John responded before the rest of us.

"Alright then. Come on, Natalie. Let's go fetch some food for these boys." The two women hurried off to their RV, the men following behind, grinning. The one dressed in fishing garb was just shaking his head, mumbling something to his buddy. It wasn't long before the women were back with groceries in hand. There was over a dozen eggs, a few pounds of burger patties, pork sausage links, and a loaf of bread.

Natalie walked over to Lucky, now tied up to a picnic table, and got down on the ground to pet her. She looked like your typical grandma; the white hair and all. She had on a polyester grey pant suit and the most obnoxious bright red shoes with at least a two inch heal! She hardly looked like she was an outdoor type. But she had a heart of gold as did her friend, a sweet lady who I never did get her name.

The two women seemed to take a grandmotherly interest in us and wanted to know all the details of our trip. They asked if we were calling home enough, which I assured them we had. They laughed when John told them we were almost broke and his and my parents were wiring us some money to a Western Union in Sioux City, Iowa, which we hoped to find in the next couple days.

We had a great dinner that night, while the sky turned shades of pink and purple. It was cool and the fire felt especially satisfying. We were sitting there around the fire, John and Tim sitting up against a large oak tree, and I could tell what they were thinking just from their faces. Each one of us went through it at different times, except perhaps Steve. That feeling of just wanting to be off the river, done with the trip, back in the real world, unlimited food and cold drinks, bathrooms, etc. Up to that point in the trip, I had gone through it once or twice, but that night it was Tim and John's turn. We were seasoned River

Rats now though. There was no mention of giving up or turning back. They both just sat there sipping their tea, staring at the fire, but I knew the look. I don't think Steve had ever experienced it yet. An adventure like this was just perfect for his childlike enthusiasm.

We all really should have been in a great mood. We had survived the lakes and everything they had thrown at us. We had been stranded many days by ferocious winds, scared to death in waves much too large for open canoes, had snapped both sail masts, and had eaten quite a unique assortment of foods in the last weeks. But that was all history now. I would never look at a map of those lakes and all the empty space around them without remembering the windswept beaches, the days of carefree sailing, the terrifying storms, the incredible starlit nights and awesome sunrises and sunsets. We hadn't just seen it but had lived it all.

As we sat there, I looked at the map of the river. We now had 810 river miles left to go. We all knew things would be different now. The river was navigable from this point on. In other words, we would now be dealing with commercial barge traffic up and down the river and a whole lot more civilization. We would pass through cities like Sioux City and even Kansas City. Now we would have a current again, one that would allow us to make some serious distance each day, though we still didn't know how much.

None of us could deny the changing of the seasons, sitting around the fire with long pants, jean jackets and chamois shirts on. Those blistering hot days in Montana seemed so far away, so long ago.

Perhaps John and Tim had sensed something that night that Stave and I had missed. It was an ending of sorts, saying goodbye to the glorious wilderness river we had each come to love. What we had experienced and even grown accustomed to was now behind us. Looking back now, it was sad in a way. Things would be different now, yet we didn't really know how.

I gazed downstream, a habit of mine that had developed over the months. Many nights, in the stillness and silence along the river, I would think about what we had experienced and wonder what lied ahead around the next bend. It had been a good day, a pleasant evening. We had covered some miles, made it to our last dam, enjoyed great weather, and had met some really nice folks. Life on the river was good. It had become just about that simple.

On August 29, 1804, a very different meeting took place just down-river from where we were camped that night. The men of the Corps of Discovery made camp on the north side of the river, at the mouth of the James River. A large band of Yankton Sioux camped on the southern bank. It was a large group with about seventy warriors and a number of women. It was the first time the men had seen cone-shaped shelters covered with buffalo skins, what we all know now as teepees. It was agreed that the parties would have a council in the morning.

Though the Yankton Sioux could not begin to understand the European culture of the captains, they too, couldn't begin to relate to the culture of the Sioux. They were from two very different worlds. But both worlds would come together through the efforts of a strug-gling translator.

The next morning, with the captains decked out in their formal dress uniforms and the Sioux chiefs in their ceremonial garb, they met and sat together. They discussed the opportunity of trade, the Indians having a new Father in Washington, the need for gun powder and ball. Though the Sioux were disappointed with the gifts and trinkets they received, there was still a spirit of alliance among them all. After the council there was celebrating and dancing and exhibitions of bow and arrow skills. The festivities continued through the night by the light of camp fires.

As they say, if only the rocks could talk. Unfortunately, as I gazed into the night, just upriver from that eventful meeting, alive almost two centuries away from 1804, the same hills and the rocky bluffs that wit-nessed it all remained silent, sharing nothing of what they had seen.

In the morning Natalie and her friend stopped by to see us off. Natalie of course had to spend some time with Lucky before I placed her in the canoe just in front of me. Natalie's friend was snapping pic-tures and asked for my address.

"I'll send you a copy!" she said excitedly.

I jotted down my post office box back in Yellowstone, never believ-ing I'd ever see any pictures, but appreciating the thought. We turned around and waved at the camera, heading downriver to take on the next challenge that lay ahead.

The story of these two sweet ladies does not end there on the river-bank in South Dakota. In fact, many months later a bulky letter would show up in Box 191, Mammoth, WY, Yellowstone National Park, addressed to me. Inside were a handful of photos, most a bit blurry but still very special. There were our two canoes headed down the river, the only photographs we had of both boats on the river together with all the River Rats. There was also, of course, a picture of Natalie and Lucky. Unfortunately, if there had been a return address it has long since been lost, and today I am really sorry about that. I should have written her and thanked her for her kindness, but as a typical nineteen year old, at the time I didn't think to do it. The photos were stuffed in a box like most of my other "junk" until many years later when I was much older and feeling a bit nostalgic.

When I pulled the photos out and started looking through them, I instinctively turned them over to see if I had written anything on the back. What I found was such a surprise. I don't know how I hadn't remembered seeing it before. There was handwriting on the back of a few of the photos and it wasn't mine. On the picture of Lucky and Natalie it read:

> Natalie and Lucky, Canoe Trip, Gavin's Point Dam, Yankton, SD. 1979

> Sorry I cut off the top of Natalie's head. She has such beautiful snow white hair.

But it was the picture of both canoes heading down the river that made me stop and spend more than just a few minutes reminiscing. On the back of that photo, in the nicest handwriting, it said:

> Glenn–1979 off we go into the wild blue yonder! Have to admit I had tears in my eyes when I knew you were gone. We thank God for you, filling an empty little spot in our hearts.

I reread it a few times, partly feeling blessed by the words after such a long time, but also ashamed. Had I never seen what she had written before? Did I see it back then but just dismiss it as a silly old woman? I hoped not. But if I had not appreciated it then, I surely did now. She had been so nice, so enthusiastic about our trip and so concerned about our welfare...even Lucky's.

The sad thing was, somehow I had never learned her name. If she even mentioned it, I didn't recall ever hearing it. I don't know what we did or said that touched her heart in such a way. Perhaps we didn't do anything. She just had a big heart and God had caused our paths to cross. Now as a Christian, years later, I have to wonder if she and perhaps Natalie prayed for us on that final leg of our journey, with all the hazards we faced.

I couldn't help but think of all those other folks along the way that had offered us help and asked for nothing in return. People that gave us rides into town and around the dams, gave us food, and sometimes just a word of encouragement. I'm sure we had thanked them all but now years later I felt an overwhelming desire to somehow thank them again, to let them know how we appreciated them, to let them know we had made it with all their help, to let them know even now I appreciated them, perhaps even more.

I suppose when we're young we don't realize how important people are to us or how vital relationships are to our mental and spiritual well being. I suppose it takes years of experience and perhaps having lost a few of those people before you realize what impact they had or how precious they really were.

There were many people that came into my life, even if for a very short time, that shared the truth of God with me and helped me realize I had turned my back on manmade religion, but not God. Many of them were used by God, especially those that I mocked and ridiculed without mercy, yet they shared their faith and gave me answers to all my ridiculous charges and questions.

There was a certain Private O'Brian who witnessed to me constantly in basic training at Fort Leonard Wood, Missouri, while I mocked him relentlessly for eight weeks. I can just imagine how shocked he'll be to see me in heaven one day! I look forward to seeing the look on his face and seeing him rewarded for his faithfulness.

Having recently picked up and moved our family across the country from Syracuse, NY to Colorado Springs, CO, just two short months ago, my whole family and I know what it is like to leave the fellowship of dear Christian brothers and sisters who had become a part of our lives. I had taught an adult Bible study in our church for over ten years, and also led a small group of ten to twelve adults every Sunday night for a number of years. We had all experienced life together, celebrating births, raising our kids, mourning deaths. We laughed, cried, and worshipped together. We had all seen the best and worst of each other. Good Christian friends are a blessing I will never again take for granted.

Every Christian has heard or read that the Christian life is not to be lived alone. It also must be stated that spiritual warfare is not to be fought alone. Scripture makes it very clear we are to fight as a band of brothers, not as Rambo's. We've all seen a movie like Rambo, when one guy, with no weapons and no supplies, takes on a whole army and single handedly defeats them. Bullets fly, bombs explode, but our man just gets a bloody scratch on his bulging arm for dramatic effect. In real combat, it doesn't happen that way.

I think back to the men of 1st Squad of 1st Platoon that I spent many days and nights with in the field. I was the medic in charge of everyone's safety and health, but every other soldier had a specialty as well. There was the radio man, who constantly shadowed the lieutenant. There was the heavy machine gunner who handled the awesome M60 machine gun, and an assortment of other specialties other soldiers were responsible for.

We were a bunch of guys from different parts of the country, different races, different social and economic backgrounds, different talents and abilities, but we came together and had been transformed into one cohesive unit committed to one mission. Though still individuals, we now found our identity in the group. We were never alone.

Isn't the church of Jesus Christ much the same way? Though many unbelievers and so-called religious people consider the church a particular building or a specific congregation or denomination, the holy scriptures tell us that the church is simply those people called out of the world that belong to God's family by faith in Christ. We are from all races, with a wide variety of cultures and socio-economic backgrounds, with a wide variety of talents and abilities, brought together as one.

> For as we have many members in one body but all the members do not have the same function, so we, being many, are one body in Christ, and individually members of one another.
> Romans 12:4

Paul compared the many members of our own physical body to the many members that make up the body of Christ. Though still individuals, they now are one with one purpose as a body, even to the point of being members of one another.

There are many times "one another" is mentioned in the scriptures concerning how we are to treat our fellow brethren. We are to care for one another, comfort, edify, serve, and have compassion for one another. We are to admonish and forgive one another in the same way Christ has forgiven us. We are even called to confess to one another. The scriptures tell us we are to pray for one another and bear one another's burdens. All of these are represented in the command that Jesus gave His disciples at the Feast of the Passover, His last meal before going to the cross.

> A new commandment I give to you, that you love one another, as I have loved you, that you also love one another. By this all will know that you are My disciples, if you have love for one another.
> John 13:34,35

I suppose with all the talk of "one another" and "one body" someone might believe a person's individualism could or even should be lost in it all. But the scriptures reveal just the opposite. Paul specifically wrote that we were individually members of one another and most importantly that we all had different functions.

> Having then gifts differing according to the grace that is given to us, let us use them.
> Romans 12:6

This wonderful truth can release men and women from the bondage of man-made religion where everyone is supposed to look and act alike, producing a false form of unity, much like the Pharisees of Jesus' day. Instead God declares we are all made unique, with different gifts and different purposes. Instead of trying to be like another person, no matter how godly or wonderful that person might be as a role model, God has created each member of the body to be different and unique, with our own purpose.

> And the eye cannot say to the hand, "I have no need for you";
> nor again the head to the feet, "I have no need for you."
> 1 Corinthians 12:21

Perhaps some believers in Corinth who had the more prominent gifts of teaching or prophecy were feeling prideful, thinking they were more important than others. There is a lesson there for those with such high visibility gifts. For others, perhaps most of us, the lesson is that not all of us are called to be a preacher or pastor or have a large ministry. In a world that measures success by popularity or size or numbers, Christians, especially Christian men, can miss the fact that success for us should be measured by our faithfulness to what God entrusts us with. The results will always belong to Him, so He gets the glory. As Paul told the Corinthians, it is God who has placed the different members in the body, as He desires. I must confess in my own life of lay ministry over the years I have had to learn to not be proud by any successes and not to be discouraged by what seemed to be failures. I did learn over time to just be obedient and leave the results to God.

> And if one member suffers, all the members suffer with it;
> if one member is honored, all the members rejoice with it.
> 1 Corinthians 12:26

How blessed is the Christian who has that kind of relationship with other believers. If there were ever a verse to support the idea of small groups, that may be the one. In a large church it is too easy to get lost in the crowd, to be invisible in the pew. Only in a small group can true fellowship occur, where suffering, honoring and rejoicing are truly experienced together.

> But speaking the truth in love, may grow up in all things
> into Him, who is the head,-Christ- from whom the whole
> body, joined and knit together by what every joint supplies,

according to the effective working by which every part does its share, causing growth of the body for the edifying of itself in love.
Ephesians 4:15–16

Paul is not simply talking about being sincere or honest when he says to speak the truth in love. The body will grow up in all aspects of Christ, the head, when we speak sound doctrine, which he mentioned in the preceding verse 13. Sound doctrine will enable each member of the body to work together properly, which will not only build us up individually but the whole body, the church.

Paul makes it sound so simple. Unfortunately, we very often remain individuals and don't find our identity in the church, in the position we now have with Jesus. We are far from a cohesive unit committed to our mission. We too often remain alone, especially Christian men.

Ironically, when things are going well we are more apt to enjoy fellowship with other Christian men. We are more willing to share our successes, our victories, how the LORD has blessed us. We enjoy being a Christian band of brothers. But when the storms hit, when the trials come, when we find ourselves in the valley, we are prone to shy away from our brothers. Perhaps it is pride, perhaps fear. Who knows? But most men I know, including myself, have that natural tendency.

In a real sense, we find ourselves in a terrible spiritual battle and resort to being a Rambo. Not only is that deadly, but it is also sinful. God has not designed us that way.

> Let us hold fast the confession of our hope without wavering, for He who promised is faithful; and let us consider one another in order to stir up love and good works, not forsaking the assembling of ourselves together, as is the manner of some, but exhorting one another...
> Hebrews 10:23–25

We've all heard it before. "I love God, I just don't like church." Or worse, "I love God. Its people I can't stand!" Such statements, though sincere, are not Biblical. If we choose to forsake coming together for worship and "the equipping of the saints," there is no encouraging one another and any one of us, all alone, will become a casualty in the battle.

I remember a raw, overcast day in February when Joshua and I were driving through Lamar Valley in Yellowstone. Up on the northern slope, about 150 yards away, a lone elk calf stood in the cold. She seemed fine just standing there but when she moved, it was obvious her one hind leg was broken. Obviously she could not keep up with them, so the herd moved on without her. She was now alone. I knew it would not be long before the pack of wolves that lived just to the southeast found her. We learned later that day that they were busy with a buffalo they had brought down that morning, but they would not pass up such an easy kill for very long.

That doomed animal was no more defenseless and vulnerable than a Christian all alone in this world. Whether the prowling lion Peter spoke of, the world and its anti-Christian culture, or simply the sinfulness of our own flesh, our spiritual health, even our spiritual survival depends on one another.

> For I long to see you, that I may impart to you some spiritual gift, so that you may be established; that is, that I may be encouraged together with you by the mutual faith both of you and me.
> Romans 1:11,12

Even the Apostle Paul, someone we would consider a pillar of faith, someone with an incredible relationship with Jesus, found encouragement being with his brethren. If Paul needed such encouragement, why would we think we don't? We can even go back to Adam, the very first man created. He shared a close relationship with Almighty God in the garden that we have a hard time even imaging. Yet God still declared it was not good for him to be alone. Adam needed another human being. And all of us still do.

Perhaps the worst danger in not fellowshipping with other believers is that we will eventually begin to fellowship with unbelievers. Instead of sharing our lives with people that share our faith and encourage us, we will find people that are of this world. Instead of keeping our perspective on spiritual things and eternity, we will settle for the temporal things of this world.

Do not be deceived: Evil company corrupts good morals.
1 Corinthians 15:33

It is interesting that right in the middle of a chapter where Paul is explaining the resurrection of the dead, he makes such a statement that almost seems out of place. We must realize Paul was dealing with those in Corinth that were denying the resurrection of the dead. He was concerned these false teachers would deceive and confuse believers, taking their focus off spiritual truth and settling for all kinds of lies. Without a healthy spiritual perspective we each can easily become worldly and carnal.

In a more general sense, when a Christian isolates himself from his brothers, he tends to find those who will offer no spiritual perspective and no Biblical accountability. We might think these relationships are spiritually neutral but as Jesus said, you are either for Him, or against Him. He never allowed any middle ground.

For Christian parents, we know all about the dangers of peer pressure and how good kids get in trouble with the wrong crowd and bad influences. Yet as adults, we can just as easily fall into the same trap, especially when we are hurting or confused. For adults, the question is so simple. Do my relationships with different people draw me closer to God or do they pull me further away? It's the same question we need to be asking our sons and daughters, not allowing the answer to be neutral. It may take some conversation to help remove that neutrality. Another question that might help clarify things is to ask if that relationship with that person is more important than their relationship with God.

With that in mind, we must realize that a Christian without meaningful fellowship doesn't simply miss out on the blessings and joys in his Christian life, but puts his Christian life in needless peril, exposing himself to all the curses and sorrows this world has to offer.

Therefore if there is any consolation in Christ, if any comfort
of love, if any fellowship of the Spirit, if any affection and
mercy, fulfill my joy by being like-minded, having the same
love, being of one accord, of one mind.
Philippians 2:1,2

When Paul speaks of being like-minded, he means being in agree-
ment with sound doctrine revealed in God's Word. What a comfort and
encouragement it is to be around those who believe and trust in the things
we do. That's why fellowship doesn't simply mean hanging out with other
Christians and talking about Monday night football or the weather, but
sharing spiritual things with each other to build each other up.

Paul also says to have the same love. The love of God that binds us
together as His children is something we should all cherish. We can all
be reminded to express that love that we have more often. In our busy
world, we can easily forget to do that. And we must also, as difficult
it is to do as men, be willing to receive Christian love from others.
Again, that Rambo complex can make it difficult and we just want to
help others and not accept help when we need it. That only comes with
closeness and trust. I have heard it said that the quality of our relationship with our brothers and sisters in our lives reveals the quality of our
relationship with God. I believe it.

And Paul speaks of being one in spirit and purpose. Christians
share a purpose that is eternal, a purpose that transcends time and
space. As soldiers in the 3rd battalion, 325th Airborne Infantry, we
never lost focus of our mission, the cause we were willing to fight and
die for. As spiritual soldiers, we must do the same. The Gospel of Jesus
Christ is the most precious, most noble cause.

It is because of that gospel that I am now part of an eternal band
of brothers, many of whom I consider heroes in their own right. They
probably don't view themselves as heroes at all. In our culture a hero
fights in wars or saves a child from a burning building, or even simply
punches out the school bully who picked on the weakest of kids.

Those men certainly are heroes and there isn't a man alive who
hasn't fantasized at some time in their lives of being one of them, but I
have seen another type of hero.

Peter represented the typical kind of hero when he was in the

Garden of Gethsemane where the soldiers came to arrest Jesus. Peter drew his sword and was willing to die for his LORD as he had stated not long before. He showed bravery, loyalty, total self-sacrifice, much like the soldier who jumps on an enemy grenade to save the lives of those around him. But we all know the story. It was part of God's eternal plan of salvation that Peter's calling was not to fight and die in that garden that night.

For Peter, he was called to live a heroic life of faith, braving all kinds of trials, dangers and suffering, until finally murdered for his faith. I once heard a pastor say, "There are many men that would be willing to die for Jesus. Where are the men willing to live for Jesus?" It is a sobering, humbling thought. Did Peter show what kind of man he was when he bravely, quickly drew his sword to fight, or when he spent many years faithfully serving God? Did Peter show the power of God in a man's life when he drew that sword or when he ministered to others sharing the truth of salvation with them in the midst of danger and peril?

One could ask the same thing of the Apostle Paul. While he was still Saul, persecuting the Christians, one could say he was quite a powerful guy, a man's man. But when one looks at the incredible life he lived once he accepted Jesus as Messiah, it was only then that he showed true heroism; heroism throughout the rest of his life.

I suppose you could go all the way back to Noah. Was he a hero for building that ark and saving not only his family but the entire human race? I believe Noah was a hero long before then. In Genesis 6:9 it states that Noah was a righteous man, blameless in his generation; Noah walked with God. He had already showed bravery and true heroism by taking a stand and not being conformed to an evil culture. I'm sure Noah wasn't perfect, but he was a hero.

It is because of that Gospel that people who were once strangers to me are now close brothers and sisters who I will spend eternity with. I have had the privilege of being around men that never went to war or saved children form burning buildings, yet they lived each day, quietly giving all they had to their families, their work, their churches, their brothers and sisters in the LORD. They were faithful to their calling as husband and as father. I learned much and was often encouraged and inspired by such men. Were they perfect? No. But they were heroes just the same.

In another garden, some six thousand years ago, if Adam had been

Eve's hero he would have pulled a knife like Peter and cut that serpents head right off, or perhaps better yet, not only quoted the words of God but actually honored them!

Until Jesus returns, He is calling for men to be heroes.

And finally, it is because of that Gospel that I trust I might one day see that sweet old woman from that South Dakota campground again to let her know how she had touched my heart. Perhaps not back then on the river when my arrogant heart was still stone cold toward spiritual things and the love of God, but now, years later, with a heart that is alive with His love.

The Missouri River Rats had to admit they were running low on cash so John and I called home while in Pierre and arranged for our parents to wire money for us to pick up at a Western Union office at a truck stop in Sioux City. They were told the truck stop was along a highway adjacent to the river and easily seen. Hopefully, they were right. We reached the outskirts of Sioux City on a gray, cloudy day. As we went along, that grayness seemed to drain the colors from the trees. Even the water looked gray, though sadly it was getting dirtier and the color really couldn't be blamed totally on the overcast skies.

The banks were dominated by trees, blocking our view of anything beyond them. We paddled past a few more duck blinds and some more ducks and geese that seemed to be avoiding them. They didn't seem to care about us. It was almost as if they knew we weren't hunters. It made me wonder if duck hunters should give up their blinds and invest in canoes.

It never really rained but the sun never came out and everything remained damp and cold throughout the day. It appeared to be getting darker in late afternoon as we finally saw buildings and a highway come into view. Houses started to appear on our right as we made our way through town. From talking with my dad, we knew the truck stop would be after Interstate 129 passed over the river. The Western Union people had told him that, but not much else. Finally the interstate bridge came into sight. On such a dreary day we must have looked pretty pathetic to folks looking out at us coming down the river.

We paddled under the left side and then landed. There were fields with some trees, the highway now a few hundred yards back from the river. As it was getting darker, the lights of cars, trucks, and businesses lit up the horizon.

It was decided Tim and Steve would stay with the boats while John and I would venture out to find the truck stop and hopefully the Western Union office. We walked through some trees, then across the open fields, crossing a railroad track. When we reached the interstate, we could see all the businesses were on the other side on a frontage road. We didn't have much of a choice, so when the traffic thinned out a bit we made a mad dash across two lanes, then some grass median, then the opposite two lanes.

The commotion and noise around us felt disturbing and I found myself just wanting to go back to our quiet river. It was useless to try and hitch-hike since we really didn't know where we were going. We walked down the road and were amazed when not even a half mile down the road we found a truck stop with a Western Union logo on the building.

We walked into the place, nervous they might be closed this late in the afternoon, but found the desk open. Within minutes both John and I had our money and were heading back down the street feeling like we were rich. Dad had wired me seventy-five dollars and I forget how much John got, but we both agreed it was time to eat a real meal in a real restaurant. We wanted some good food and also a dry, warm place to sit in soft chairs. We almost ran back to the guys and helped them stash the boats in some bushes along the water. We put Lucky in her box so she'd stay dry. On a night like that, there was no danger of someone coming across the boats.

The restaurant was one of those typical shiny metal diners from the 50s. The inside was decorated in gaudy red velvet sections on the walls and a glass case up front with various mouthwatering desserts. The woman who sat us gave us a strange look as we walked in. As she led us to our table it seemed like the patrons couldn't take their eyes off us and we couldn't take our eyes off all the food on their plates. We felt awkward and wonderful at the same time. The aroma of the food was incredible and the warmth of being indoors seemed to sooth my body almost immediately. I hadn't realized how cold I had been all day while paddling.

Water that hadn't sat in plastic bins for days tasted wonderful. We all ordered the largest cheeseburgers they had with heaps of French fries. The waitress kept filling our coffee cups as fast as we drank it down. When we were done devouring our burgers she came back and asked if we wanted dessert. John announced he was buying us all a slice of pie from the glass case. It was the best tasting pie I ever had.

We had such a great time but, as tough as it was, it eventually was time to get back to the boats. When we walked out the front door, it was now dark and a slight drizzle was falling. A cold wet wind hit my face and I really just wanted to go back and have another piece of pie. Reluctantly we made our way back across the interstate, dodging the cars and avoiding the cold spray that shot out from them as they whisked by.

It seemed like a longer walk back in the dark. As we made our way across the field and over the railroad tracks, we discovered an old railroad boxcar not far from the boats. With everything around us wet, the inside of that boxcar was the only dry place we would find. It didn't take long to decide we'd never get a fire going so we'd just sleep in the boxcar. We wouldn't have any heat but at least we'd be dry.

We got our sleeping bags and Lucky's box and, after inspecting the railroad car for any unwanted roommates, made ourselves at home. We sat down to get comfortable and talk awhile while Lucky hopped around inspecting the place, but it wasn't long before we were all too cold and decided to just get in our bags and go to sleep. I soon realized that was easier said then done. The floor was made of metal and it wasn't very long till the damp coldness made its way through my sleeping bag and three layers of clothes. The numbing cold made my muscles ache and after the few times during the night when I actually fell asleep I would quickly wake up almost shivering. I spent most the night staring out the large doorway of the boxcar, listening to the light rain fall, waiting anxiously for the light of morning. I had no clue what we would do if the rain didn't stop.

It had been an unpleasant night for the River Rats back in October of 1979, but less than a mile from where we spent the night, it had been a very sad time for the men of the Corps of Discovery. In camp on that night of August 20, 1804, they were mourning the loss of one of their own. On August 19th, Captain Clark wrote that Sergeant Floyd had become dangerously ill. Historians believe he suffered from a ruptured appendix that led to peritonitis. Sadly, even back east, there would have been no medical understanding of the disease for another twenty years. There was nothing anyone could have done for him. Captain Clark recorded around midday on the 20th the young man of perhaps twenty or twenty-one years of age died calmly and with dignity.

The men buried Sergeant Floyd on a bluff overlooking the river. He received full military honors with Captain Lewis performing the service. The captains named the bluff and a nearby river in honor of the only man that perished on that epic journey.

This young man's life was cut short, at least by man's standards, but the man that was chosen by the men to replace him was Private Patrick Gass. Ironically, Gass would live a long life, dying in 1870. At the age of almost one hundred, he would become the last surviving member of the Corps of Discovery.

⚶

Barges, Braves, Bullets, and Buildings

October 9 - 18, 1979

I don't know how much sleep I actually got that night in that freezing boxcar but as soon as it was light enough, I woke the others. Judging from how quickly they got up they seemed just as anxious to get going as I was. It was still a gray and wet morning but the rain had finally stopped. Fog hung in the higher trees, thick and wet.

My back was sore and every joint ached as I climbed out of the railroad car, my sleeping bag under my arm. I walked over to the canoes. A slight film of frost coated the boats and paddles so we had to wipe them down before we could shove off. We all decided to skip breakfast. I just wanted to start paddling to get my body moving and generate some body heat.

Over the next few hours we paddled through flat lowlands with trees lining the river on both sides. It seemed to be getting warmer and though the sun hadn't come out at all, it did seem just a bit brighter. Even the trees had some of their color back. The layers of clothes started coming off and it even got warm enough to take my sneakers off and tie them to my seat as I had done every day since leaving Three Forks.

The right bank now was Nebraska, the left bank, the state of Iowa. The current was steady and fast and paddling was easy.

One afternoon we had just finished lunch, just letting the current take us along, when we overheard the faint sound of some type of engine. At first I thought perhaps it was an irrigation pump. We had passed many of those in the last few months. It was only a few moments later that a large tugboat pushing an even larger barge came around the bend just a few hundred yards behind us.

"Whoa, look at that!" Steve exclaimed.

I turned around to see what appeared to be a massive metal wall, pushing its way through the water, right at us! I instinctively started steering to the right side of the river, not willing to share any river space with what was heading toward us.

"Right side!" I yelled to the other boat.

It turned out that the barge was moving slower than we anticipated and we easily made it to the side of the river with plenty of time to spare.

We were all out of the boats when the massive metal barge started passing in front of us. The front was just a solid wall of metal pushing the water up and around it, creating a powerful wave on each side. We all stood there watching the length of the barge go by, then finally seeing the tugboat in the back, pushing it along. The engines of the tug were creating turbulent waves that extended out behind it. Now with it so close, we were surprised at the speed of the huge mass of metal as it passed by us.

The waves generated from the barge rolled away from the side walls, causing the river to sink then swell as the wave rolled toward the shore. What we didn't realize was how the swelling wave gained size and strength as it headed toward the bank, toward us!

As the first wave of water rolled toward us, the knee deep water I was standing in suddenly dropped to my ankles, the boat scraping the bottom. Then, without any warning, the boat lurched forward toward shore as the wave lifted it violently. John and I grabbed at the boat frantically, trying not to get knocked over by it. Steve grabbed the rope on his boat but not before it slammed into ours with a crash. The next wave hit the bouncing canoes and sprayed cold water into our faces and up into the boats. When the third wave hit we had gained some control of the boats and the impact was less. The waves diminished till we just stood there, dripping wet, amazed by what we had just seen.

We paddled for a few more hours till we found a flat area of grass, perfect for a campsite, and called it a day. Decatur was probably less than five miles away. That evening as we made camp, we talked about our barge experience. How many more would we run into over the next 700 miles?

We had just started collecting wood for the fire when we all heard the distinct sound of horses' hooves coming toward us. I was just picking up driftwood in my arms when I looked up and saw five riders on horseback coming over the slope behind our camp.

As they got closer, it was easy to see they were all young Indian boys. They were riding bareback, wearing jeans but barefooted and no shirts. A few had long black hair blowing in the wind as they rode while others had almost buzz cuts.

I have to admit the moment was a tense one. It seemed to me to be a scene right out of a western. We could have camped on the Iowa side of the river, I thought to myself. We must have been on a reservation. Thankfully, these Indians had no visible weapons and they all seemed to be between ten and maybe sixteen years old. They turned out to be very friendly.

Like everyone else they were curious where we had come from and where we were going. Their horses weren't very big but they seemed strong and healthy. I stroked the neck of a pretty gray mare while we talked with the boys. They told us we were on the Yankton Indian Reservation. We asked the oldest boy if it was alright if we camped there for the night. He made it quite clear we could stay as long as we liked. As abruptly as they had shown up, they said goodbye and galloped away, leaving us standing there, not sure what to do. They hadn't told us to get off their land. They didn't seem to mind at all that we were there. Judging from the map the reservation land was huge so what was the harm in us camping along the river? If we hadn't already unloaded the boats we could have just gotten back in the water and found another sight on the other side of the river, but we decided we would just stay put.

I have to admit as it got darker we became a bit more uncomfortable, wondering if anyone would come back in the darkness of night to teach us not to trespass or at least to harass us some. We stayed up late around the fire that night. We also moved the boats in closer. We talked about each of us taking a turn with guard duty through the night but we were all too tired to convince ourselves that was necessary. As it turned out, the beautiful fall night would be peaceful and our sleep would be undisturbed. Our friendly visitors had been just that.

Though we had our unexpected meeting with the Omahas on that day, the Corps of Discovery had in fact tried to meet with this same tribe. The captains sent five men out to bring an invitation for a council, but unfortunately the Omahas, who had a village just west of the river, were out hunting bison so the meeting never occurred.

A beautiful campsite nestled in thick colorful trees became home the next night. The ground was grassy and soft. There was plenty of firewood, and we had five hot dogs each for dinner.

Lucky seemed extremely energetic, constantly hopping away from camp and having to be rounded up by one of us. She seemed to know she wasn't behaving, darting away as we tried to grab her. After a few too many times, we put her back on her leash.

We were camped on the Nebraska side of the river again, far from any town or Indian reservation.

On day 74, October 11th, we came upon the town of Fort Calhoun. It was at this site that the Corps of Discovery had their very first council with native people. It was held beneath a bluff along the river that the captains called "Council Bluff." Because of the meandering of the river over the past 200 years the bluff is now a few hundred yards from the river. With all the historical sites of the Lewis and Clark expedition, with monuments and fine museums, this famous bluff sat for years among the trees and bushes with probably very few visitors. This wonderful historical site had no marker or any designation until only a few years ago, when a monument was finally erected there.

Though probably everyone has heard of Council Bluffs, Iowa, I'm sure very few have ever heard of Fort Calhoun, Nebraska. Most people probably figure the rock bluffs just outside the modern town of Council Bluffs would be the actual site of the council, but they would be wrong. The town of Council Bluffs was actually Kanesville, Iowa, until 1853, when the residents incorporated and renamed the town.

The men had arrived at the "council bluff" site on July 30th, and set up camp. It would not be till August 3rd that they would have a council with the Oto and Missouri Indian chiefs. The days they waited, the men enjoyed a plentiful variety of fruit but also suffered with harassing mosquitoes.

The chiefs seemed happy with the idea of a new government, most likely due to the fact they were already familiar and eager to trade with the white man. The council was not very long but it seemed to be successful. As we paddled through the area, we were unaware of the rich history that had occurred there.

After a little over an hour, a major highway started following the left side of the river. We knew we were close to Omaha but the trees were still very thick along the river so it wasn't until we came around a bend that Omaha came into view. There was a large grain elevator, a typical sight, but we were all surprised by the downtown area in front of us with office buildings that had a few dozen floors. This was the first large city we had encountered. We indeed were not in Montana any longer.

If we felt out of place we must have surely looked it. Busy highways with noisy traffic buzzed all around us. There was simply too much activity for my senses to take it all in after months of stillness and a very simple existence on the river. In one sense it seemed familiar and almost welcoming but at the same time it was too much too fast and I found myself just wanting to get to the other side of the city, where we would be back alone with our river.

The decision was made to see if we could find a place to take showers. It had been awhile and there was little debate. The weather had been too cold and the water was now too dirty to even think about bathing in. Again, just another reminder we weren't in the western wilderness any longer.

The nights were definitely getting colder. I was starting to wake up each night with the cold seeping through my army surplus sleeping bag. Some nights were so cold that I was grateful when the light of day finally arrived.

For two months of the trip getting splashed or getting your hands or feet wet was no big deal and very often simply relief from the heat. Now getting wet meant being cold. The shoes were now staying on, along with long pants, shirts, and jackets. Now getting in and out of the boats was different and more difficult, trying to keep your feet dry. The passing of the season was changing our behaviors. Staying dry and warm was something we didn't even consider back in August and September.

And in a very real sense, the river had changed, too. Oh, she was still faithfully carrying us along on our way but the cities and eastern woods made the plains and mountains of the west seem so far away. It was hard to imagine one could just turn around and paddle back upstream and get back to places like Gates of the Wilderness or Lake Sacajawea.

As we paddled that day, I know all our thoughts were on making it to St. Louis. The question now was not if, but when. Nothing was going to stop us now. We were a day or two from the Missouri state line, the seventh and last state we would paddle through. From there at Kansas City, the river would turn straight east, cut across Missouri and finally pour into the Mississippi. At that point we would paddle down the Mississippi to the Arch in St. Louis. After so long, it was starting to seem like it was going to happen.

One early morning while we were paddling, John suddenly turned around and looked at me. "Do you hear that?"

I stopped paddling and listened. "Yeah," I said, looking up river.

This time the barge was coming at us from our front. Tim and Steve's boat was about fifty or sixty feet in front of us. Steve called to us and headed for the left bank. I started paddling, following them. The barge looked like some kind of grain container with large doors on top. As it came down the river toward us, I could see the wave coming off each side. The tug boat was large, a white craft with two stories and the pilot house on a small third floor. It had the typical shape of a tug, with red trim and the name "River Queen" on her side.

I was carefully stepping out of the boat while John steadied it just as the barge started to pass us. This time we were ready for the onslaught of water, but as the waves started to roll toward us we could see they were very small and were just gentle swells when they reached the shore. I have to admit we were almost disappointed after what we had seen days before. We would have two more barges pass by us that afternoon with the same results. In fact, no other barge we encountered ever created such waves as that first barge.

Judging from the map, on October 13th our left bank changed from Iowa to the state of Missouri. Though it surely didn't look anything like St. Louis, just knowing we were in the same state was quite a feeling.

Campfires were now different than back in Montana and the Dakotas. We now had trees at our camp sites and very often a canopy of branches and leaves above our heads as we sat around the fire. For weeks we had the open space and the brilliant stars all around us. Now very often you would need to walk over to the river's edge to look up and see the stars. Where we once saw a dozen shooting stars in a night, we now hardly saw any through the leaves.

Even on the narrow river with a current the wind could make paddling difficult. Though progress at times was slow and hard, the scenery was simply beautiful. Rocky bluffs protruded out from steep banks covered in trees and bushes now fully transformed into autumn colors.

We were getting used to seeing the tug boats and the barges and it seems they were getting used to seeing us. One morning everyone was slow getting up out of our tents. It was a sunny day and the warmth in the tent felt great. I was stretching, still in my bag, when I heard a loud voice call out, "Get up boys, it's getting late!"

"What the...?" John rolled over and looked at me with a puzzled look.

I shrugged and unzipped the door of the tent. Out on the river, a large barge was just going by, and from the window of the pilot's cabin someone was waving. Steve had just stepped out of his tent and waved back, laughing. I guess we were becoming a fixture on the river.

There was one day when we had heard the distant sound of gunshots somewhere. It didn't seem strange since it was hunting season and we had heard many shots in the last few weeks, but this was more of a steady pattern, more like someone target shooting with a .22-caliber rifle.

We were just a few miles upriver from St. Joseph, Missouri. We had gone forty miles so we decided to stop, rather than having to paddle past the town to find a campsite. There were plenty of nice spots under all the trees with soft grass and plenty of firewood, whether we camped on the Kansas side or the Missouri side.

We decided on a nice clearing on the Kansas bank. As we pulled the boats ashore, we were surprised how close the gunshots seemed. We all agreed the shooting had been going on for quite a while and whoever was shooting had used at least a few hundred rounds. There was nothing we could see except for woods, but perhaps a shooting range was nearby.

Collecting firewood was the first thing we did, as we did every night. John and I were collecting driftwood along the river's edge while Tim and Steve were collecting pieces along the wood line. We were looking forward to a pleasant evening, some River Rat Stew, a baked potato, a soothing fire. We didn't just look forward to it, but after two and a half months on the river, we came to expect it. No one was prepared for what came next.

As John was bending over picking up wood, he waved his arm above his head, swatting at some bug. At the same moment I too heard the distinct buzzing of what I assumed must be a huge bumble bee flying around us. But it was mid-October and we hadn't seen any bees in quite awhile. This must be one hearty bumble bee, I thought.

At the moment I was thinking all this, John and I both noticed the reeds and plants along the edge of the water looked like they were dancing and twitching. When we watched them more closely we realized they were being torn up. The buzzing by our heads was not a bumble bee but bullets! The shooting we had been hearing was now directed at us!

John and I hit the dirt instantly and instinctively. We started yelling into the woods, "Stop shooting! There are people over here!" Tim and Steve came running and dove down beside us. "Hey, hold your fire! Hey!"

My first reaction was concern for the boats. What in the world would we do if a boat took a few bullet holes out here in the middle of nowhere? Then the reality set in that bullets were flying toward us and someone could get killed!

"Get the gun!" someone shouted. Steve was the closest to the canoe so he crawled over and reached for one of the water tight bags. We hadn't used the pistol in so long that he had to dig feverishly through the bag to find it. When he finally pulled it out, he pointed it in the air and squeezed off a few rounds while we all continued to yell.

When the shots kept coming we yelled to Steve to shoot into the woods, in the direction of the shooter. He looked at us and seemed to hesitate for a moment, but then aimed into the Kansas woods and started shooting till he emptied all the chambers.

While he reloaded the pistol the rest of us kept yelling.

It felt like a very long time before the shots finally slowed down. We all stayed as low to the ground as possible, still looking around for where rounds were hitting. It was almost dark when the final shot rang out and after a few more minutes we felt safe enough to get up. Amazingly, there were no holes in the boats and no holes in any of us!

We slowly resumed our wood collecting and got an extra large fire going, still trying to take in all that had happened so quickly. It was a strange feeling not knowing whether the shooter knew we were there or not. Didn't he hear us yelling? Did he even know we were shooting back in his direction? Without really knowing, dinner was a bit uneasy. We kept the pistol nearby just in case. Once darkness had set in, it was hardly the relaxing evening we had planned.

But by the time we were ready for bed we were laughing and joking over what had happened. After all, we were young and still had that feeling of invincibility. But to this day I have never forgotten the sound a bullet makes as it flies by, way too close for comfort.

We made it to St. Joseph, Missouri, on Day 79, October 16th. Most of the town was up on a hill on our left side. We didn't know it at the time, but near the top of the hill was a small, modest white house, the last home of the notorious Jesse James. It was there he was shot in the back and killed by one of his men.

St. Joseph was a town full of history. The Pony Express started there, taking daring young men on wild journeys into the new frontier of the Wild West. This was the place where those seeking gold or those seeking to homestead would join a wagon train and start their trek west. The rest is history. Concrete pillars and four-lane highways now stood where wagons, tents, and campfires once littered the landscape. What used to take months in a wagon now can be done in days, by plane in literal hours.

Decades before those crowds would arrive, the Corps of Discovery would spend a long hard day here, pushing ahead during rainstorms with thunder and lightning and fierce winds. The world had changed much over those almost two hundred years, but that old Missouri River still flows through that same history drenched land.

As abruptly as the noisy civilization appeared, we quickly were back in the woods with no one around. Paddling was easy and pleasant.

By mid-afternoon we could see Atchison, Kansas, just ahead.

We had always paddled past a town to make camp, away from any people, avoiding any potential trouble, but that day we decided to paddle the canoes to the highway bridge that crossed the river. We would pull the boats up under the bridge and camp there.

It was a mild night so we decided not to bother with the tents. We ate our dinner, sitting around our tiny fire. The atmosphere was awfully strange. Cars and trucks drove back and forth over the bridge above our heads, making a droning noise that ended with a metallic thump where the bridge ended and the road began.

On the near side of the street, right in front of our tiny camp, was a factory that turned out to be a foundry of some type. When it got late and we climbed into our sleeping bags, the noises from the foundry seemed to get even louder. Small engines pulled railroad freight cars slowly down tracks, just on the other side of a chain link fence. Sparks flew and machinery ran all night. The traffic over the bridge seemed to lessen but through the night many large trucks thundered through, sounding like they were coming right over the bridge and through our camp.

All night long I would wake up now and then to a truck or a railroad car being moved, sparks flying in the metal building, or loud machinery sounds. It was a restless sleep, much like a night in the wilderness during a thunderstorm. The loud noise just never allows you to fall into a deep enough sleep. Sometime during the night, in the middle of all the endless racket and activity, I became convinced we should never try camping in such a place again.

Of course, this was not such a place when the Corps of Discovery camped just upriver from here, near a small creek they named Independence Creek, which still bears that name today. We hadn't even noticed it as we paddled by, but the captains named it such a name because when they reached this spot it was 4th of July, Independence Day, 1804, the 28th birthday of a still very young United States of America.

They camped just upriver from the creek, just outside present-day Atchison. That night more than one man from the group wrote of how beautiful the landscape around them was. Sadly, the beauty and tranquility they enjoyed that warm July night was very different than the night we had spent almost 200 years later on that mild October night.

The next day high bluffs rose on our right side. We started seeing buildings high above us and knew we must be coming up on Leavenworth, Kansas. We actually first passed Fort Leavenworth, the oldest active military post west of the Mississippi.

We passed a few grain elevators and before we knew it, the town was gone. More trees and farmland occupied the next few hours. When we were at 40 miles for the day, we tied both boats together and floated along.

Kansas City was probably less than ten miles downstream so we decided to camp before we reached civilization. We could see jets coming in for a landing up ahead but other than that there was no clue that such a large city lay just ahead. The lights of aircraft continued to pass across the night sky. Clouds were slowly moving in, causing the lights of the planes to disappear and reappear. Fewer and fewer stars were visible as the clouds to the east of us glowed from the city lights below.

With the threatening sky, we decided to put up both tents. It was a good thing we took the precaution. During the night the temperatures dropped as a light rain began to fall. It wasn't enough to penetrate the tent walls so my bag remained dry, but by the middle of the night, it wasn't enough to keep me warm.

The light rain continued all night and I awoke to a gray, wet morning. The air was cold and damp, and though I just wanted to roll over and go back to sleep, I climbed out of my bag, dressed, and put on my rain gear. Everything was wet so we decided to just pack up and get going. We were anxious to get past Kansas City and we were just hours away now.

The rain continued and it seemed to get even colder. My hands were wet and cold and water would run up my arm as I paddled. The wind had worked the rain into the collar of my raincoat and water found its way down my back and down my chest in more than a few places. My legs were soaked and my sneakers were slowly getting drenched as well as water accumulated in the bottom of the boat. When a breeze hit my face, the rain would hit me and I'd have to wipe my eyes now and then. All I wanted was a warm fire and a cup of hot coffee.

In front of us we could see the mouth of the Kansas River pouring into the river. The Kansas was just about a third smaller in width than the Missouri. As we paddled, the canoes passed into the faster current of the converging rivers.

As our canoes passed under a highway bridge and a railway bridge beside it, the sights and the sounds of the city made an incredible impression on me. Never before had the reality of how far we had traveled really sunk in. The majestic high mountains and imposing white cliffs were now replaced by steel and concrete buildings that were even higher and more imposing. The eagles and the pelicans that took off, soured over, and landed effortlessly among us for months were now suddenly replaced by twin engine Cessnas and jet airliners. The soothing motion of the tall grass of endless prairie blowing in the Dakota winds was now replaced with cars and trucks speeding by on highways going in every direction. The clear, clean water, melted snow from the mountains that we paddled, drank and bathed in was now replaced with brownish, polluted industrial water. The incredible silence that can only be heard in the wilderness, miles from civilization, was now suddenly replaced by harsh sounds that seemed so disquieting right down to my soul.

Lewis and Clark and their men had spent a few days camped at the mouth of the Kansas River. It was mid June and the weather was warm and sunny. The men spent the time drying out clothes and gear among other chores. Ironically, there would be no dry clothes for the four River Rats. As difficult as it is to imagine the place where the city now stands as pristine wilderness, how more impossible for those men to have imagined what it would look like as a 20th century city.

Perhaps if it had been a warm, sunny day it would have seemed different, but as the grayness of the day settled in around us, with the cold steady rain soaking our clothes and chilling our bodies, our long-awaited arrival to the big city had an unexpected result. Though no one spoke it then, I know I was not the only one that day who was ready to have our Missouri River adventure end. I was cold, wet, hungry, and I was no longer on the river that flowed through the western Rockies and the plains. It was as if she had made a wrong turn somewhere, though the map said this is where we should be.

Strangely enough though, as I missed those days back in August among the White Cliffs, the hot sun and gorgeous starlit nights, I couldn't help but look around and now long for civilization. Restaurants, music, plumbing, warm beds, even television looked good. I watched the cars going by and thought that in less than an hour they would reach what would take us almost two days to reach by canoe.

Our daily life on the river had slowed to a pace most people never get to experience. We had enjoyed it and I am grateful I got to experience it, but that day sitting in that tiny canoe as the large city loomed above us, I began to miss the faster pace. I suppose as a young man I had no way of knowing how precious that slow pace was and how in the future as I grew up and got older, life would become much faster, a speed and pace that could ruin your life if you weren't careful.

So, as we slowly paddled through this strange new landscape, I felt myself torn between two worlds. As I shivered, paddling along, I suppose I was too uncomfortable to think much about it, but looking back now, Day 81, with less than 400 miles to go, we now knew enough of the river and of ourselves to know we would indeed make it to St. Louis. It would take another week to ten days, but we'd make it.

The fun and adventure that was our priority in the beginning of the trip had now been replaced with one priority. Get to St. Louis...and get home. It would be many years later, while reading Steve's journal from the trip, that I would learn that he too on this day decided he'd had enough. Steve, the eternal optimist, the guy that enjoyed every minute of every mile on the river...was ready to go home.

A Soldier's Discipline

Day 81 through Day 90

October 18 - 27, 1979

We paddled through downtown Kansas City and finally reached the trees and farmland on the east side of town. I was grateful I was paddling because I probably would have been shivering if I had been sitting still. The rain had finally stopped but there wasn't much of my body that wasn't wet and cold. I figured everyone else was as miserable as me but no one complained. I suppose we all realized it wouldn't do any good. Even Lucky kept under the tarp in our boat, nestled between the bags, trying to stay dry.

We didn't paddle far out of Kansas City before we passed under an old steel bridge and noticed a park on the right bank. We could see a row of parking spaces with picnic tables and small grills on poles in the ground. Both boats headed toward shore without anyone even saying a word. There had been enough paddling for one day, especially under the conditions we had faced. It was getting dark again. All I wanted was to get into some dry clothes and get a fire going.

The park was deserted except for one lone old pick up truck parked in one of the spaces along the dirt road. A couple probably a few years older than us got out of the truck to greet us. Glenn and Carol were their names.

If the day hadn't been bad enough, Glenn told us they had been listening to the radio in the truck and there was more rain expected, heavy at times, with a tornado warning for the county.

"Where exactly are we?" I asked. We had kept the maps safely tucked away in plastic to keep them from getting damaged in the rain.

"Well," Glenn said, pointing over his shoulder and across empty fields, "Independence, Missouri is just over there."

When a light rain started falling again, Glenn and Carol offered to give us a ride into town to buy some dry firewood. It hardly seemed right to spend money for what had been in unlimited supply for months, but it was pretty obvious after all the rain, we weren't going to find much good fuel. A fire would feel so good.

Tim jumped in the pick up while the rest of us set up camp. There was a gazebo in the middle of the park with a cement floor and a wooden roof. It was perhaps twenty feet wide and long. We decided we'd spend the night under that roof and would tie the boats to one of the large wooden posts holding up the roof structure. There really wasn't much else we could do.

It didn't take Tim long to get back with some store bought wood and after we found some semi-dry kindling, including some pages from our magazines, we managed to get a fire going. While dinner cooked we changed into dry clothes. Being warm and dry was a wonderful feeling after such a miserably cold and wet day.

After some small talk Glenn and Carol said their good byes and headed down the road, leaving us alone again. It was getting dark and cooler but at least it wasn't raining. We pulled two picnic tables into the gazebo so we could actually sit comfortably for dinner. As we ate, we all noticed in the darkness that the leaves in the trees were rustling more as the wind was picking up.

We made some hot tea, but with the chilly breeze blowing, it didn't stay hot very long. It just wasn't one of those nights to sit around the fire relaxing. We all decided to make it an early night and get in our bags. At least the cement floor in the gazebo was dry.

I must have been awfully tired because I fell asleep quickly on the hard surface. The next thing I knew I was hearing shouting and rain. As I started coming to my senses, I realized the wind was howling and there was a driving rain pouring down. Streams of water flowed off the roof all around us. Steve was yelling that a river of water was beginning to run across the center of the floor. I quickly looked around my bag, relieved to see I was still dry.

"We better get up on the tables!" Steve shouted as he and Tim climbed out of their bags. I really didn't want to give up the warmth of my sleeping bag but I could easily see that the gazebo floor was about to be flooded. In a sleepy stupor, I unzipped my bag, climbed out, feeling the chill of the damp night air, and threw it on top of the other picnic table while Tim and Steve were getting settled down on theirs.

"John!" I yelled, as I slid back into the sanctuary of my bag. He looked up at me sleepily and waved his hand, as if saying, "Yeah, I know."

Once in my sleeping bag I looked out into the darkness of the night. The wind blew the water running off the roof, sporadically sending it in all directions. It was too dark to see anything beyond that but I could hear the wind blowing the trees. I couldn't help but wonder if the roof of the gazebo could withstand a tree falling on it. I decided to pull the sleeping bag over my head and just try to sleep.

I simply was tired of hearing wind blowing all around me, always wondering if a tornado was going to touch down or something was going to slam into me. It reminded me of the sound of the wind on the lakes and I was just tired of it. I had heard it enough and I just wanted to hear quiet. I must have been exhausted, because I fell asleep again almost immediately.

Tim, Steve, and I remained dry during the night and I actually woke up in the morning having had a good night's sleep. That's more than I could say for John. He never had gotten off the cement floor and at some point during the night a flood of water invaded the gazebo and soaked him and his sleeping bag. Somehow he got a small fire going and spent the night trying to stay warm. How he got a fire going, I'll never know.

The next day was a cold, miserable paddle to Waverly, Missouri. Everything was wet. Everyone was cold. I'm sure on another day with sunshine we would have enjoyed the scenery of endless farmland and autumn trees, but not that day.

The town was way up high on a hill, most of it not visible from the water. The right bank was full of bushes and trees with a railroad track running along it. The usual suspension bridge ran across the river. We couldn't find a good place to pull in till we were past the bridge, almost past the town. There was a small park with some old children's swings, and a row of tall grain elevators along the railroad tracks. There wasn't a soul around so we decided we could probably get away with camping in the tiny park. There was a small road that led up the hill into town. Surely there had to be a laundromat somewhere up there.

We had been out of the boats probably less than a few minutes when a car drove down the road and pulled up beside us. It was as if they were just waiting for us to get there. Two men, maybe in their thirties, asked us if we needed any help.

"Yeah, know where there's a laundromat?" Steve laughed, as he lifted up a handful of wet clothes from his boat.

As usual, these guys offered to give us a ride into town to get our things dried. It was just amazing all the wonderful people, young and old, from Montana to Missouri, who went out of their way to help us. The whole trip would have been very different without their help. This time I stayed behind with the boats, giving John some of my stuff to dry. I had fared much better than Steve, who didn't have one dry piece of clothing left.

While they were gone, I started to collect wood to get a nice warm fire going. No one else came down to the river the whole evening. I walked over and sat on the metal swing set, looking out on the river while Lucky foraged around in the grass.

The other side of the river was still more farmland, difficult to see in the dimming evening light. It was extremely quiet, except for the squeaking of the old metal swing as I slowly swayed back and forth. Somewhere out there in the dark, the Corps of Discovery made camp on June 17, 1804. The men made twenty oars from the ash trees that grew along the north bank. They also spent time making a tow rope for the keelboat for when it had to be pulled from shore. On their warm night here they were really just getting started on their journey, knowing little of what lay ahead for them. On that chilly October night, I knew we were soon reaching the end of our journey, still not knowing what lay ahead or when we would reach the Arch. All I knew was, after 82 days on the river, with my feet on Missouri soil, it wasn't that far off now.

Lucky and I didn't stay long. The sun was down and it was getting chilly and the growing fire looked welcoming. I stood over it for quite awhile, letting the warmth penetrate my clothes and warm my hands. I hoped the guys would get back soon. I was getting hungry.

Pancakes were on the menu for the night. We didn't have much food left as we were trying to run out right as we arrived in St. Louis. How we were going to get back to Yellowstone was now weighing on our minds. John planned on wiring home for money and getting a bus back to New Jersey, so Steve, Tim, and I would have to sell the canoes in St. Louis for enough cash for three bus tickets back to the park. We didn't give much thought at that point as to how we would do that, but it seemed to be our only plan.

It was dark when I finally heard voices. The guys were walking down the hill, easily led by the fire, the only light in the area, dry laundry in their arms. It was late by the time we ate so we all hit the sack pretty quickly. The chilly windy days always seemed to take more out of us and sleep came more easily.

None of us could believe it but the next day a terrible headwind came up after only a few hours of paddling and we were stranded yet again. We were surrounded by large trees, many dropping their leaves with the gusts of wind whipping around. With no bugs and a sunny, warm day, it was actually nice to just relax for a bit. Perhaps in the early evening we could make up some miles.

There wasn't much to explore around camp. The flat farmland just seemed to go on forever so we stayed close to camp. I woke up from a short nap and noticed Steve gazing up into a particular tree. I looked and tried to see what it was he was staring at.

"What are you looking at?" I finally asked.

"I'm looking at one leave, waiting to see when it falls from the tree," he said.

"Huh?"

"You always see leaves falling from trees but have you ever seen a single leaf release from a tree?" He continued just staring.

"How long you been watching that one leaf?" I asked looking up again, wondering which leaf he had his eye on.

"Man, quite awhile."

I looked up in the tree, leaves blowing everywhere. I grinned at him. "I think you've been on the river too long, buddy."

"Yeah," he smiled. "Maybe."

Steve later told me he never did see that leaf fall. Perhaps it is more difficult than I ever thought to see a leaf when it actually falls from a tree.

The wind never did let up and we ended up doing only thirteen miles for the day. It had been a long time since we did such a short distance due to wind. Hopefully, it would be the last.

The weather was about to take a turn for the worst but little did we know we would have shelter from it and travel some easy miles at the same time! On the morning of October 21st there was a chill in the air and the sky was overcast and looking threatening.

We came around a bend and came upon a small tugboat on the north side of the river. There were two small grain barges tied next to it. The tug was awfully small compared to the huge ones we had grown accustomed to on the river. It just had a flat deck with one enclosed cabin area, including the pilot cabin. Steve and Tim got in a conversation with an elderly gentleman on shore while John and I paddled up to the side of the tug. There was a younger man looking out the window at us.

"Good morning, fellas! How are you doing this morning?" he asked, obviously surprised to see canoes on that section of the river and in late October.

"Good morning. We're headed to St. Louis," John answered.

"Really, quite a ways to go."

"Well, we started in Montana a few months ago," John continued.

"That's quite a haul!" our new friend exclaimed. He took off his greasy baseball cap, scratched his head with the same hand, and then fitted it back on.

I couldn't help but notice there was space on the deck for a few seventeen foot canoes.

"How about a ride? You guys headed down river?" I asked, trying to sound nonchalant.

"Well, we've got to transfer our load from that damaged barge to the other one so that's gonna take a good part of the day…but after that we're headed downriver to Mile 219. You're welcome to come along if you'd like. The weather's supposed to get pretty nasty later on."

Since the river became open to barge traffic, every mile was posted along the bank. We were at Mile Marker 279 which meant this tug would take us 60 miles! The four of us talked about it with big grins on our faces and decided, "Heck, yeah!"

It was difficult pulling the boats up onto the deck of the tug, but once that was done we went in the cabin where there was warm coffee and buns that we were welcomed to. There were a couple small bunks to sit on and magazines to read. While the other few workers were busy outside, the River Rats just relaxed in what we considered paradise, a greasy, grimy metal tug boat.

The insurance examiner came by in the afternoon with a bag full of hamburgers and fries. There were plenty for all of us, the workers taking a break to eat and hear all about our adventure. They were a bunch of really great guys.

After lunch I was lying on one of the bunks when the engines of the tug started up. At first it sounded like an explosion from underneath us, shaking the entire boat. As the engines revved the bunk vibrated and it seemed a giant monster underneath the boat was growling and grumbling. It seemed like it took all of the engine's strength to just barely nudge the boat forward. I looked out the small vibrating window to see we were finally heading downstream. I glanced back inside and saw John looking back at me with a big smile. "Now this is the way to travel!" he said.

I went out on the deck in the back of the tug and watched the churning wake. I thought about what it would be like to be in a canoe back there. Watching the banks go by so quickly made the whole river look so different. You're much more removed from the river when you're up in a boat with a motor carrying you along, less intimate than paddling right there in the water.

There really was no quiet spot on the boat but the cabin was the most comfortable. We played cards most of the afternoon, looking out the window now and then, watching the banks go by and watching the sky get more threatening by the hour. By late afternoon rain was running down the windows. The great thing about it was we were warm and dry!

The only other thought was that soon we'd have to get back out there in it. Or so we thought.

We pulled into a small steel dock as it was getting dark. There were just woods but the town of Glasgow must have been nearby. We figured this is where we get off but the captain of the boat stepped into the cabin as soon as the tug had come to a stop.

"We're gonna be leaving her here tonight. Going just a bit further tomorrow. You boys are welcome to stay put tonight if you'd like." He glanced over his shoulder out the door as the raindrops bounced on the deck and the canoes. "It ain't really a night for camping."

There was no arguing about that offer. We agreed and thanked him for such hospitality. Well, that was just the beginning. In a small building near the dock the guys came out with two electric heaters to get us through the night and an electric frying pan to cook up the stew, potatoes, and spaghetti that were in one of the cabinets. We really didn't know what to say. There didn't seem to be anything these new friends of ours wouldn't do for us.

They had trucks parked nearby and as they headed home for the night, one of the older gentlemen kidding not to take her for a ride. When the last truck drove away we just hooted and howled at our good fortune. Who ever would have thought?

We ended up turning on one of the heaters while we played cards into the night. Lucky roamed around the metal floor sniffing at all the strange new smells. We figured she had to be one of a very few rabbits to ride in a tugboat. She lay down not far from the heater and stretched out her body, relaxed as could be. I slept like a baby my first night on a tugboat. Lewis and Clark never had it so good.

Early in the morning the first truck pulled up outside the tug. It was either still a bit dark or it was terribly overcast. It had rained most of the night. The few times I woke up during the night I could hear the rain hitting the metal roof, so grateful I had a roof at all. It didn't seem right to keep sleeping as the workers showed up so we all got up. A pot of coffee was started right away. One of the men brought an apple for each of us, a simple but thoughtful gesture.

This time I was now ready for the loud engines as they turned over. I sipped my coffee as we headed down the river, slowly at first but then gaining to a steady speed. It wasn't long before the windows had lines of rainwater running down them, slanting and twisting like silver snakes. A fog hung over the water and in the upper reaches of the trees. It was as ugly a day as the day we passed through Kansas City, the only difference being we were still warm and dry!

Within a few hours we reached Mile Marker 219. We were informed that the barge would be unloaded tomorrow and the crew would be heading back upriver. With that news, we again were invited to spend the night onboard due to the weather and head out in the morning. Again, we humbly accepted. Probably at any other time in our lives we would have gone stir crazy in the tiny cabin of that tiny metal tugboat, but we were seasoned River Rats now. Just the simple pleasures of being dry and warm were things to truly be appreciated.

The rain poured down and the wind blew all day as the electric heater and the dim light of the cabin made us feel at home. We watched the dismal weather from the comfort of our little metal sanctuary. By evening, when we couldn't read any more magazines or play cards any longer, we finally went to bed.

I lay there in the warm bag realizing in the morning we would have to climb into wet, cold canoes, most likely in the rain, and spend another day like Kansas City. Of course, it wasn't that we had much of a choice. It wasn't as if it would take an incredible amount of self discipline on our part. We had absolutely no say in the matter. If we had a choice, I suppose it would have taken quite a bit of self discipline to get back in those boats, a self discipline I didn't really feel I possessed at the moment, warm in my sleeping bag.

THE IMPORTANT ART OF SELF-DISCIPLINE

Self-discipline is a funny thing. The longer I live the more I realize what a wonderful gift it can be. I know people that are extremely self-disciplined and so are their parents. It makes me wonder if it is simply genetic or is it the upbringing they got under the authority of disciplined parents? Perhaps it is a combination of both, but I can think of some self-disciplined parents who have children that are very undisciplined, and some undisciplined parents with children that seem to be naturally self-disciplined. Either way, as a parent I cannot escape the fact that I am commanded to train up my children God's way and God does speak of discipline in the scriptures.

And you have forgotten the exhortation which speaks to you as to sons:

"My son, do not despise the chastening of the LORD, Nor be discouraged when you are rebuked by Him; For whom the LORD loves, He chastens, And scourges every son whom He receives." If you endure chastening, God deals with you as with sons; for what son is there whom a father does not chasten? But if you are without chastening, of which all have become partakers, then you are illegitimate and not sons.
Hebrews 12:5 - 8

God, as our Heavenly Father uses chastisement and discipline as proof of His love for us, His children. In the same way, we as earthly fathers must use discipline in a loving way as well. The writer of Hebrews even goes so far as to say a son that is not chastened and disciplined is illegitimate, and not a real son.

Furthermore, we have had human fathers who corrected us, and we paid them respect. Shall we not much more readily be in subjection to the Father of spirits and live? For they indeed for a few days chastened us as seemed best to them, but He for our profit, that we may be partakers of His holiness.
Hebrews 12: 9 - 10

It is obvious from the text that as earthly fathers we are to discipline our children. We are to do our best even though as imperfect fathers we will make mistakes. Yet God, as our perfect Father does not make those mistakes, so His discipline always has our spiritual good in mind that we might profit from it.

Probably the worst act of passive fatherhood is avoiding the responsibility of disciplining our sons and daughters. We just would rather not have do deal with the conflict. Perhaps we're tired or we're just too busy. The fact is our children will learn there are consequences for their actions. The question is whether they will learn that on their own when it is too late and the consequences are grave or as they grow up, learning from the loving discipline of their fathers and mothers.

I believe disciplining our children may be the most difficult responsibility God has called us to. I also believe it can be one of the most challenging aspects of marriage. A father may very well have a very different perspective on how his sons should be disciplined and for what actions, than his wife. I find mothers have their own perspective when it comes to their children. I'm not even hinting that one might be right and the other wrong, but acknowledging they are sometimes very different.

Having two sons first, I find myself very willing to let my sons experience certain hardships to help them grow, both spiritually and physically. I am much more willing to have them take certain risks. Karen seems much more protective and cautious, more motherly, I suppose.

I know that scenario will be very different when my precious little Emma is in her mid teens! I find myself somewhat willing to let my sons deal with this world we live in but I can't imagine sending my daughter out into the world. I am certain there are dads agreeing with me right now and some of you who have walked down that road already are probably nodding your heads knowingly.

Some might say it's a double standard. Call it what you will, but there are two standards when it comes to my sons and my daughter. I am not speaking of a difference in expectations, behavior, respect, responsibility, etc. But unlike the world, I recognize there are very clear differences between men and women and the roles God has designed them for. As a godly father, I must acknowledge and respect that.

It is easy to see why parents, even with our differences as dads and moms, must present a united front to our children. If we are both Christians, you would think that wouldn't be difficult, but most of us know our children have learned the military strategy, "Divide and Conquer." Obviously God designed parents to be a mom and a dad with different perspectives, and somehow, with all our differences as men and women, He expects us to be a team. The effective discipline of our children depends on it.

> Now no chastening seems to be joyful for the present, but painful; nevertheless, afterward it yields the peaceable fruit of righteousness to those who have been trained by it.
> Hebrews 12: 11

Discipline can be painful at times, for both the one being disciplined but also for the one having to impose the discipline. Yet scripture makes it very clear that we all benefit from that very discipline and we all suffer when discipline is lacking.

> My son, hear the instruction of your father, and do not forsake the law of your mother; for they will be a graceful ornament on your head, and chains about your neck.
> Proverbs 1:8

> A wise man makes a glad father, but a foolish son is the grief of his mother.
> Proverbs 10:1

King Solomon had much to say about wisdom, especially in the first ten chapters of the Book of Psalms. The dictionary says wisdom is understanding what is true, right, or lasting, common sense, good judgment. Why is it some people seem to gain wisdom easier than others while for some it seems to elude them their whole lives? There are some that can watch the actions and decisions of others and the consequences that befall them and learn from other's mistakes. Yet there are others that need to make those same mistakes in their own lives, suffer the consequences, and sometimes still not gain any wisdom at all. I believe wisdom is the prize won from the training discipline brings.

To me, I have always thought knowledge and wisdom were two very different things. As Christians, we can have lots of Bible knowledge. We can read all the books, listen to the tapes and CDs, and watch all the DVDs. We can also live our lives with all that knowledge while it has no effect or impact on our lives. I believe wisdom is simply applying the knowledge we have. That application takes discipline. And that discipline takes time. Perhaps that is a good definition of spiritual maturity, which is an ongoing process for all of us, a destination we will never reach in this world, yet always the goal.

The military would never be able to accomplish any of its missions and objectives without the discipline it demands. Any veteran will tell you that if they learned anything in their time in the military, it was discipline. Though I would never want God or Christian parents to discipline the way the army or marines do in boot camp, one cannot argue with the results of such discipline. The military has just a few months of basic training to instill such discipline. As parents we have a whole childhood, so we don't need to use such drastic measures.

⸎

Most people probably forget that the expedition of Lewis and Clark was a military mission. The men weren't simply adventurers or mountain men. They were soldiers. There were only a few times, but men were court-martialed and faced punishment during the journey. There was one desertion. There was one man who fell asleep on guard duty and another that broke into the whiskey while guarding it. The captains knew the importance of military discipline to accomplish their mission and to keep them safe, as well as keeping morale high.

If any of us are to achieve much while in this world, we and our children must accept the fact that we need to be disciplined in whatever we do, from academics, to athletics, to our professions, and even in our spiritual service to God.

I awoke the next morning to the voices of the men showing up right at the crack of dawn. The first thing I did was to look at the small window above me and see it was dry. The rain had stopped sometime during the night.

We walked out onto the deck and though there was a slight chill in the air, the dampness of the last few days was gone. There was no fog on the river, and it even looked like the clouds were ready to break up. We carefully emptied the water out of each boat and while having some small talk with the men, slowly slid the canoes off the back of the tug, into the water. We shook hands with everyone, thanking them for all their help and hospitality. We each climbed into the boats and got situated, Lucky sitting just in front of me. Just as we paddled out of sight, the tug boat engine roared to life, a now familiar sound.

High rocky bluffs would appear now and then, especially on the left side of the river. The light colored rock made the colors of the trees and shrubs stand out even more brilliantly. The blue sky helped finish the perfect scene. How different from the previous days of cold rain and gray skies.

Breakfast now consisted of whatever was left in the food bags. Each time we ventured into those bags we would find remnants of opened packages, crumbled food, nasty mold spores growing everywhere, and everything seemed to be sticky with sand stuck on it. Knowing the trip was nearing its end, there were now some things even River Rats refused to eat.

Jefferson City appeared one day, high up on a hill on our right. As the state capitol, the dome-topped capitol building could easily be seen from the river. We debated going ashore but it would have been quite a walk just to get up to the main part of town, and we really didn't need any supplies anyway. A train passed by, a long lumbering freight train on a track that ran right along shore.

We camped near the mouth of the Osage River. Where the rivers converged, the surrounding banks were thickly wooded. There was a high bluff on the right side of the Missouri that dominated the land-scape. The high hill was named Clark's Hill. Captain Clark had writ-ten in his journal that he had climbed that very hill to get a better view of the area. He remarked at how pleasant a view it was, looking out over the rivers and the hills. The Corp camped there on June 7, 1804, and then again on their return trip in 1806.

Our campsite was a pleasant one in among the trees. It was a calm evening, much warmer than usual. We built an extra large fire to enjoy and cooked up yet another unique version of River Rat Stew.

It stayed unseasonably mild all day. For the first time in quite a while, I didn't wake up shivering in the middle of the night.

On Day 88 we pulled into the town of Hermann. I had enjoyed many of the small towns we had seen along the river, but I think this old German town was my favorite. The quiet streets and antique build-ings made me feel as if I had stepped into a Mark Twain novel. With the dramatic autumn colors as a backdrop, it was like walking through a Thomas Kincaid painting.

There was a bed and breakfast just down the road so we stopped in to see if we could take showers. The manager in charge was a stocky man, probably in his thirties. He wasn't much of a talker but he agreed to let us take showers for two dollars each. Somehow, after our showers, we con-vinced him to let us stay in one of the rooms for free. Actually, the room he offered us was hardly bigger than a walk in closet. It was an old room that hadn't been updated and remodeled, but we accepted his final offer.

After almost three months on the river, sleeping inside was a bit strange, especially in a room so small. There was one thin mattress that somehow I got to sleep on. The other guys put their bags right on the floor. There was no TV or phone, just four bare walls. We opened the one small window we had just so we could feel and smell the outdoors that had become so familiar to us.

We went to sleep that night knowing we were now just a few days away from reaching the Arch in St. Louis. It was finally that close.

On the morning of October 27th, our 90th day on the river, we packed the boats the same way we had for three months now. It was now so routine we could probably have done it blindfolded. In no time at all we were pushing off. We had only fifty-four miles to the end of the Missouri and about another 15 down the Mississippi to the Arch.

St. Charles was the last town before St. Louis so we decided we had to get past there for the day. The paddling was easy and the sun kept us comfortably warm even though the temperature was awfully cool.

By mid afternoon we made it to St. Charles, going ashore in a small park with a walking trail and benches. We pulled the boats onto shore. It always felt great to get out and stretch our legs. Sometimes my feet would be totally asleep if I forgot to uncross my legs now and then to get the blood flowing.

We would be in St. Louis tomorrow, looking up at that beautiful Arch, reveling in the fact we had finally made it. Yet now I couldn't help but wonder how we were going to sell the boats while stranded in a city and somehow get back to Yellowstone. Our focus had always been on getting there with little time spent on how to get home.

Little did I know the good LORD had His own plan. Just as I got back to the guys, an elderly couple was walking by. They were dressed in winter coats, he with a brimmed hat and she with a scarf around her hair. They seemed a bit overdressed for the temperature, but they both had warm smiles and greeted us. Looking at the canoes, they couldn't help but ask where we had come from and where we were headed. It felt really strange after all the times we had told folks about the trip to now be saying we would be done tomorrow. They were very sweet and just couldn't stop telling us what a great feat it was to canoe the whole river and we should be very proud. They asked us when we thought we'd make it to the Arch tomorrow. I told them that if we did another fifteen miles today, we should be there by one o'clock or so. They almost made it seem like they were going to come and welcome us to the city.

We all seemed to run out of things to say and it was time for us to get back on the water. We said our goodbyes as we had done so many times before over the last three months to so many kind people all along the river.

When we got past Mile Marker 9, we decided it was time to stop and make our final campsite of the trip. To think of all the beautiful places we had been and had camped at, it was impossible for this last campsite to measure up to that standard. The trees along the river were now mostly bare; the brilliant color we had enjoyed was now past. The banks were flat with about twenty or thirty feet of muddy ground, strewn with driftwood, but also tires, construction debris, and various garbage. We found a spot where a new bridge was under construction and decided it would have to do.

It was our last campsite of the trip. My mind had images of the mountains and white cliffs of Montana, the incredible lakes of the Dakotas, the endless prairie and farmland of Kansas, Iowa and Nebraska, the autumn colors and limestone bluffs of Missouri. As I stood there, looking downriver as I had done for now ninety days, all I could think to myself was that the Missouri River Rats had indeed come a long way.

A Soldiers' Uniform

The Boy's Third Day

August 21, 2002

On our left, the bank was a steep eight or ten foot embankment of dark earth cut out by the river. It made a wide turn to the right, entering into an area of faster water. After two days of paddling on flat water, the boys and I enjoyed the feeling as the boats sped up and bounced over the small waves that carried us along.

"Follow me!" I yelled to Dustin in the other boat. I steered the boat toward the left bank where the water was the swiftest and where the most waves were. There were very few obstacles, logs or rocks to avoid. The river gave us a fun ride for a few hundred feet and then all too soon the quiet, flat water returned.

Josh turned around and grinned. "That was cool."

The hills were a golden color with tall grass covering most of them. Here and there the rugged shards of rock jutted out, as if trying to rip their way through to the surface. Long rows of layered limestone formed natural walls, as if part of great fortresses; some straight, others at various angles, evidence of the massive upheaval of the land spoken of in the Scriptures.

If I needed another reason to love the west, I love how the evidence of the worldwide flood of Genesis is so visible in the landscape. Where else can you see such vivid results of the flood, creating layer upon layer of sedimentary rock? Where else can you see the evidence of the earthquakes and volcanic activity that tore the land apart, creating massive mountains and valleys, which in turn caused enormous movement of water that carved out places like the Grand Canyon and such marvelous rock formations as in Arizona and Utah? What better place to see the millions of dead things found in those rock layers, from ocean plants to large dinosaurs?

The unbelieving world has built its theories around its bias and refusal to look at the evidence with an open mind, refusing to even consider the pages of the Bible to be actual history. Events like Mt. St. Helens showed the world that cataclysmic forces could produce the geologic results that before we assumed had to take millions of years. The foolishness of man will continue to lead the unbelieving world down the wrong path as they continue to bend and twist their ideas, all in the attempt to deny the obvious.

The world will call us religious fanatics if we take a stand and acknowledge the authority of the scriptures over the foolish ideas of man. It takes a spiritual soldier to stand up for the authority of God's Word, and as our American culture becomes more and more secular, even anti-Christian, it will take the best soldiers to stay the course.

"Hey, guys! We need to do one last swim!" I shouted loud enough for Dustin to hear in his boat ahead of ours.

"No way!" Dustin yelled back. I could tell from his voice there was no changing his mind any time soon.

"How 'bout you, kiddo?" I asked Josh.

He seemed to hesitate for a moment but then said, "Maybe later when I get hot."

Well, it looked like I was going in the frigid water alone this time. I pulled off my shirt and quickly before I had enough time to reconsider how cold the water was, I slid over the side.

Again, the water's chill took my breath away. Josh was grinning as he watched me trying to catch my breath. I couldn't feel the bottom so I hung onto the side of the canoe and floated along. When I think about it, it wasn't that I really wanted to go swimming that day. I surely didn't enjoy the feel of that freezing water. But all I could think of was the question of when I would get another chance. Somehow it had become twenty-three years since my last swim in my beloved river. At my age of forty-three, I didn't want to think about when or even if the next time would ever come. All I knew was I was there at that moment and I didn't want to miss out on any part of the experience, whether the heat of the afternoon sun or the cold of the water. I was consciously living in the moment, something most of us don't really do very often in our busy lives, with our minds on other things rather than the moment at hand.

It wasn't long before I had to climb back into the canoe, allowing the warmth of the sun to relieve the numbing that I was starting to feel. I didn't bother drying off but picked up my paddle and Joshua and I started back down the river, with Dustin about a hundred yards ahead.

A few miles further we were coming around a slow wide bend in the river when I noticed a wooden structure on the right side of the river. The right back was a steep four or five-foot earthen wall up to a level field of golden, dry prairie grass.

"What is that, Josh?" I asked. "Up there on the right."

He had spotted it about the same time I had. "It looks like it was a house."

We had passed a few old buildings in the last few days, but most were farther from the river. We had taken pictures of some of those that still resembled at least a hint of what they once were. A few looked very tempting and we had thought about stopping to investigate them but had decided not to. This old house, or I should say, what was left of it, was too close to fight the temptation.

Dustin and I steered the boats to shore. The steep bank prevented us from seeing anything. We carefully climbed the bank. When we reached the top the remnants of the house again came into view.

It had collapsed back onto itself, what was once the peak of the roof still protruding above the mass of splintered, sun bleached planks of wood. Square window frames with no glass lay among the pile. The front door frame of the house was lying flat beside a section of what was once the roof.

The tall grass came up to my knees, even higher on the boys. It seemed to be trying to overtake and consume what was left of the wooden structure. With just shorts and water shoes on, I realized it wasn't the smartest thing to be sloshing through that grass, totally vulnerable to any rattlers that might be there, impossible to see until it was too late.

We carefully walked around the side of the collapsed building, stepping slowly and deliberately. I found an opening in the ground that turned out to be a root cellar or perhaps a storm shelter. As with everything else, the wooden steps and frame had caved in some but it was still possible to see down into the dark opening. My mind raced as I thought about what might still be down in there. I didn't want to consider how many decades of river travelers had also stopped to investigate the house, even back when it stood straight and intact, taking whatever interesting treasures they found.

I tried to imagine what the house looked like in its day, whenever that was. Had there been a barn or at least a corral? Had there been a swing set somewhere in the yard? Was there an old, rusted bicycle lying out there somewhere in that sea of grass?

I couldn't help but wonder who these people were who built this home and then tried to scratch out a life here. Were they a young couple in love just starting out? Was it a large family? If only those wooden planks could talk.

What kind of people would be willing to try and make a life out here in the middle of nowhere? What was their motivation? Were their dreams and their fears much different than yours and mine? I'm sure in so many ways they were no different than you and me, yet I have to believe their being alive at a very different time and in such a very different place produced a very different mind set. I really couldn't tell how old the house was, but it surely had no electricity, no plumbing, no phone or radio.

I thought about the dad who had put so much hard work into building a home for his family. How long had they lived here before they had to move on? How heartbreaking it would be for him to see the house now, reduced to a pile of scrap wood.

I couldn't help but wonder if today there was an old great grandma somewhere who had memories of this house as a little girl, perhaps peering out one of those old window frames when it still held glass, gazing up at the stars, yearning to be grown up.

It reminded me again of what really is important in life. I hope the man that built this house worked as hard at raising his kids as he did at building them a house. I hope he had been the type of father that helped make it a loving home. Whenever that was, the time of opportunity for him to shape future generations had come and gone. His legacy of children, grandchildren, and great grandchildren now lives on.

I won't even begin to try to figure out how much of the legacy we leave with our kids and grandkids is genetic and how much is a result of our choices and actions as parents. I can just watch my own children and see there seems to be a mixture of both.

As I slowly walked among the grass and the boards, I wondered how well this father had done. He was long gone now, but he had implanted ideas and behaviors in the others that followed. Were his descendents as strong willed and independent as he? Were they as hard working as he was out here in the wilderness? Did they still have a spirit of adventure and courage as he had? Did he ever think about this day when he would be gone, no worries, no worldly demands, no worldly possessions left, just what he had passed on to his children, for them to pass on to theirs, and on to theirs. Did he pass on the things that mattered most? Do we spend much time thinking about that day for ourselves? Probably not, though each of us knows that day is coming.

We carry much of our past and our family's past with us as we live out our lives. Some people call it "baggage" and choose to focus on all the negative things that occurred, perhaps back in our childhood. We think of it as the stuff we carry around with us and never get rid of. Since we all come from imperfect parents who had their own share of baggage it is only logical we would end up with some ourselves. It's the stuff that keeps psychologists and psychiatrists in business.

Though I don't dispute our sad condition, I also am aware of the positive that can be passed on. Yes, positive things even from imperfect, sinful people. Many of us carry around with us a strong work ethic, a sense of justice, a generous heart, a sustaining faith, all due to someone in our past. We can choose to carry those things around with us. They become a part of who we are on the inside, as we choose to wear them as clothing or even a uniform to show the world who we are. In a very real sense, we choose what we will clothe ourselves in, not unlike a uniform.

I used to love wearing my dress uniform while I was in the service. I made sure my jump boots were spit shined to perfection; my silver wings on my chest, my red beret cocked just right on my head. I was proud of what I had done to earn the right to wear such a uniform but even more than that, I was extremely proud of what it represented.

There weren't many young men my age that noticed but those of previous generations from Vietnam back to World War II, would notice the patch of the 82nd Airborne Division on my shoulder. They knew the history of the famous airborne unit that had been called upon to fight in every major and minor conflict our country was involved in. Some would simply give me a friendly nod, while others wanted to buy me a drink or lunch. Some would start telling me of when they were a paratrooper during World War II, jumping into France, not any older than me. They would tell me their incredible stories and I would wonder why they were buying me lunch instead of the other way around.

Every American owes them so much. All those brave young men sacrificed so much. Many suffered and bled and many died for all of us. It was the bravery and the blood and sacrifice of these young soldiers that brought honor to the uniform I was privileged to wear. I was a twenty one year old paratrooper who had never been to war yet these heroic war veterans treated me as if I had flown in those C-47 transport planes with them and fought along side them across Europe. They treated me as one of their own, though I most certainly didn't deserve the honor.

It was in the early spring of 1981, not long after arriving at Fort Bragg, NC., that I received another uniform, one that I most definitely did not deserve to wear. It was a warm evening and I decided to go for a walk. If anyone had asked me where I was going I would have told them nowhere in particular, but I know in my heart of hearts, I went out that night looking for the chaplain's office. If someone had stopped me in the street even then and asked me I would have told them I didn't believe in or need their God.

Military installations have signs everywhere so it didn't take me long to find the small building. As I walked around to the side door that was propped open I could hear singing. I looked around, almost as if all those people who had shared their faith with me and had endured my brutal attacks were now somewhere watching me. For some silly reason, I just didn't want anyone to know where I was.

As I reached the door, another song started to play. I peeked into the room, still not wanting to be seen. There were five soldiers, all clad in camouflage with hymnals in their hands starting to sing another song. The chaplain, also in camouflage, was up front leading, while a woman played a piano in the corner.

As the men sang, I listened to the words I had never heard before.

Amazing Grace, how sweet the sound, that saved a wretch like me,

I once was lost but now am found, was blind but now I see.

After years of rebellion and rejecting God, I realized those words were describing me. I was that wretch who had been so lost. From childhood to young adulthood, I had known nothing of the amazing grace of God. I had only seen manmade religion that seemed to oppress and judge people. It was like a system of doing certain things and not doing other things in order to somehow please God enough and perhaps get a shot at heaven. The relationship that God speaks of in the Bible was never shared with me, and I came up with all kinds of reasons to believe the Bible was simply a story book and God really didn't exist. I truly was blind to spiritual truth, consumed with myself and the world around me. That night everything changed as my spiritual eyes were opened and my heart was softened.

I now understood the amazing, loving, forgiving grace that God had bestowed upon me. Through my rebellion and rejection of God I had been judged and that sin came with a death penalty, separating me from God now and forever. Jesus said He did not come to judge the world, because the world had already been judged. He said He came to save the world. God, in all His love and mercy, became a man, lived a perfect, sinless life, and willingly paid the death penalty for sin by dying on that wooden cross. He then proved to the world how He had conquered sin and death by rising again on the third day.

God demonstrates His own love toward us, in that while we were yet sinners, Christ died for us.
Romans 5:8

I was as unworthy as anyone else, deserving eternal punishment from God, yet instead I received loving forgiveness.

> For the wages of sin is death, but the gift of God is eternal
> life in Christ Jesus our LORD.
> Romans 6:23

After all the years of hearing I had to do certain rituals and perform in certain ways, I now understood that forgiveness and salvation were freely given by Jesus. Instead of trying to work for it, to somehow pay my way into heaven, I finally realized Jesus had paid it all. What I needed to do was surrender my life to my LORD and Savior and believe.

> For by grace you have been saved through faith, and that
> not of yourselves; it is the gift of God, not of works lest
> anyone should boast.
> Ephesians 2:8,

It is sad that we have a world full of religious people trying all different ways to earn their way into heaven, yet rejecting the wonderful eternal life God so freely offers. How sad for those that have rejected religion and now are convinced there is no God, missing out on the greatest love they could ever experience

> For God so loved the world that he sent His only begotten
> Son, that whoever believes in Him should not perish but
> have everlasting life.
> John 3:16

I received Jesus as my Savior that night. I didn't know much yet of the nature of God or what the Holy Scriptures really said, but I knew my life would never be the same. It might sound silly now but the first time I jumped out of an airplane as a Christian I remember saying a short prayer just as the green light was illuminated. I simply offered myself into His care and committed my soul to Him.

I will greatly rejoice in the LORD, My soul shall be joyful in my God;

For He has clothed me with the garments of salvation.

He has covered me with the robe of righteousness...
Isaiah 61:10

If I felt unworthy wearing my uniform among those heroes of World War II, how so much more unworthy am I to wear garments of salvation and a robe of righteousness before God? How could I not be brought to my knees in grateful humility over such love from my Creator?

My military uniform carried with it authority and honor. I was privileged to enjoy and partake in that honor, but it was others who paid for it with their own blood long before I was even born. In somewhat the same way, I now wear garments of salvation with all the authority of the King of kings, the LORD of LORDS, the Creator of the universe. All the honor of my robe of righteousness is His righteousness, not my own, and paid with His own blood, again long before I was born.

My old uniform hangs in a closet now. I pulled it out every couple years to wear at church a few times for Veteran's Day services, relieved to see it still fit, though much tighter than back when I was a young paratrooper. The beret didn't fit exactly right with a head full of hair, but it still felt great to wear.

I can't help but wonder if sometimes as Christians we tend to take off our Christian uniform, our garments of salvation and our robe of righteousness. In reality, we really can't take them off, but we surely can act as if we have. The world mocks the need for salvation and ridicules even the mention of righteousness. There are those times it becomes too easy to conform to this world. We sacrifice righteousness and honor for the sin and corruption of the world. We forget we are soldiers and back away from the fight. We go AWOL in a very real sense.

Not only do we hurt ourselves but very often we hurt those we love and care about the most. AWOL (Away With Out Leave) can be most devastating to our children, who need us the most. The sad fact is it doesn't necessarily mean the father has physically left. We can leave emotionally as well. You can be home yet emotionally be a thousand miles away. In doing so, you are unintentionally adding some more weight to the baggage your kids will carry, affecting even the next generations.

Our military uniforms may grow old and obsolete, packed in moth balls. They eventually get to the point they don't fit anymore. As spiritual soldiers we can't allow our spiritual uniforms to grow old or obsolete. We mustn't willingly take them off and put them in moth balls. In God's army there is no discharge, no retirement, not even an inactive reserve. We have been called to serve for eternity.

When the boys and I had seen enough we carefully walked through the tall grass back to the river. We slid down the crumbling embankment and climbed back into the boats, pushing back out into the slow current. We drank some juice from the cooler, everything still cold inside even on the third day.

We were almost at the end of the trip and I tried as best I could to take it all in. I wanted to remember every sight, every sound and smell. I would close my eyes and listen to the sounds and breathe in the scents of the river and the land. I'd then open them and take in the beauty all around me.

This had been the long-awaited trip down the Missouri River with my sons. That dream of a lifetime that had actually come true. It had been better than I could have ever hoped for. In less than an hour it would all be great memories, a part of our family history. It would be a gift to both my sons that they could hold on to for a lifetime.

It was a wonderful gift for me as well.

We paddled past a few more white sandstone cliffs that morning and saw more pelicans and eagles. It was another perfect day with a warm sun and a gigantic clear blue sky. We came around a slight bend in the river and a highway bridge came into view, our cue that Judith Landing was coming up on the left, just after the bridge. As our canoes floated under the bridge I looked to see if I could spot anyone waving to us, but no one was around. We made our way over to the left side of the river, looking for the landing and the campground. About half a dozen cars were parked in a rugged parking area, and maybe five or six tents were scattered under a grove of large cottonwood trees. On the opposite side of the river, we spotted a large mule deer standing by the bank cautiously watching us.

Dustin pulled up on shore first and steadied our boat as Joshua and I climbed out. There were a few other canoes parked there along the boat ramp and sitting in the grass. A small log structure with a big sign, "General Store" was about thirty yards away, tucked under a few trees for shade beside the makeshift campground. I looked for our vehicle but it wasn't among the few SUVs and vans parked nearby.

While the boys took a stroll over to the store, I dug out my cell phone just to see if there was any reception. After taking it out of the plastic bag and turning it on, I was again disappointed to find no signal. I looked at my watch. It was 11:32. We were early. I felt a bit anxious, but it wasn't as if they were late. It was a long drive, almost three hours from Great Falls so I really shouldn't have been surprised they weren't there early. I decided to just go check out the tiny general store and relax.

The store was a 19th century log cabin, but it did have electricity. There were coolers with a variety of cold drinks and ice cream, just about the best items to have for sale out in the middle of nowhere on a hot, dry day. There were some other snacks on the shelves, along with camping necessities such as matches, toilet paper, and bug spray. By the register there was of course a selection of books on Lewis and Clark. There were a handful of paddlers sitting around, talking about their trip, enjoying the food and drink.

The boys and I sat on the wooden porch of the cabin, enjoying an ice cream. "So what did you guys think of the Missouri River?" I asked.

"It was cool," Josh said as he worked on his cone.

"We should do it again someday, Dad," Dustin added. I was pleased with their answers. It really had been a great three days.

"That was three days. How would you like to spend ninety-one days on the river?"

"You guys were nuts!" Josh responded quickly, shaking his head.

"Yeah, maybe we were," I answered, as I glanced out at the river, looking downstream. I couldn't help the fact a part of me wanted to continue down the river, get around the next bend. The remote badlands of the river were further downstream, then Fort Peck Lake. North and South Dakota with the gigantic lakes would be next. The great plains of Nebraska, Iowa, and Kansas would come next, followed by downtown Kansas City. The beautiful trees and little towns of Missouri would be the final leg until the Mississippi River and the Arch in St Louis. "Yeah, I guess we were a little nuts," I said with a grin on my face.

It got to be 12:30 and Karen and Dad were thirty minutes late. I joked to myself that Karen was rarely on time and I let that thought reassure me for awhile. I just had to be patient. Surely they would be showing up any time now.

The outfitter showed up in a large pick up truck to collect the canoes. Ron was a pleasant, mellow guy, the type that belonged out in the rugged wilderness.

"So how'd you fellas do out there?" he asked, walking around the pick up and shaking my hand.

"It was great! The boys had a great time," I said.

"How about that storm last night? What a doosy that was!" he chuckled.

"Yeah, well, we didn't stay dry but we survived," I answered back. After a few more minutes of small talk our canoes were headed down the gravel road, the road I was really hoping to see Karen coming down any time now.

At 1:15 I decided I'd walk up the road to where I could see out over the flatlands. I wanted a better view of the road. The boys decided to stay by the river while I ventured up out of the river valley. When I reached the top of the hill, I could see the distant snowcapped mountains on the horizon with miles of prairie before me. The road snaked out of the valley and across the flatlands. I could probably see a few miles of the road stretched out toward the south. If a car came, I'd spot the dusty cloud way before I could make out what kind of vehicle or which color it might be. I tried the cell phone again, another failed attempt.

I sat down on the gravel road, not having to worry about any traffic. I looked back down on the river and the cabin in the trees. On the opposite side of the Missouri, the Judith River flows in. Captain Clark had named the river after his young cousin, Julia Hancock.

Eventually the two would marry three years later. The Clarks would have five children, the eldest named Meriwether Lewis Clark, a testimony to the respect and admiration Clark had for Lewis. Tragically, they would only enjoy twelve years together, before Julia would become ill and die in 1820.

Joshua came walking up the hill at one point. "Where are they?" he asked, obviously knowing I had no idea.

"They should be here any time now," I said, trying to sound reassuring. The fact was I was now getting somewhat nervous. If Karen missed the one turn on the road that would bring her down to the river she could be driving for hours before she reached any civilization. What if they got a flat tire? It's not like you could call Triple A. Would she and Dad be able to find the jack and the spare tire? I hadn't looked. What if the spare was missing? That happens with rental cars sometimes. I should have checked before we left.

Josh hung around for awhile but then went back down to the river where our gear was.

It was almost 2:00 and it was difficult to not imagine all the things that could have possibly gone wrong. I was starting to feel awfully guilty of planning the trip and having Karen do such a drive through such desolate, unknown territory. I prayed that everything was alright. "What do I do if she doesn't show up soon?" I asked myself.

The End of the Journey

October 28, 1979

I awoke that morning and immediately realized this was it. We would reach the Arch in St. Louis by the afternoon. We all must have been thinking the same thing because we all awoke early, ready to go. We didn't bother with a fire, eating whatever was left in our food bag that didn't need to be cooked. We packed the boats and joked that it was finally the last time we'd have to do it. I think it felt strange for each of us. Perhaps it just wasn't sinking in. We were half a day's paddle away and then we would be done. It took us three months but we were about to do what we had set out to do. I don't think any of us knew exactly how we felt that morning. We all were ready to go home. That was for sure. Yet after so long on the river, it was hard to sort out the feelings of accomplishing our goal of reaching the Arch.

After St. Charles, the river returned to trees lining the banks, now mostly bare of leaves, revealing rolling farmland beyond. After a few hours we passed under our last highway bridge, meaning the confluence with the Mississippi River was probably less than an hour ahead. The weather was pleasantly mild and it promised to be a warm day, a perfect way to finish our journey.

Surprisingly, we didn't talk much those last few miles. I told John a few times it couldn't be much further but other than that we just kept paddling. I suppose we were all lost in our own thoughts. In the back of my mind was the reality we would soon be in a very large city with nowhere to stay, two canoes to sell, and very little money. We had discussed it a few times on the trip and never came up with too much of a plan. Even last night we were still more interested in reaching the Arch and dealing with it when the time came. I was now realizing that time was literally a couple of hours away.

Up ahead the river made a turn to the right, heading south. I glanced at the map and knew just around that bend, the last bend of so many over the last ninety one days, we would see the Mississippi River flow in from our left and the Missouri River would come to an end.

"Just around that bend, John." I said it with a big smile on my face.

"Oh yeah," he replied, without turning around.

Steve and Tim paddled their boat up next to ours. We had started out together on that small mountain stream back in Three Forks, Montana. We would finish together at the end, seven states and 2,500 miles later.

As we rounded the bend, the trees came to a point on our left and the distant bank revealed an even wider river entering. The water of the Missouri converged on the water of the Mississippi as if not willing to give up its claim on the river. The canoes were tossed a bit as the turbulent waters fought it out for supremacy. Water swirled in circles in both directions. We stopped paddling and let the current turn the boats this way and that. It didn't matter for the moment. We had accomplished paddling the entire length of the longest river in the United States.

When the Mississippi had finally won over and the steady current headed straight south, Steve stood up and let out a howl, waving his paddle. It was impossible to not let out a shout of some kind. I leaned back in the boat laughing and just enjoying the moment.

"Hey, John, grab Lucky! I wanna get a picture!" John lifted up Lucky high in the air as in victory, and I took the shot, one of my favorite of the trip. That crazy rabbit had made it, traveling over 900 miles by canoe. How many rabbits could say they've done that?

Though it was a time to celebrate canoeing the whole Missouri River, we still had about fifteen miles left to the Arch in St. Louis. The Mississippi River was wider than the Missouri and had an even faster current. It surely wasn't any cleaner. We started paddling again, enjoying the speed. It wouldn't take us long now.

Though we were just miles from a large city like St. Louis, the banks of the river were still mostly trees. Some buildings slowly started appearing, most looking like warehouses or factories. A few roads and railroad tracks seemed to appear out of nowhere, but still no sight of a city.

We were surprised when we ran into our last obstacle, what we later learned was called "The Chain of Rocks," a wall of rugged rocks extending the width of the river, turning the flat, calm water into a deadly mixture of white water and jagged rocks. The drop was not as steep as back in Great Falls but there was no safe chute to paddle through. If we had attempted it blindly, it appeared neither boat would have made it through. We carried the boats for the last time. As the water calmed down, up ahead just a few miles away, we could see the skyline of St. Louis and just a few minutes later, glistening in the mid day sun, was a shining sliver of steel that didn't look like any other building: The Gateway Arch.

We passed rows of barges tied up on both sides of the river as the tall buildings grew taller up ahead on our right. Beyond two highway bridges, we paddled under an old railroad bridge. Just past it the giant Arch towered over most of the buildings. After three months of long days of paddling we were now paddling the last few minutes. This was it. That time on a journey when you realize you're doing certain things for the last time. We had already spent our last night on the Missouri River. We had packed the canoes in the morning for the last time. The last sunset. The last full moon. What is it about doing something for the last time that brings such special lasting meaning and importance?

We were approaching the Arch from its side so at first it looked like a tall silver column. Now, as we got closer and in front of it, the Arch began to take shape. John and I had never seen it before. After three months of anticipation, it was a beautiful, spectacular sight, larger than I had imagined. I stopped paddling to take a few pictures before we were too close and it was too big to fit in the frame.

A large ship, the SS Admiral, was docked on the right bank in front of the city. It reminded me of a giant Twinkie painted silver. It had rows of windows and open decks, obviously a cruise ship of some kind.

The Arch stood majestically on a grassy hill. As strange as it seemed, now it was time to simply turn the boats and come ashore, yes, for the last time. A small, old fashioned steamboat, with its two high steam smoke stacks and its wooden paddle wheel in the back, was docked on the river, so before we passed it, we steered for shore.

The waterfront bank was paved cobblestone right down to the water, at a slight incline. The canoes scraped on the cobblestone bricks as we hit land. Tim and John got out and steadied the boats for Steve and me to climb out. Then we all pulled the boats up out of the water.

The funny thing was we all just stood there, saying nothing. We stared at the Arch, than looked around to discover tourists staring at us! Surprisingly, though people stared, no one asked the usual question, "Where did you guys come from?" or "Where are you guys headed?" I stood there, my hands in my pants pockets, looking around. Though no one seemed willing to ask it, we all had to be thinking it. "Now what?"

Before anyone had a chance to say anything a white van pulled up on the road up at the edge of the cobblestone. On the side in bright red letters it read Channel 4 News. A stocky man got out of the driver's seat, opened the back door and placed a large camera on his shoulder. An attractive black woman in a smart business suit stepped out of the passenger door and walked over to us. She extended her hand. "Hi, my name is Robin Smith. Congratulations! We'd love to hear about your trip." She had a contagious smile and though none of us had ever been interviewed live on TV, she made it very easy.

Of course, we had to ask her how she knew who we were. How did she know we had just arrived in St. Louis?

As it turned out, that sweet old couple back in St. Charles had called Channel 4 and had set in place events that made our time in St. Louis both an adventure and a real blessing, much like the whole trip had been. With Robin Smith, a local celebrity, interviewing us on camera, curious passersby stopped and watched. When she was done, many came up and had their own questions. We even met some folks who offered to take us a few blocks to an Irish pub where they would buy us a meal and let us watch ourselves on the news. How could we turn down such an offer? We decided to paddle the canoes out into the river and tie them on the river side of the old abandoned steamboat. Lucky would just have to stay put.

The small pub was just a few blocks away, full of people who had just finished work. When our story started, everyone cheered so loud it was difficult to hear each of us talking. The whole place cheered even louder when our story was over. It was great fun, a great way to celebrate the end of an unforgettable adventure, but unfortunately we weren't home yet. Our new friends had to head home and as we stepped outside of the pub, it was now dark. One thing was sure: we weren't going to be pitching a tent in downtown St. Louis.

A man who had watched us on TV stepped up and congratulated us on our trip. He mentioned there was a Salvation Army shelter for transients less than ten blocks from there. Well, I don't think I would have thought of that term, but I suppose that night the term fit. We were indeed transient. We decided to give it a try. I hoped Lucky would just sleep in the canoe and not try anything stupid. If she fell into the Mississippi current we would never see her again.

We walked down the city sidewalk, a very different environment for us. Crossing city streets after three months in a canoe was almost intimidating. It didn't take long to find the building and check in.

Years later, a bit older and wiser, I would learn to appreciate the people that ran such facilities, those who helped reach out to the needy with such love and compassion, but that was not my perspective that night. We were led into a gray, dark room that had at least twenty sets of bunk beds. Instead of mattresses, we had plastic mats about four inches thick. We were each given a pillow and a blanket. I would have preferred my lifejacket that I used for the last three months over that pillow. Well, at least I would be warm.

John took the lower bed and I climbed into the upper bunk. I threw the blanket over myself and laid there, the white ceiling that appeared gray in the dim light was barely a foot from my nose. After weeks with a million stars above me, that ceiling seemed to be closing in on me. Instead of the fresh air of mountains and prairies, the room had a strange smell, a combination of pine cleaner and body odor.

The men that started claiming beds were both young and old, but all looking depressed, desperate, hopeless. I found myself watching them but wanting to look away.

I don't know exactly what it was but I just felt I had to get out of that room. I was like a claustrophobic in a stalled elevator. I slid down off the bunk and leaned over John. "I can't stay here. I gotta go."

John propped himself on an elbow. "Where?"

"I don't know. Anywhere but here."

Tim and Steve were watching and listening. "You sure?" Tim asked me.

"Yeah," I assured them. "I'll see ya at the boats in the morning."

I walked out to the front door that was now locked. I found an attendant and explained I needed to leave. "You can go if you want," he said, "but you can't come back in tonight. There's about thirty guys out there wanting that bed."

"They can have it," I said to him, standing in front of the large metal door. The attendant fumbled with a large collection of keys, then opened the door.

He was not kidding about others wanting that bed. I stepped out the door and into a crowd of men and boys that looked even worse than the ones I had seen inside. I walked quickly through the crowd and down the street, back toward the river.

The air was crisp and cool and though in the middle of a city, it smelled and felt great. I felt good, just walking and feeling the wind on my face. It felt like I was back on the river again. All I could think of was to go back to Lucky and the boats. When I reached the park the Arch was in I looked for a place to camp but it was simply too populated. I walked up to the north base of the Arch. It looked even more impressive in the evening. I ran my hand over the smooth, cold steel. The arching form high above me was silhouetted against the starry night sky.

I walked over to where I could look down at the waterfront. The white 19th century steamboat sat dark and quiet. I had an unsettling feeling about Lucky. All of a sudden I regretted leaving her there in the canoe. Was she still there? Were the boats still there?

I walked down the grassy hill, over the cobblestone to the steamboat. I looked around to make sure no one was looking, feeling pretty safe in the darkness. I climbed onto the boat and walked around the deck to get to the other side. In the darkness of the night and the water, I could see the canoes were safely tied. I still felt anxious as I reached down and pulled back the tarp. There she was, lying comfortably, waiting for us to return.

"Good girl," I said soothingly as I picked her up. "Let's find a place to sleep." I don't know why we hadn't thought of it but the old steamboat was perfect for us. The first floor was all gutted and construction supplies were everywhere, but there was a set of small stairs that led up to the pilot house where the boat is steered. Up there I found a small room with a wooden bunk, perfect for a good night's sleep.

"Looks like we're home, Lucky," I said, as I gently put her down, closed the door and went back and got my sleeping bag and life jacket for a pillow. I had stuffed some lettuce in my pocket from my meal at the pub so Lucky munched on that while I lay down, staring out the dirty windows at the night sky. Warm and dry, all a River Rat could ask for. The Missouri River adventure wasn't over yet, I thought as I got comfortable and quickly fell asleep.

During the night I awoke to the sound of howling wind. Though I now was no stranger to hearing the wind, it sounded quite different in the rickety old boat, whistling through cracks in the wood and around the windows. The boat rocked gently back and forth. I looked over at Lucky, lying down by my feet. She didn't seem concerned.

I looked out the window to see it was still a clear night. In my sleepiness, my thoughts drifted to the Corps of Discovery and their return. They arrived back in St. Louis on September 23, 1806. Captain Clark wrote that it was around 12 o'clock noon, just around the time of day we had arrived, not more than about a hundred yards from where I laid. Back then there was no crowded city, no highway bridges, and no giant silver Arch. It was a quieter, much slower world that I struggled to imagine.

Captain Clark wrote that he had trouble sleeping that first night back. I would have thought after all they had been through, he would finally have slept like a baby, but perhaps I had just a glimpse of the mixed feelings and the flurry of emotion he must have felt. Perhaps the celebrations kept him up most of the night.

I hadn't realized the rocking of the boat was quite relaxing and before long it lulled me to sleep once more. Unlike Captain Clark, I slept soundly the rest of the night.

St. Louis, Missouri October 29–31, 1979

The next day people who had watched us on TV came down to the waterfront to see us. Some folks brought food while a few others even gave us money. A car salesman from a Chrysler dealer brought helium balloons to hang on the boats and ladies from the USS Admiral walked over with a homemade For Sale sign. When a police officer came by we figured we were in trouble but he just congratulated us. Just like everywhere else along the river, people went out of their way to help us and it showed me there are lots of wonderful people in the world.

As planned, John was wired money and caught a Greyhound bus back to New Jersey. We spent a lot of time on the pay phones trying to find a store interested in two used canoes but we were coming up with no luck. We were still sitting out by the boats when the sun went down. We all spent that night on the steamboat.

The next day we tried the newspaper for some help. The Globe-Democrat interviewed Tim and Steve while I stayed with the canoes. It turned out to be about a quarter of a page article with the headline "Big Adventure Over: Canoes For Sale" and would be in the 7PM edition.

That late afternoon while we were sitting around playing cards, a young intern we had met from Channel 4 came to the river and invited us to dinner at her mom's home. We didn't hesitate! We piled in her car and drove to a nearby St. Louis suburb. Margaret's uncle had been out hunting squirrels that day and had decided we were just the kind of guys that would enjoy a squirrel dinner. We all looked at each other when we realized our first home-cooked meal in three months would be fresh squirrel! The rattlesnake actually tasted better! When her mom insisted we spend the night in their guest room, which had two double beds, again we couldn't refuse. Our first night in a real bed with clean sheets and fluffy pillows was a wonderful experience to say the least.

The next day back at the waterfront, the sweet lady from the Admiral, who had been providing us with drinking water and rabbit food, asked if she could adopt Lucky. I hated to see her go but I realized we weren't in the position to keep her. She had been a great Missouri River Rat and I was happy to see her go to a good home.

A few more people came by but by nightfall we climbed aboard our steamboat for yet another night. We were really starting to wonder what to do next.

Thankfully in the morning a man came and offered us just enough money for three bus tickets. "There's history in those canoes!" Steve stressed, throwing in the life vests and paddles. I protested and kept my paddle, which to this day hangs on our living room wall.

It was 7 p.m. when we finally boarded a Greyhound to Livingston, Montana. We had a 44-hour bus ride ahead of us so we each took a whole seat since the bus was half empty and we planned on sleeping the whole way.

Instead of lying down, I sat there staring out the huge window. The engine started and it reminded me of that little tug boat that had been home for a few days and I smiled. I heard the driver put it in gear and we pulled out of the station.

It was a dark night and the glare of the city lights danced and bounced off the glass. I tried to get one last glimpse of the Arch or the river, but there were too many buildings. Within minutes we were on Interstate 70 headed northwest, back to Yellowstone.

In the light of day I might have noticed the large wooded cemetery off to the right. I had no way of knowing, out in that cemetery, near the center in a clearing, was a 35 foot granite obelisk, marking the final resting place of Captain William Clark.

Unlike Captain Meriwether Lewis, who suffered from depression and sadly, allegedly took his own life less than three years after the expedition, Captain Clark lived a full and successful life. He was appointed Superintendent of Native Affairs and then was made territorial governor by President Madison in 1813. He died in St. Louis at the home of his eldest son, Meriwether Lewis Clark, in 1838. He was sixty eight.

One could say that the mission of the Corps of Discovery was a failure. The hope was that they would find a northwest passage to the Pacific Ocean. They didn't find any because unfortunately it didn't exist. Yet they made incredible discoveries of new plants and animals, started peaceful relations with more than a few Native American tribes, and paved the way for the westward expansion that was to come. In the end, they achieved far more than hoped for.

It's funny how life is like that. None of us have lived this life without failures and disappointments. None of us are spared no matter how gifted we might be. It is the human condition. Yet through the disappointments and failures we continue on, and if we do, we achieve things and find success in other areas of our lives, that sometimes are even greater than our original goals.

As I relaxed, my eyes grew heavy, my mind slowing down, but still filled with images of mountains and prairies and rivers. Our wonderful adventure was over. We were heading home. God only knew the failures and the triumphs, the trials and joys that lay ahead for each of the young Missouri River Rats. Little did I know there were many more adventures yet to come, just around the bend.

LUCKY B. SPRINGFIELD

A few years after the river trip of '79, my wife and I were driving through St. Louis, my first time back. I couldn't resist stopping at the Arch. This time we were tourists and we took the elevator to the top, looking out at the incredible view. The USS Admiral was still docked in the same place on the waterfront so I walked over to see if the woman who had adopted Lucky still worked there. She did and we recognized each other right away.

It turns out Lucky was doing great and her favorite activity was running around in the backyard being chased and even chasing their German Shepherd. She said they had become inseparable best friends! Lucky B. Springfield, the fifth Missouri River Rat, had indeed turned out to be one lucky bunny.

A Soldiers' Weapons

Our Rendezvous The Boy's Third Day

Aug 21, 2002

There was still no sign of Karen. I kept telling myself there were still over five hours of daylight left. Everything would be fine. I tried to convince myself but I knew all too well the empty miles of driving that lay out there in the Montana prairie. If they took a wrong turn….I felt a deep sense of helplessness as I realized with no cell phone there was no way for me to reach them and no way for them to reach me.

I thought about how well the boys had acted on the river with each other and with me, how well they had performed with the different challenges we faced, and especially how well they had enjoyed the land and the river. They had done great and I was very proud of them both. Their great Missouri River trip was now over and I started thinking of all those adventures that lay in store for both of them. They still seemed so young, yet seemed to be growing up so quickly. There they were, just two kids skipping rocks in the water with not a care in the world, but in just those few days on the river I noticed unmistakable signs of manhood appearing. My boys were growing up. With that thought came a strong sense of pride, along with a feeling of trepidation.

I knew all too well what they soon would be facing as young men: the world, with all it's dangers and traps, their own flesh with all the desires and impulses that fight against the spirit and the soul, and of course, the ultimate spiritual enemies of every Christian, Satan and his demons. As I watched them playing, I asked myself whether they were really ready for those spiritual battles that lay ahead. Did they understand what they were up against?

> For we do not wrestle against flesh and blood but against principalities, against powers, against the rulers of the darkness of this age, against spiritual hosts of wickedness in the heavenly places.
> Ephesians 6:12

I thought about my boys fighting in a spiritual war much more destructive, more horrific that the world wars, even greater and more insidious than the war on terror. Were they ready? Did they have the weapons necessary to fight and be victorious in the end?

> For though we walk in the flesh, we do not war according to the flesh. For the weapons of our warfare are not carnal but mighty in God for pulling down strongholds, casting down arguments and every high thing that exalts itself against the knowledge of God, bringing every thought into captivity to the obedience of Christ.
> 2 Corinthians 10:3–5

We live in a physical world so it is only natural we, as men, are ready to fight with physical weapons. Most of us seem to have a natural attraction to guns, knives, even explosives. I must confess my boys and I enjoy an occasional great shoot'em up, blow'em up movie where the good guys get the bad guys in the end. Yet God's Word tells us we do not war in the flesh but with spiritual weapons that have the power of God. Instead of shooting or blowing up the bad guys, we are to pull down and destroy the ungodly strongholds that have been built by the world that oppose the knowledge and truth of God. Man's ideas and philosophies such as humanism, moral relativism, evolution; the list goes on. The world will call it enlightenment or being open-minded, but at the core, it is simply man's rebellion against the clear divine revelation of God found in the Holy Scriptures.

Every Christian is aware of Paul's description of the Armor of God described in his letter to the Ephesians. It is interesting that the only offensive weapon the apostle mentions is the Sword of the Spirit, the Word of God.

…and the sword of the Spirit, which is the Word of God.
Ephesians 6:17

Perhaps most Christians don't see the Bible as a weapon, but that is exactly what it is. Jesus understood that better than anyone. He battled Satan in the greatest spiritual sword fight ever recorded. Satan understood that God's Word was a weapon. He tried to use it against Jesus, yet Jesus fought back with the same Sword and beat Satan at his own game.

Then Jesus was led up by the Spirit into the wilderness to be tempted by the devil. And when he had fasted forty days and forty nights, afterward He was hungry. Now when the tempter came to Him, he said, "If you are the Son of God, command that these stones become bread."
Matthew 4:1–11

Satan knew Jesus was hungry and weak. What better time to attack Him? I'm sure in His physical hunger, to Jesus those smooth round stones in the Judean wilderness resembled fresh loaves of bread. Satan was not questioning Jesus' authority. He knew all too well who Jesus was.

But He answered and said, "It is written, "Man shall not live by bread alone, but by every word that proceeds from the mouth of God."

No matter what He was going through Jesus knew God's Word had absolute authority over all things. Though He was weak and hungry, God's Word still stands. He fought Satan with the only weapon Satan had no defense against.

Then the devil took Him up into the holy city, set Him on the pinnacle of the temple, and said to Him, "If you are the Son of God, throw yourself down. For it is written, 'He shall give His angels charge over you,' and 'In their hands they shall bear you up, lest you dash your foot against a stone.'"

Again Satan takes a swipe with the same spiritual sword. Isn't it interesting how well Satan knows the Word of God?

Jesus said to him, "It is written again, "You shall not tempt the LORD your God."

Jesus doesn't flinch, coming back with a response that answered Satan's twisted use of the scriptures. The sword fight continued and intensified.

Again the devil took Him up on an exceedingly high mountain, and showed Him all the kingdoms of the world and their glory. And he said to Him, "All these things I will give you if you will fall down and worship me."

Perhaps Satan was becoming frustrated but at that point he showed his hand, revealing what he was really looking for. He wanted God's chosen One to worship him. He was going for broke!

Then Jesus said to him, "Away with you, Satan! For it is written, "You shall worship the LORD your God, and Him only shall you serve." Then the devil left Him, and behold, angels came and ministered to Him.

Jesus took that sword and swung with a deadly blow. Satan had no choice but to retreat. Do you notice the pattern Jesus used? He repeatedly said, "It is written…" How much more effective we would all be as spiritual soldiers if we fought the same way with the same weapon. Yet Satan knew that man doesn't fight very well with the Sword of the Spirit. He learned that all too well with his encounter with Eve in the Garden.

> Now the serpent was more cunning than any beast of the field which the LORD God had made. And he said to the woman, "You shall not eat of every tree of the garden?" And the woman said to the serpent, "We may eat the fruit of the trees of the garden, but of the fruit of the tree which is in the midst of the garden, God has said, "You shall not eat it, nor shall you touch it, lest you die." Then the serpent said to the woman, "You will not surely die."
> Genesis 3:1–4

Again, it is interesting that Satan knew very clearly the commands of God. And sadly, Eve seems to have known them, too. Why she mentions that they should not even touch the tree is a curious mystery. Had she and Adam agreed it was wise to not even get near the tree? Was she just being legalistic even way back then? Whatever the case, the fact is Satan was able to shed doubt on God's Word and Eve fell for it. And worse, Adam gave in just as easily.

Nothing has changed over thousands of years. Satan uses the same weapon against us. As soon as the authority of the scriptures is questioned we open ourselves up to all kinds of theories and foolish thinking, which is really nothing but rebellion against God.

> Now the Spirit expressly says that in latter times some will depart from the faith, giving heed to deceiving spirits and doctrines of demons.
> 1 Timothy 4:1

Today we find more and more churches watering down the gospel, neglecting sound doctrine, not teaching the Word of God, opting for mere entertainment and more contemporary ideas in hopes of "not offending" or being "more relevant." I can't help but believe Satan is well pleased with such churches. I believe those churches are giving heed to spirits and are in fact teaching doctrines that come from Satan.

> Be diligent to present yourself approved to God, a worker who does not need to be ashamed, rightly dividing the word of truth.
> 2 Timothy 2:15

Today in America there is very little dividing the word of truth. We are in an age where you can cherry pick verses that promote a new idea and write a book that Christians will flock to buy, even though it is filled with man's ideas and not God's. We form small groups to study and discuss those books, yet too often have little time or interest in studying the actual scriptures.

> All scripture is given by inspiration of God, and is profitable for doctrine, for reproof, for correction, for instruction in righteousness, that the man of God may be complete, thoroughly equipped for every good work.
> 2 Timothy 3:16

Though no professing Christian would disagree with Paul's statement here, we need to ask ourselves just how equipped we really are. I believe the most humbling experience for a Christian is to have a knock on their front door from the neighborhood Jehovah's Witness or those clean cut young men in the white shirts and ties. These missionaries of error will run circles around most Christians, twisting and misinterpreting the scriptures to suit the doctrines that deny the truth of God. Most Christians politely close their doors because very few know enough of God's Word to lovingly challenge them. Though I am not recommending the coercion that these cults use on their members, it is still sad to think that people caught up in these groups spend more time studying their doctrines than the people of God who have the truth and spend so little time being equipped by it.

> These were more noble than those in Thessalonica, in that they received the Word with all readiness and searched the Scriptures daily to find out whether these things were so.
> Acts 17:11

Luke tells us that the Bereans didn't simply believe what Paul was preaching, but went to the scriptures to see if what he was saying was true. Sadly that concept is not practiced much in America any longer. Today, if it sounds right, if it makes people feel good, if the speaker is dynamic enough, it often times is accepted as truth. We must realize, just like with any other type of weapon, you need to use it safely and correctly. Otherwise it can bring more harm than good. I believe there are many Christians today that treat the scriptures with little care, not realizing the consequences can be devastating.

It is clear in the scriptures that the Bible is indeed a powerful weapon. I believe it is equally clear that we as spiritual soldiers have a secret weapon. Sadly, if it is true we neglect the Sword of the Spirit, the Word of God, we perhaps neglect this weapon even more. That secret weapon is prayer.

Though we may not understand all the details of how prayer works, we know that we are commanded to pray and that it should be an important part of our Christian life. Jesus was a man of prayer. He took the time to be in fellowship with His Father every day, in everything He did. He took time to teach believers how to pray.

Unfortunately, and I include myself in this, most of us men tend to want to be men of action rather than men of prayer. We seem to be much more comfortable in doing something, almost anything, whether right or wrong, than to be still and go to God in prayer.

Judging from his letters, it is obvious that the Apostle Paul knew the importance of prayer and prayed often.

> For God is my witness, whom I serve with my spirit in the gospel of His Son, that without ceasing I make mention of you always in my prayers, making request if, by some means, now at last I may find a way in the will of God to come to you.
> Romans 1:9, 10

> ...praying always with all prayer and supplication in the Spirit, being watchful to this end with all perseverance and supplication for all the saints, and for me, that utterance may be given to me, that I may open my mouth boldly to make known the mystery of the gospel...
> Ephesians 6:18–19

It might seem surprising that the Apostle Paul, perhaps one of the boldest apostles of Christ, would be asking for prayer from the brethren in Ephesus, that he would have boldness to preach the gospel. Paul reminds us that we are indeed dependent on God for any spiritual service we perform. Perhaps that is precisely why Paul was so effective. Another lesson, much more personal, might be that it is natural for us to sometimes question our abilities or even our worthiness in serving God. We must remember that the humble realization that we can do nothing apart from Him helps us rely on Him and do incredible things through Him.

> Epaphras, who is one of you, a bondservant of Christ, greets you, always laboring fervently for you in prayers, that you may stand perfect and complete in all the will of God.
> Colossians 4:12

One can only assume the early Church was full of those who prayed fervently, judging from the scriptures and from the actions of the early believers. They knew the importance of prayer.

There is a fascinating passage of scripture most Christians are well familiar with: the raising of Lazarus from the dead. Though it is easy to simply focus on the miracle itself, there are so many other lessons found in those words.

Right before Jesus cried out for Lazarus to come forward, He prays out loud so the crowd could hear Him.

> Then they took away the stone from the place where the dead man was lying. And Jesus lifted up His eyes and said, "Father, I thank you that you have heard me. And I know that you always hear me, but because of the people who are standing by I said this, that they may believe that you sent me."
> John 11:41

I suppose a critic could say His prayer was almost staged, at least speaking it out loud, but Jesus makes it clear it was for the crowd's benefit that they would know and understand what God was doing and that Jesus was in fact the Son of God, the Messiah. He wanted to show us that God does indeed hear our prayers. In this case, Jesus is praying a prayer of thankfulness more than petition, very different than our prayers most of the time. I'm ashamed to admit it, but my most fervent prayers are when I or someone I love is in desperate need, not prayers of thankfulness. It wasn't that His prayer was staged or even fake, but its purpose here was for all those there to hear it.

I can think back on all those times in my life when I should have been praying but for whatever reason didn't. Why is it at times we don't even feel like praying, especially when we need it the most? Is it that we really don't believe God is hearing us, even though Jesus reassures us in His prayer at Lazarus' tomb?

Perhaps when we pray we forget the compassion and love that God has for us. The truth is we are not praying to some distant, cold god that dominates the universe, but as the passage in John 11 reveals, a wonderfully compassionate, loving God.

> Now a certain man was sick, Lazarus of Bethany, the town of Mary and her sister Martha. It was that Mary who anointed the LORD with fragrant oil and wiped His feet with her hair, whose brother Lazarus was sick. When Jesus heard that, He said, "This sickness is not unto death, but for the glory of God, that the Son of God may be glorified through it."
> John 11:1

The disciples must have felt reassured that Lazarus would recover since Jesus had stated the illness would not result in death. They did not, perhaps could not understand yet that God would be glorified not in Lazarus' healing but in his resurrection.

> Now Jesus loved Martha and her sister and Lazarus. So when He heard that he was sick, He stayed two more days in the place where He was. Then after this He said to the disciples, "Let us go to Judea again."
> John 11:5

Probably every believer has at least one time in their lives questioned God's timing. I know I have. What an example of God's timing being very different than what the disciples would have expected, and certainly different than what Martha and Mary wanted. Yet, though sometimes so hard to understand, God's timing is always perfect.

The text is clear that Jesus loved Martha and Mary. I believe that is important to remind us that when God's timing seems so wrong, it is not because He doesn't care or doesn't love us anymore. It is precisely because He loves us. I admit that is sometimes the most difficult thing in the world to accept.

> These things He said, and after that He said to them, "Our friend Lazarus sleeps, but I go that I may wake him up." Then His disciples said, "LORD, if he sleeps he will get well." However Jesus spoke of his death, but they thought He was speaking about taking rest in sleep. Then Jesus said to them plainly," Lazarus is dead. And I am glad for your sakes that I was not there, that you may believe. Nevertheless let us go to him."
> John 11:11

Jesus finally begins to reveal God's plan to His disciples. It is easy to miss the fact that He did not just simply delay for a day or so, but for four long, sad days.

> So when Jesus came, He found that he had already been in the tomb four days. Now Bethany was near Jerusalem, about two miles away. And many of the Jews had joined the women around Martha and Mary, to comfort them concerning their brother. Now Martha, as soon as she heard that Jesus was coming, went and met Him, but Mary was sitting in the house. Now Martha said to Jesus, "LORD, if you had been here, my brother would not have died. But even now I know that whatever you ask of God, God will give you."
> John 11:17

Martha says just what you or I would have said; "LORD, if you had only been here…" Don't we sound just like that at times? "LORD, if you would have only done this or done that! LORD, if you had only been

here!" Whether we say the words or not, haven't we all felt that way?
Even in her pain, Martha makes a wonderful statement of faith, but
even she is not prepared for what Jesus is about to do.

> Jesus said to her, "Your brother will rise again." Martha said
> to Him, "I know that he will rise again in the resurrection
> at the last day." Jesus said to her, "I am the resurrection and
> the life. He who believes in me, though he may die, he shall
> live. And whoever lives and believes in Me shall never die.
> Do you believe this?" She said to Him, "Yes LORD, I believe
> that you are the Christ, the Son of God, who is to come
> into the world."
> John 11:23

Jesus declares truth to Martha; clear Biblical doctrine. Unlike sterile, cold doctrine being taught by a stuffy old seminary professor, sound
doctrine is neither sterile, boring nor cold. Jesus doesn't just try to make
Martha simply feel better, but comforts her with the true knowledge
of God. The world may offer flowery speech and comforting philosophies, but believers will find peace and strength in God's Word where
they can know the truth.

> Then, when Mary came where Jesus was, and saw Him,
> she fell down at His feet, saying to Him, "LORD, if you
> had been here my brother would not have died." Therefore,
> when Jesus saw her weeping, and the Jews who came with
> her weeping, He groaned in the spirit and was troubled.
> And He said, "Where have you laid him?" They said to
> Him, "LORD, come and see." Jesus wept. Then the Jews
> said, "See how he loved him!"
> John 11:32

I used to ask myself why Jesus would weep. After all, unlike Martha and
Mary, He saw the whole picture. He knew He was about to raise Lazarus
from the dead. Everyone was about to see a wonderful miracle. Lazarus was
about to be reunited with his sisters. He should have been chuckling under
His breath, anticipating everyone's joy. Instead, Jesus is weeping.

Commentators have different opinions about Jesus' tears. Some say He wept seeing the suffering Martha and Mary were experiencing. Others say he was weeping for the world and the awful consequences of sin. I agree with the latter.

In His divinity, as the Son of God, Jesus knew all too well the consequences of sin in the world. He knew how mankind was created in God's image and how we were formed to have a close personal relationship with our Creator. In His divine wisdom, He knew the incredible chasm that now separated mankind from God.

I don't know if it was in His divinity or His humanity but I believe Jesus didn't simply weep over the consequence of sin in general that day. I believe He wept for every tear we've ever cried, every pang of pain we've ever felt, every sorrow we've ever suffered, every tragedy we've ever experienced, very much in the same way that He would soon pay with His own blood for every sin ever committed, past, present, and future.

I believe Jesus didn't simply see the suffering of Martha and Mary that day. I believe in His heart He saw the suffering of the whole world; the hungry, the homeless, the lonely, the discouraged, the diseased and disabled, and especially those spiritually lost.

I believe Jesus' tears on that day were as much for you and me as they were for Martha and Mary.

> And some of them said, "Could not this man, who opened
> the eyes of the blind, also have kept this man from dying?"
> John 11:37

"Couldn't Jesus do this one thing?" Again, haven't we said the same thing at times in our own lives? "If God can do anything, why can't He do this?" The Jews didn't understand what God was up to and many times in our own lives we may not know what God is up to, yet He asks us to trust Him. Not with a blind trust, but trusting in His nature and His promises recorded in the Holy Scriptures.

> Then Jesus again, groaning in Himself, came to the tomb.
> It was a cave, and a stone lay against it. Jesus said, "Take
> away the stone." Martha, the sister of him who was dead,

said to Him, "LORD, by this time there is a stench, for he has been dead four days."
John 11:38

Even though Martha had wonderful faith in Christ, to her it must have seemed illogical, perhaps even cruel, to ask them to remove the stone. It had been four days. She knew her brother's body had begun to decompose. Could we blame her for questioning Jesus?

Again, I can't help but identify with Martha. How often do I look around me, my sights on my circumstances, trusting in my own limited understanding and logic, forgetting that God is working in all those situations, even when I perhaps can't see? It wasn't that Martha didn't have faith. She surely did. Yet, just like you and me, it's so easy to take our eyes off God, focusing on the physical and ignoring the spiritual.

Jesus said to her, "Did I not say to you that if you would believe you would see the glory of God?" It was at this point that Jesus prayed out loud to the Father for all to hear.
John 11:40

"Be anxious for nothing, but in everything by prayer and supplication, with thanksgiving, let your requests be made known to God, and the peace of God, which surpasses all understanding, will guard your hearts and minds through Christ Jesus."
Philippians 4:6,7

I believe our prayers, a wonderful spiritual weapon the LORD has given us, would be much more effective if we better understood the nature of the God we pray to. We can only be thankful if we truly realize all we have to be thankful for. We can only understand the sinful condition of our hearts if we truly understand the holiness of God. We can only experience the peace of God that guards our hearts and minds when the truth of who God is has been revealed to us.

Are you as guilty as I am of ignoring this wonderful weapon we have in our spiritual arsenal? What better use of such a weapon than the safety and the salvation of the children God has entrusted us with?

If men have a problem praying, I believe young men have an even worse time of it. Why is it women seem to be wired in a way that prayer is more natural for them? I of course can't speak for all men, but I believe I have some idea why men struggle so.

Prayer is not simply talking to God, as we often hear. Yes, we are communicating with our Heavenly Father but true prayer goes much deeper and has a profound effect. When we pray we realize God is not simply our spiritual genie waiting to grant all our wishes. He is not sitting around in heaven waiting for our many commands and requests.

The power of effective prayer is that it reminds us that God is in charge; not us. I believe Christian men have a problem praying as often as they should because they simply have a hard time submitting to God's will in many situations. We are so often focused and fixed on our own plan, our own agenda, that we ignore His. Praying to God is a way of accepting our dependence on Him. It is an exercise of agreeing with His sovereignty and His will in all things.

Submission and dependence are not natural for men, especially young men. Perhaps overcoming both obstacles is what spiritual maturity is all about. Perhaps the young men of the church would be surprised and even encouraged to know the battle of the wills is a battle that rages no matter what your age. The only difference is that the older men have been in the battle longer and have hopefully learned through experience. They have a lot to offer the young men if they would only speak and the young men would only listen.

Right before the Apostle Peter wrote of our adversary, the devil, that roaring lion that walks about seeking whom he may devour, he wrote to the older men of the church, then the young men. Though writing to the elders, the spiritual leaders of the church, I believe his words are just as true for fathers, the spiritual leaders of their own families.

> Shepherd the flock of God which is among you, serving as overseers, not by compulsion but willingly; not for dishonest gain but eagerly; nor as being LORDS over those entrusted to you, but being examples to the flock; and when the Chief Shepherd appears, you will receive the crown of glory that does not fade away.
> 1 Peter 5:2

How easy and how natural it is to take any position of power, no matter how small or insignificant, and LORD over others. There are examples of men doing that all over the world. It is all too common. How much more difficult it is to decide to be an example; to live your life with that purpose always in mind.

> "Likewise, you younger people, submit yourselves to your elders. Yes, all of you be submissive to one another, and be clothed with humility, for God resists the proud, but gives grace to the humble. Therefore, humble yourselves under the mighty hand of God, that He may exalt you in due time, casting all your care upon Him, for He cares for you."
> 1 Peter 5:5

Humility is not something found in most young men. Perhaps Peter was writing remembering his younger days as well. How difficult it is to teach our young men that God will exalt them in His perfect timing, when they have learned to resist pride and have received grace in their humility.

They will learn to accept His will and depend on Him when they realize how much they are loved by their Creator and Savior. That dependence will enable them to fight as the spiritual soldier God intended.

As fathers, we need to do our best to let our children know how important prayer is. Our young children need to hear us pray. Our older children need to know how dangerous it is to neglect, even if we are guilty ourselves.

I was indeed praying when something caught my eye and I looked back toward the road. A cloud of smoke appeared far off. I watched carefully until I was sure. It was a white vehicle. "Oh yeah!" I shouted out loud to no one, feeling a rush of relief and thankfulness. "Oh yeah!" As it got closer, I could tell it was a white SUV. It had to be ours! I whistled and waved to the boys and they came running. The Explorer kept coming and I was sure it was ours. I waved my arms high and wide. The boys made it to the top of the hill just as Karen came pulling up to me. Once I saw she was smiling, I could finally feel a great sense of relief.

She rolled down her window as she came to a stop. "You made it!"

"Yeah! And you made it, too!" I laughed, still filled with relief.

There were lots of hugs and kisses to go around. The boys started right away telling mom all about their adventures while I tried to find out how the drive had gone. As it turned out, they had made a stop in Fort Benton to get a coffee mug as a souvenir, but they weren't there very long. Karen and Dad both admitted they were starting to get just a bit worried on that gravel road for hours with no signs at all. They too were relieved when they came over the crest and started down into the valley and saw the river and then me waving.

The boys and I loaded the cooler and our bins into the Explorer while Dad and Karen stretched their legs walking by the river and exploring the general store. Emma just wanted to throw rocks into the water.

"So did you miss me, Emma?" I asked, kneeling down beside her.

"Yes, I did, Daddy! Why couldn't I come with you?" she asked with pleading eyes.

I scooped her up in my arms. "Well, honey, you're still a little young."

"Can I go when I get bigger?"

"Well," I looked into those beautiful blue eyes of hers, "The next time I come down this river, you're coming with me. How's that?"

Her eyes widened. "Promise?"

"I promise." She gave me one of those great bear hugs, throwing her little arms around my neck and squeezing as hard as she could.

It was starting to get late and we still had a few hours of light to get some driving done on our way north to Glacier National Park. We were meeting up with an old friend there. Ron, the guy that had driven up from Yellowstone to drive our canoes around the falls at Great Falls back in '79, was going to meet us there. I had found him through the internet a year before and we planned to get together. Ron had stayed in his beloved Montana and had made a career as a wildlife photographer. We hadn't seen him in twenty-three years.

After that, we would drive south to Yellowstone to meet up with Steve, my fellow River Rat, and his family. Somehow, though it was hard to believe, I hadn't seen Steve in twenty-three years as well.

When it was time to go, the boys and dad climbed into the Explorer as Karen buckled Emma into her car seat. I shut the hatchback and walked around and opened the driver's side door. I paused before getting in, glancing over my shoulder one last time at the river. I watched the smooth, gentle flow of the current passing by me. I looked up, my eyes drawn to the horizon, where the river meandered to the right and disappeared into the lovely Montana hills.

I felt extremely blessed. After all these years, it was nice to know the river was still calling me.

EPILOGUE

JULY, 2006

It was a business meeting in Kansas City that has brought me back to Kansas. It would have been a straight shot west across I 70 to Topeka but when I picked up the Grand Prix from the Avis lot, I headed north on I 29. I was just too close to the river to not make a detour up to Atchison, Kansas, to look around.

It took less than an hour, driving through tiny towns and fields of cows. I arrived there as the sun was just barely above the horizon. Unfortunately it would be dark soon.

I drove over a rusty, narrow bridge and realized it was the very bridge we had slept under on Day 79 of the trip, back on October, 16, 1979. After a quick right turn off the bridge I started to recognize the place, though there were some changes. There was now a Veteran's Memorial Park along the river. Manicured grass and a paved path with picnic tables led to a concrete gazebo that honored all the branches of the armed forces. There were also historical markers telling the story of Lewis and Clark. I was certain none of that was here back in '79.

The foundry was still there, though now strangely quiet compared to the night I remembered trying to sleep in my sleeping bag with all the noise. The railroad tracks remained, now with "No Trespassing" signs posted.

I walked up the street, one block from the river. New buildings were being built here and there, but the old YMCA where we took showers was right where I remembered it. The old neon sign was gone now and it was twice as large but the old red brick section was still standing.

I walked along the river bank over to the highway bridge and discovered the town had leveled the ground under the bridge. The slope to the river where our original campsite had been was now about ten feet underground. It was buried, much like the original Lewis and Clark campsites that had disappeared under the huge lakes or where there was no record of them.

I thought about the Corps of Discovery camping just upriver at the stream they named Independence Creek, way back on July 4, 1804. That campsite was now long gone too. At the age of forty-six I felt the strange sensation of being as old as Lewis and Clark.

Time marches on for all of us. It was less than two weeks till the anniversary of the River Rats heading out from Three Forks, Montana twenty-six years ago. It had been four years since the boys and I paddled the river in Montana. Dustin would be twenty-one in a few months, Joshua, sixteen. My little princess Emma was now 7 ½! Each one of them had grown and changed so much over the last few years.

I can't believe it's been three years since I first started writing down my memories and my thoughts recorded here on these pages. Now that I'm finally finished, I find I'm asking myself what my motivation for writing actually was. At first, I just wanted to have a record of the wonderful adventure and nothing more, but once I started, I came to realize I wanted to include the trip I had done with the boys since it was now even more important to me. As I wrote and reflected on those two river trips, I realized it was those years in between that meant so much to me. A journal of the '79 river trip would have no mention of faith or fatherhood. Those years were highlighted by both.

At times I felt like I was writing things I wanted my children to understand, at other times I felt like I was writing to my future grandchildren, telling them things I wanted them to know just in case I don't get the opportunity to share those things in person with them.

At some point in the writing, I started thinking about other dads like me and felt I was sharing my thoughts with them as well. I thought of the good men I was privileged to call "friend." Over the years fatherhood had indeed made us a "band of brothers."

If you're a brand new dad and the birth of your child is still a recent event, you remember that feeling when you gazed at that little infant, totally helpless and dependent, lying there. You know that overwhelming feeling of realizing that little life was counting on you. You were responsible for everything in his or her life. If you were like me, it brought you to tears.

If that's you, especially if your baby is a son, I hope some of the thoughts I have shared here will help you to be the best father you can be, or at least encourage you in that direction. If you concentrate on your fatherhood now, you will not be so overwhelmed when your child has grown and is not helpless or very dependent any longer. I know you've heard it already many times but it really won't take long. Make the commitment now to be a great father to your children and get in the fight.

If you're a dad who has traveled that road already and perhaps your children are even parents themselves now, I'm sure you'd say you never stop being a father no matter how old your children are. You have been through it all and are still learning. Let me encourage you to be a mentor and help those young dads that come into your life. Perhaps God has you there for a specific reason. You know young dads need the wisdom of men that have gone before them. You may not feel wise enough. You might feel that you weren't the father you had wanted to be. Don't let that stop you. Let a younger father perhaps benefit from your own experience, even your own mistakes.

Perhaps you're a dad like me, right in the thick of it all. Maybe it's not going the way you pictured it when your little one was still just that. Perhaps this book has you regretting things you did or didn't do as a father, doubtful things can change. That's probably why most men don't read books on fatherhood. We feel like we don't want to be reminded of how poorly we're doing.

The honest truth is I have gone back and read the chapters that I wrote myself over these last three years and must admit I find myself struggling to do those very things. In the last few years as a father I have continued to make the same mistakes with all three of my kids.

If you have had restless nights, lying in bed feeling you don't have what it takes to be a good father, you're not alone. If you've had those moments when you were ready to throw in the towel and just give up, you're not alone. If you've ever felt fatherhood was the loneliest job in the world, you're not alone. I've been there, done that.

The one thing I know is we can't give up. Too much is at stake. If we quit on ourselves, we're quitting on our sons and daughters. We're quitting on the mission that God has called us to. That is something I know I couldn't live with. And I'd hate for any dad out there to live with it either. You have a battle to fight and win, fellow soldier. Your brothers are with you and so is your God.

I leave you with the words of the Apostle Paul, written to our fellow soldiers in Corinth.

> Watch, stand fast in the faith, be brave, be strong. Let all that you do be done with love.
> 1 Corinthians 16:13, 14

The battle continues.

GLENN FRONTIN has taught Adult Sunday School and small groups for the past fifteen years. He lives in Colorado Springs with his wife, Karen. They have three children, Dustin, Joshua, and Emma.